iOS 17 App Development for Beginners

Get started with iOS app development using Swift 5.9, SwiftUI, and Xcode 15

Arpit Kulsreshtha

www.bpbonline.com

FIRST EDITION 2024

ISBN: 978-93-5551-585-8

Distributors:

BPB PUBLICATIONS
20, Ansari Road, Darya Ganj
New Delhi-110002
Ph: 23254990/23254991

MICRO MEDIA
Shop No. 5, Mahendra Chambers,
150 DN Rd. Next to Capital Cinema,
V.T. (C.S.T.) Station, MUMBAI-400 001
Ph: 22078296/22078297

DECCAN AGENCIES
4-3-329, Bank Street,
Hyderabad-500195
Ph: 24756967/24756400

BPB BOOK CENTRE
376 Old Lajpat Rai Market,
Delhi-110006
Ph: 23861747

Published by Manish Jain for BPB Publications, 20 Ansari Road, Darya Ganj, New Delhi-110002 and Printed by him at Manipal Technologies, Manipal

www.bpbonline.com

Dedicated to

My Daughter

Anaya Kulsreshtha

About the Author

Arpit Kulsreshtha is an accomplished Developer, Team Lead, and Architect with an 11 year track record in Mobile Application Development. His expertise lies in Data Structures, Software Architecture, and Machine Learning, and he has successfully worked on a wide range of platforms, including iOS, Android, Symbian, macOS, tvOS, and watchOS. Arpit is well-versed in various programming languages and technologies, such as Swift, SwiftUI, Objective-C, J2ME, C#, Xamarin, React Native, and Flutter.

Throughout his career, he has demonstrated his versatility by developing mobile apps for diverse domains, including business, e-commerce, education, health and fitness, lifestyle, entertainment, and medical. His deep knowledge of software architecture, analysis, application integration, and development make him a highly skilled professional. Beyond his technical expertise, he is also a passionate blogger, an avid traveller, and enthusiastic about all things related to the latest technology.

Acknowledgement

I am immensely grateful to the many individuals who have significantly brought this book to life. Their continued and unwavering support throughout the writing process has been invaluable.

First and foremost, I would like to express my deepest gratitude to my mother, Mrs. Anita Kulsreshtha, for her continued support and encouragement, and to my wife, Akanksha Khare, for her constant inspiration, which has been instrumental in motivating my writing endeavors. I am also thankful to my dear family members - Ankit Kulsreshtha, Pallavi Raj, Mukesh Khare, Sandhya Khare, Aadya Kulsreshtha, Aayush Khare, and Sarthak Khare - for their incredible support and for being an integral part of my life.

I would like to express my sincere gratitude to everyone I have been honored to lead, follow, or work with. Their mentorship, leadership, and collaboration have contributed significantly to my professional journey and played a vital role in shaping the foundation of this book.

I am indebted to Dheeraj Takyar, Ravi Tailor, and Nayyar for their invaluable support, guidance, and assistance throughout the writing process. Their contributions have been truly remarkable.

Lastly, I would like to express my sincere gratitude to Mr. Nrip Jain and the entire team at BPB Publications for granting me the opportunity to write this book for them. Their belief in my abilities and support has been remarkable, and I am grateful for this wonderful opportunity.

Preface

Apple iOS app development is a platform to develop mobile applications with Swift for iPhone, iPad, and iPod devices. Apple will recently release its new series of iPhones with version 15 and its new iOS 17, which have updates to new APIs in Core Location, SwiftUI, Share Play, Machine Learning, ActivityKit, VisionKit, visionOS, and Symbol Framework. For years, Apple has used Xcode as their development tool and IDE, which includes the iOS SDK, tools, compilers, and frameworks that require you to design, develop, and write code for your iOS apps.

In this book, we explain how to set up and install an iOS app development environment and tools that will help you learn and practice the Swift language and how to use Swift and SwiftUI for iOS apps. We have explained iOS frameworks such as Core Location and MapKit for GPS with map-enabled applications, the AVFoundation Framework for Camera and media-enabled applications, Core Data for local database implementation, and the Core ML framework for Machine Learning and Artificial intelligence based applications on the iOS platform.

We have also covered mobile application architecture and patterns, which will help you write code with reusable and clean components that will increase the readability of the overall project. Once you can complete iOS app development, learning to publish and manage apps on the Apple Store will help you make your apps live on the Apple platform.

The primary goal of this book is to provide all necessary information and concepts with hands-on code to make you a complete iOS app developer, from which you can learn advanced concepts of the Apple platform to increase your knowledge base. We focus on the essentials and cover the material from a basic to an advanced level for you. Over the 22 chapters of this book, you will learn the following:

Chapter 1: Getting Started with Xcode- Introduces the Apple development IDE with step-by-step installation and setup of tools while learning about the playground that will enable you to practice Swift code with instant and quick results.

Chapter 2: Swift Fundamentals- We discussed the Swift Fundamentals, which include types, constants, and Variables in Swift, Operators, strings, and characters; Collection types; Control flow; Conditional statements; Control transfer; functions. And Closures. This chapter gives you the initial and firm foundation of the Swift language.

Chapter 3: Class, Structure, and Enumerations- We discussed further Object-oriented concepts in Swift, such as implementing Classes and structures. An in-depth explanation of the role of Properties in Swift classes with the types of methods. We also evaluated the Inheritance, initialization, and deinitialization of classes.

Chapter 4: Protocols, Extensions, and Error Handling- introduces protocol-oriented programming, which includes using protocols and Extensions to add new programming features to classes without changing their actual code. We explained the role and benefits of Error handling in Swift too.

Chapter 5: Automatic Reference Counting and Memory Safety- ARC is a memory management technique employed by iOS to automatically keep track of object references, ensuring that objects are deallocated from memory when they are no longer in use. This helps developers focus on writing code without worrying about manual memory management. On the other hand, memory safety is a design principle that aims to eliminate memory-related vulnerabilities, such as crashes and memory leaks, by enforcing strict rules and safeguards to prevent illegal memory access and the deallocation of objects.

Chapter 6: Implementing iOS 17 Architecture- iOS 17 Architecture refers to the underlying framework and structure that power Apple's mobile operating system, iOS. It is designed to provide a secure, efficient, and user-friendly environment for running applications on Apple devices such as iPhones, iPads, and iPods. The architecture of iOS is based on a layered approach, with different components working together to provide essential functionalities, including the kernel, frameworks, libraries, and user interface elements.

Chapter 7: User Interface Design with UIKit- Explained the UI interface design and development with StoryBoard and the UIKit framework that will enable you to learn different UI components such as tab bars, table views, collection views, etc., as well as make that design compatible and responsive for every iOS device that supports the latest development SDK.

Chapter 8: User Interface Design with SwiftUI- Discussed the SwiftUI framework, which is a declarative UI framework where you do not need to play with UI interface design and develop the UI with declarative code that takes less time compared to UIKit interface design development.

Chapter 9: Concurrency in Swift and SwiftUI- Swift introduces new features and enhancements to handle concurrent programming, allowing developers to write efficient and responsive applications. SwiftUI, Apple's declarative UI framework, leverages concurrency to create smooth and fluid user experiences. With the advent of Swift's async/await model and SwiftUI's integration with the new concurrency APIs, developers can easily manage tasks, handle parallelism, and streamline their code, resulting in highly performant and scalable applications.

Chapter 10: Storing Data with SQLite and Core Data- Discussed the local database operations with SQLite and the Core Data framework, which uses Object-relational mapping to map data to app business logic in an object-oriented manner and simplify the overall experience compared to direct SQLite handling. We also discussed the newly introduced SwiftData, which combines with SwiftUI.

Chapter 11: File Handling in iOS- Every iOS app has its container to handle files and cache in iOS. We discussed the App File Manager that makes you develop such a solution via which you will be able to manage file handling properly.

Chapter 12: Core Location with MapKit- Explains the current GPS location tracking with MapKit to track the user's geographic location and show other location references on the map to visualize in real-time.

Chapter 13: Camera and Photo Library- AVFoundation Framework, explains how to use the multimedia features of the camera and photo gallery to use photos and videos in iOS apps.

Chapter 14: Multithreading in iOS- Multithreading in iOS refers to the ability of an iOS application to perform multiple tasks concurrently, improving performance and responsiveness. It allows for the execution of multiple threads or processes simultaneously, enabling tasks to be executed in the background while the main thread remains responsive to user interactions. Multithreading in iOS can be achieved using various techniques, such as Grand Central Dispatch (GCD) and Operation Queues, which provide powerful abstractions for managing concurrent tasks and simplifying thread management.

Chapter 15: Networking in iOS Apps- Discusses the communication of iOS apps with server-side components to sync the data with Apple networking classes and the Alamofire framework.

Chapter 16: Mobile App Architectures, Patterns, and Anti-Patterns- Discusses app patterns and anti-patterns with code Architecture to make your development work more efficient and clean, enabling you to write high-end architectural code with reusability and better readability.

Chapter 17: Publish iOS App on the Apple App Store- Explains the step-by-step process to make your complete and bug-free iOS app live on the Apple app store, which requires learning App store management and understanding App Store Review guidelines to better handle rejections.

Chapter 18: Continuous Integration and Delivery with Xcode Cloud- Apple created the revolutionary cloud-based continuous integration and delivery (CI/CD) platform known as Xcode Cloud. It is designed specifically for iOS, iPadOS, macOS, and watchOS app development, offering a seamless and efficient workflow for teams and developers.

Chapter 19: Advance iOS with New Frameworks- This Chapter explains and offers advanced functionalities and features, allowing developers to leverage cutting-edge technologies in their iOS apps. From augmented reality (ARKit), vision kit, and activity kit to advanced user interfaces (UIKit) and multimedia capabilities (AVFoundation), iOS Advanced Frameworks empower developers to build immersive and innovative experiences that push the boundaries of mobile app development.

Code Bundle and Coloured Images

Please follow the link to download the
Code Bundle and the *Coloured Images* of the book:

https://rebrand.ly/1iqejxk

The code bundle for the book is also hosted on GitHub at **https://github.com/bpbpublications/iOS-17-App-Development-for-Beginners**. In case there's an update to the code, it will be updated on the existing GitHub repository.

We have code bundles from our rich catalogue of books and videos available at **https://github.com/bpbpublications**. Check them out!

Errata

We take immense pride in our work at BPB Publications and follow best practices to ensure the accuracy of our content to provide with an indulging reading experience to our subscribers. Our readers are our mirrors, and we use their inputs to reflect and improve upon human errors, if any, that may have occurred during the publishing processes involved. To let us maintain the quality and help us reach out to any readers who might be having difficulties due to any unforeseen errors, please write to us at :

errata@bpbonline.com

Your support, suggestions and feedbacks are highly appreciated by the BPB Publications' Family.

Piracy

If you come across any illegal copies of our works in any form on the internet, we would be grateful if you would provide us with the location address or website name. Please contact us at **business@bpbonline.com** with a link to the material.

If you are interested in becoming an author

If there is a topic that you have expertise in, and you are interested in either writing or contributing to a book, please visit **www.bpbonline.com**. We have worked with thousands of developers and tech professionals, just like you, to help them share their insights with the global tech community. You can make a general application, apply for a specific hot topic that we are recruiting an author for, or submit your own idea.

Reviews

Please leave a review. Once you have read and used this book, why not leave a review on the site that you purchased it from? Potential readers can then see and use your unbiased opinion to make purchase decisions. We at BPB can understand what you think about our products, and our authors can see your feedback on their book. Thank you!

Join our book's Discord space

Join the book's Discord Workspace for Latest updates, Offers, Tech happenings around the world, New Release and Sessions with the Authors:

https://discord.bpbonline.com

Table of Contents

CHAPTER 1
Getting Started with Xcode

Introduction

After a big success in Mac computers, Apple shifted their focus to consumer electronic products such as iPod, iPhone, iPad, and so on. Apple introduced their new products with the success and advancements of iOS (Apple's OS for their consumer electronic products). With the iPhone achieving an even bigger success, in 2008, Apple introduced the App Store for third party apps, which began a new era of app developments. As the consumers started moving from the Mac machines to mobiles, the application development opened a new platform for the business to acquire more consumers that can use apps on the go while they are walking, traveling etc. Apple already had an IDE Xcode which was used by the developers for Mac application development. They have now made upgrades to it and accommodated the iOS app development in the same Xcode. In this chapter, we will start our application development with Xcode and build our first simple sample application which will look like a blank app in a simulator while testing.

Structure

In this chapter, we will cover the following topics:

- About Xcode IDE
- Downloading and installing Xcode
- Xcode user interface
- Configuring Xcode project

- Running and building Xcode iOS project
- Code with Xcode playground
- Xcode organizer

Objectives

After studying this chapter, you will be able to use Xcode IDE for app development, use a simulator to test the developed applications, and create an iOS Project in Xcode IDE.

Xcode IDE

Xcode is an **Integrated Development Environment (IDE)** that contains the software development tools developed by the Apple Company for developing applications and software for MacOS, iPhone, iPad, iPod Touch, iWatch, and Apple TV.

Xcode includes the Xcode IDE, Swift, SwiftUI, and C/ C++/ Objective-C compilers, an instrument analysis tool, simulators, the latest SDKs, and hundreds of other powerful features. Swift is a programming language that is fast, safe, and modern. SwiftUI is a declarative UI language used for the interactive app user interface.

Technical requirements

To fulfill the learning requirements and coding goals of this book, we will require the following:

- An Apple system such as *Mac mini, Macbook, iMac, Mac Studio*, and so on, with MacOS 13 Ventura OS version and later.
- An Apple ID (if you don't have one, this chapter will help you create an Apple ID).
- Apple iOS device (optional) (if you have one, you can run the apps on the device; otherwise, Xcode Simulator will be enough to check how your apps work).

We will start downloading the Xcode IDE for developing iOS applications from the Mac App Store.

Downloading and installing Xcode

Before starting the development of the iOS apps, we need to download and install Xcode; the following are the steps to perform the Xcode installation:

1. Open the Mac App Store.
2. Search for the keyword **Xcode** and press the *return* key.
3. In **Search Results**, Xcode version 15.x will appear, click on **Get and Install**.
4. Now, a box will appear that will ask for an Apple ID; If you already have an Apple ID, fill in the mentioned field, and it will ask for a password for your Apple account. Refer to *Figure 1.1* as follows:

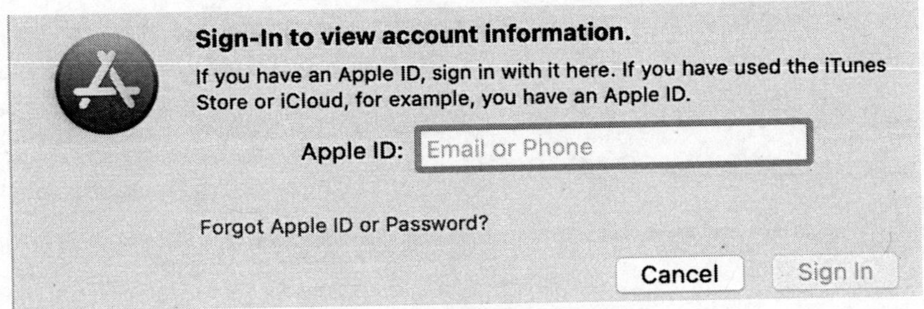

Figure 1.1*: Account information*

If you don't have an Apple ID, you must create a new Apple ID with the help of the following Apple support article:

https://support.apple.com/en-in/HT204316

1. The latest version of Xcode is 15, which includes Swift 5.9, SDKs for iOS 17, iPadOS 17, tvOS 17, watchOS 10, visionOS 1.0 and macOS Sonoma.
2. Before completing the installation of Xcode, it will ask you to select the platform environment that you would like to install. The watchOS 9.0 and tvOS 16.0 SDKs are optional to install while installing Xcode, although if required, you can download these later on whenever needed, as shown in *Figure 1.2:*

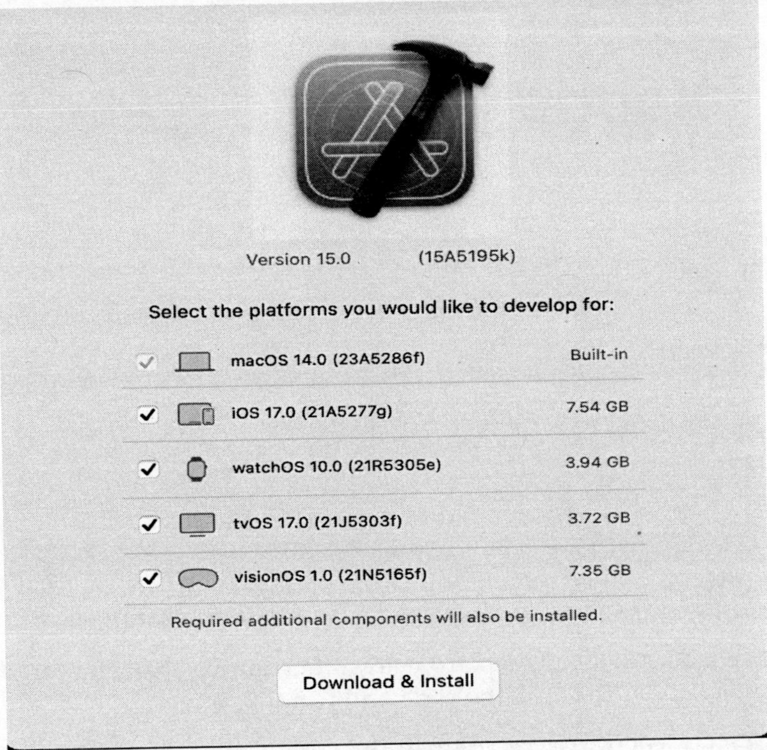

Figure 1.2*: Xcode Download SDKs*

3. Open Xcode from the App Store. This will install some supported SDK software components for some time, shown in *Figure 1.3* as follows:

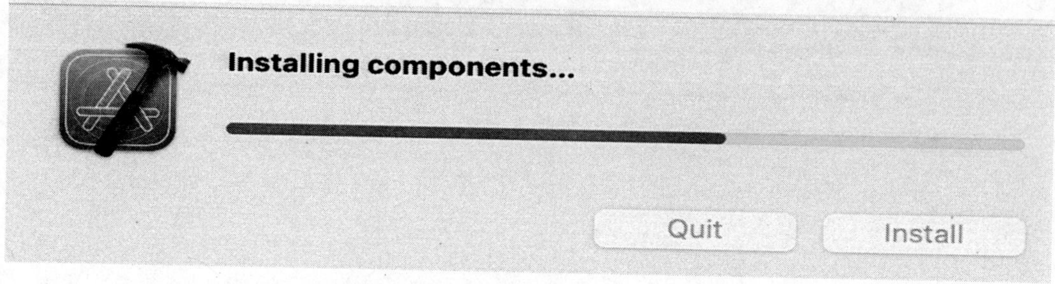

Figure 1.3: *Xcode Installing Components*

4. After installing all required components, Xcode will open with its **Welcome to Xcode** page which will have three options to start working on an iOS 16 Project, as shown in *Figure 1.4* as follows:

Figure 1.4: *Xcode Welcome Window*

No recent projects will be seen if you launch it for the first time. Click on **Create a new Xcode project** to set up a new project for iOS app development.

5. If you downloaded an iOS project from any other source, then you can select the option of **Open a project or file** to check the code and run that project.
6. When you create a new project, you will see a set of new options to choose from, shown in *Figure 1.5* as follows:

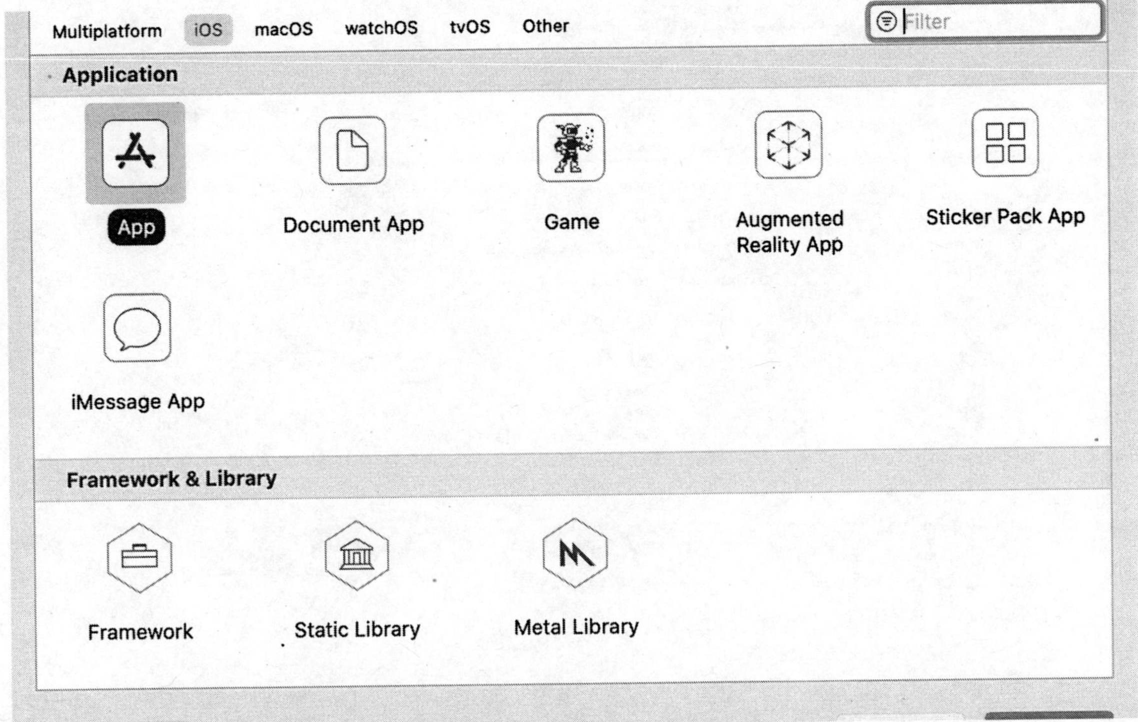

Figure 1.5: Select Application Platform

To make an app for iPhone and iPad, select the option as iOS. Similarly, select watchOS, tvOS MacOS, and multi-platform for iWatch, Apple TV, Mac apps, and hybrid apps, respectively. Then select App and click on **Next**.

7. The next screen will have some fields to fill out regarding the setting up of the project, such as product name, team name, organization name, organization identifier, language, and user interface. Let us understand what possible values these fields could have and how it would impact the project, that is going to be created, as follows:
    - **Product Name:** This will be the name of your app, which will be entered in the text field of the project name.
    - **Team:** Apple Developer account for the project. We will discuss this in detail in *Chapter 20: Publish Apps on the App Store*.
    - **Organization Name**: The name of your company that owns the development of this project. You can just put your name down for now while you learn.
    - **Organization Identifier**: This identifier is created with the conjunction of company name. For now, enter `com.organizationname`.
    - **Bundle Identifier**: This field is not allowed to be edited. It's automatically created by combining an organization name with an organization identifier. This identifier is used to uniquely identify the apps on the Apple App Store. Refer to *Figure 1.6* as follows:

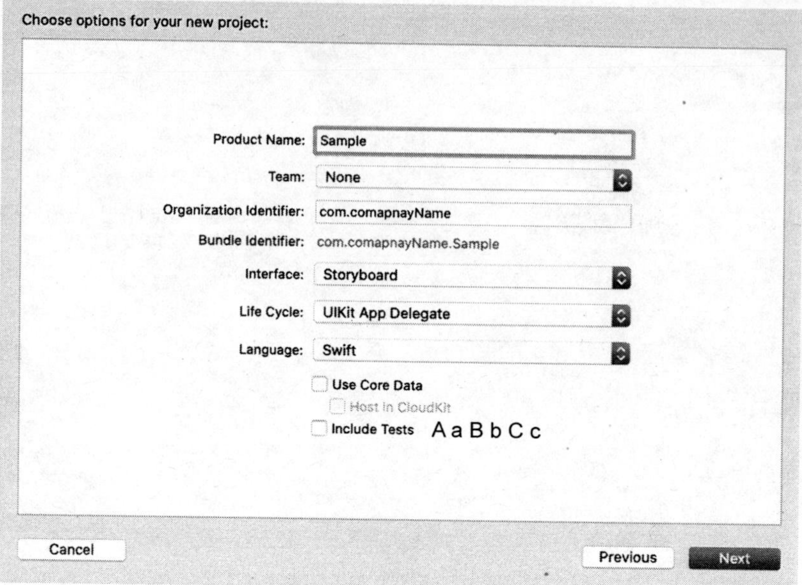

Figure 1.6: New iOS Project

- **Language**: This specifies the programming language to be used in app development. Select **Swift** from the drop-down field.
- **User Interface**: For now, set this to Storyboard. We will discuss another type of user interface selection, SwiftUI.
- **Life Cycle**: When you create a new SwiftUI Application in Xcode, you'll be given the option to choose between **SwiftUI App Lifecycle** and **UIKit App Delegate**. If the user interface is selected as a storyboard, it will be UIKit App Delegate by default.
- **Checkboxes**: These checkboxes are used to include the core data for the purposes of local database, unit tests, and UI unit test cases in the project. Keep them unchecked for now.

8. Choose the location where you want to save this project code on your Mac.

Xcode user interface

Before moving further towards app development, we first need to understand the navigation of Xcode, the tools, and the options used during the development of the iOS applications. Let's discuss the different sections of the Xcode Interface to understand clearly how we will use this IDE during app development, as follows:

- **ToolBar**: This toolbar on the top left side of Xcode is used to build, run, and view the execution progress of your app.
- **Windows pan bar**: This will help you configure the Xcode development environment.
  - **Object Library**: The addition or plus button will be used to add UI or object components to the project.

- o **Version Editor**: This will be used to check for differences of codes between two versions.
- o **Open and close buttons:** They will be used for Navigator, Debug, and Editor Area in Complete window pane.

- **Navigator area**: This provides quick access to all the parts of the project. The Navigation area is shown by default in the Xcode window.
- **Editor area**: The Editor area allows you to edit your code, user interface components, and resource files, if required in the project.
- **Inspector area**: This area will allow you to edit the information related to the items in the Navigator area and Editor area.
- **Debug area**: This area contains two portions – one for the view of variables and their values and another for the console.

Do not let all of the information about the parts and their relationships overwhelm you because we are trying to become familiar with Xcode's various components. We will study all these in detail and use each portion many times in the upcoming chapters.

Xcode search navigator

In the Project Navigator Area, when you click on the **Search** icon, it will open a search navigation bar where you can search for any text and see the results. The Xcode Editor Navigation area will show all the results of that project containing the text that was searched in the Xcode search navigation bar.

To use it via a shortcut, you can use the command *cmd + shift + F*, which will open the search navigation bar. These command operations would be helpful when you need to search multiple times and be quick. Refer to *Figure 1.7* as follows:

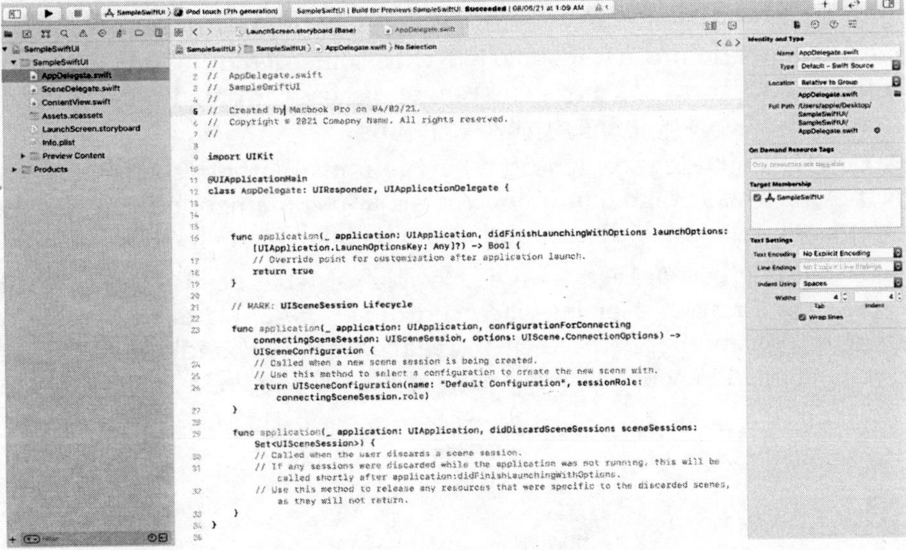

Figure 1.7: Application Development window

Xcode issue navigator

When there are some issues in the project while compiling and executing the app, the project navigation area shows warnings in the yellow symbolic icon and errors in red. A project can be built and run with warnings but not with errors. All errors need to be resolved to run a successful app.

Warnings could be potential issues in the further development of the apps, so we should not ignore the warnings that are listed down in the issue navigation. Similarly, not only in coding but also in the development of the user interface, warnings and errors could occur in the same issue of navigation.

Configuring Xcode project

The actual project configuration file is the main, or root, node of the project navigator, and it has a blue icon. In this section, all the fields are already filled with optional content, and you can also edit those fields if required to change any such configurations of the project. Let's look at what we can change here, as follows:

- You can set or change the name of the project.
- Bundle identifier-related information can be edited.
- You can allow and disallow multiple orientations of the screen for your app.
- Set the minimum iOS version below which your app can't be installed.
- If required, add additional Apple libraries and frameworks.
- App icon and launch image linkage options can be edited.

Default project setup

When you create an Xcode project, it's created with some default components from which you can start the development of your app. We will discuss the default files and components created by Xcode automatically in the project, as follows:

- **`AppDelegate`**: **`AppDelegate`** requires very minimal or no change, usually during development. This component initializes the app container and controls the lifecycle of the app, which we will discuss and use in detail in later chapters.
- **`SceneDelegate`**: **`SceneDelegate`** is responsible for what needs to be displayed on the app screen in terms of user interface and data. The app transfers some of the app handling responsibilities to the **`SceneDelegate`**. This will handle some of the app states that were handled in **`AppDelegate`** earlier in iOS 14, shown in *Figure 1.8* as follows:

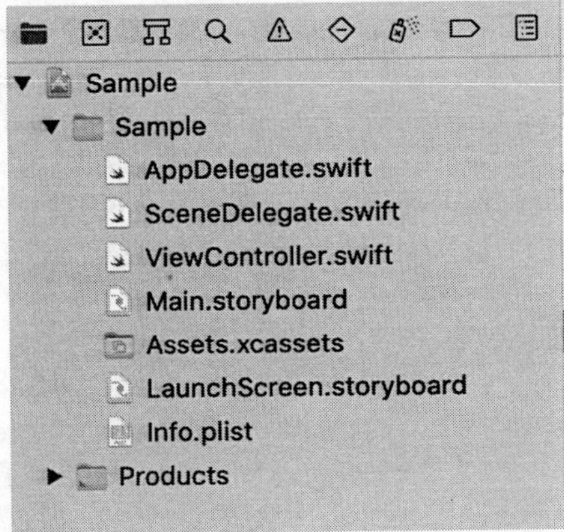

Figure 1.8: Application File Menu Window

- **`ViewController:`** Xcode created this as a default view controller. We can create a new controller if required, or we can use the default one too. The **`ViewController`** class is mainly responsible for the lifecycle and functions of that view.
- **`Main.storyboard:`** The main storyboard is used for the development of the user interface of the app, which we will discuss in detail in the User Interface section of this book.
- **`Assets:`** This component handles the images of different dimensions, such as 1x, 2x, and 3x. As we know, the same app will be run on different resolution Apple devices like the iPhone 15, iPhone 15 Plus, iPad mini, iPad Pro, and so on; therefore, we must give the respective resolution images in 2x and 3x forms, so that in any condition, the images and icons of the app do not get blurred.
- **`1x:`** It is the size (in terms of height and width) of the image component on the interface; so to get the 2x and 3x size information, we need to multiply it by 2 for 2x resolution and 3 for 3x resolution. Every item of a single image in the **`Assets`** component has three placeholders for the respective resolutions.
- **`Info.plist`**: A common property list that contains information about your project is **`Info.plist`**. Plist extension is used by Apple for file formats like XML type. We will discuss plist in *Chapter 12: File Handling in iOS*. Sometimes you need to add more information to this property list. For example, if your app wants to access a photo library, the app plist needs to contain a key which explains the reason for accessing the photo library.

Creating and adding new file

In the Project Navigator Area, when you right-click, a few options will be shown to you. To create the new code file in the project, you need to select the **Create New File** option, then a new option Pan will ask to choose the file type – as you know, we selected the Project language Swift, so you need to select Swift File type. Next, this will ask you to name the file and after naming it, this swift extension file will be added to your project.

If you want to add any existing file to your project, right-click on the project name and select the option of adding a **New File**. This will open a window for the selection of files from your Mac system. After the selection of a file, don't forget to select the copy option, because without the copy option, it will only create the reference of the file in your project, and when you change the location of the project in your Mac or any other Mac machines, that file will show as missing from the project as it never became a part of your project while adding.

Build Storyboard UI

After we created the new project, earlier in this chapter, and then selected the option of storyboard for the user interface, Xcode included the **`main.storyboard`** file. The main storyboard contains the UI screen for **`ViewController`** on which the user interface components, such as labels, buttons, and so on, will be placed to inspect or to change their properties as per requirements.

Assistant editor

To open Assistant Editor, go to the **Editor** menu and choose **Assistant**. The Assistant Editor view shows two pane views in the Xcode window in such a way that its storyboard screen and its relative view controller file can be seen together to edit or work on UI and its code efficiently. This editor will help connect the user interface elements from the storyboard view to the view controller code file, so that those elements can be manipulated via code at the time of execution as per the logic of code.

In Xcode 17, the assistant editor shows the build log timeline to help developers of iOS applications enhance the overall parallelism and identify runtime build performance issues.

Utility area

- **File Inspector** is located in the first tab of the Utility area, which shows details about the current highlighted file in the project navigation area. This contains information such as type of file and the physical location of file on the Mac machine, so that you can locate the path of the file.
- **Quick Help Inspector** is located in the second tab of the Utility area, which shows you the documentation about the method, class, and keyword that your typing cursor is currently on in the code file.
- **Attribute Inspector and Size Inspector** will only show as tabs in the Utility area when you select the user interface file's elements in the Storyboard. Using these two inspectors, you can change the properties and size of the selected element. We will further discuss these topics in detail in *Chapter 8: User Interface Design with UIKit*.

Xcode 15 multiplatform support

Applications that run on multiple platforms increase the functionality of your app to each additional platform you want to support. You can use a single, multiplatform target to share the project settings and code for your app across platforms in Xcode 15 or later.

In the case your app is already supporting the multiplatform approach and shares a good amount of code then you need to consider combining all multiple targets into a single target with the help of new settings of Xcode 15. Let us understand with an example - Use one multiplatform target if your current app uses SwiftUI and you also want to use SwiftUI for the new platform. Use different targets, however, if your current app uses UIKit and you want to use AppKit on the Mac app development. You will be able to support destination platform in app configurations as shown in below *Figure 1.9:*

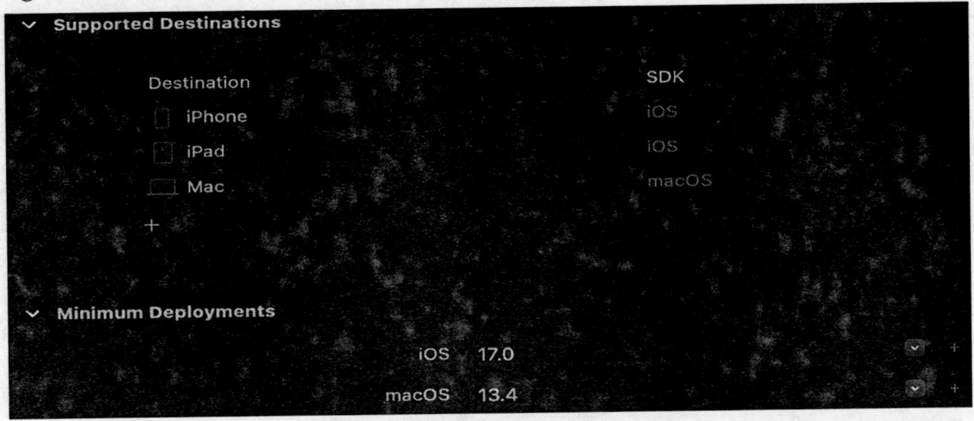

Figure 1.9: *Multiplatform support*

Another platform can help you find issues with your application's build-time. Add conditional statements around any code that makes use of platform-specific APIs or frameworks to address those problems. By including platform-specific views and features, you can make sure that the user interface and experience of your app meet the requirements of each platform. As shown in figure 1.8, a multiplatform app single target can share the code for iOS, iPadOS, tvOS, macOS but watchOS app will remain in separate target.

Adding Mac destination in multiplatform

In case if you want to add Mac OS application destination target, then you need to choose the destination type as per requirements and experience you want to give to end users. We have three options and each one of them have their own unique design characteristics and specifications.

Mac

In case you are going to start a new mac app then you will select this option while adding Mac in Supported Destinations. You may utilize all of the AppKit and SwiftUI-powered features and APIs from the macOS SDK. Multiplatform applications by default use this option.

Mac catalyst

In case you already have an iPad app, and you are bringing that to mac then select this option while adding Mac in Supported Destinations. The system modifies the way common UIKit interface components appear in your Mac application. To use Mac Catalyst, you might need to make layout adjustments in your application.

Designed for iPad

In case if you have an iPad app which you do not want to modify then select this option ton run on Mac computers with Apple silicon. The Mac version of your application keeps the common UIKit interface components in place. This option works as default Mac selection for iPad apps.

Common issues handled for multiplatform

When you are going to add another platform that can help you find problems with your application's build-time. Add conditional statements around any code that makes use of platform-specific APIs or frameworks to address those problems. The Code that makes use of platform-specific APIs or frameworks needs to be separated out. When you build your project, Xcode detects this type of build-time problem. Select the new run location for the platform you added in the scheme menu to test a build on that platform. If Xcode discovers any problems, go to each one individually and apply separate procedures to handle those cases.

Managing downloads in Xcode

In Xcode 15, Apple added a separate section to handle all downloads, Platform SDKs, and Plugins to support iOS app development. There are two types of downloads in Xcode 15:

- New platform download (if it's not installed already) 2
- New simulator downloads

Platform download

In general, there are two Platform SDKs that are part of the Xcode default environment. In case you are required to install watchOS 10.0, tvOS 17.0, and visionOS 1.0, install them from the **Xcode** menu | **Preferences** | **Platform**, shown in *Figure 1.10*, as follows:

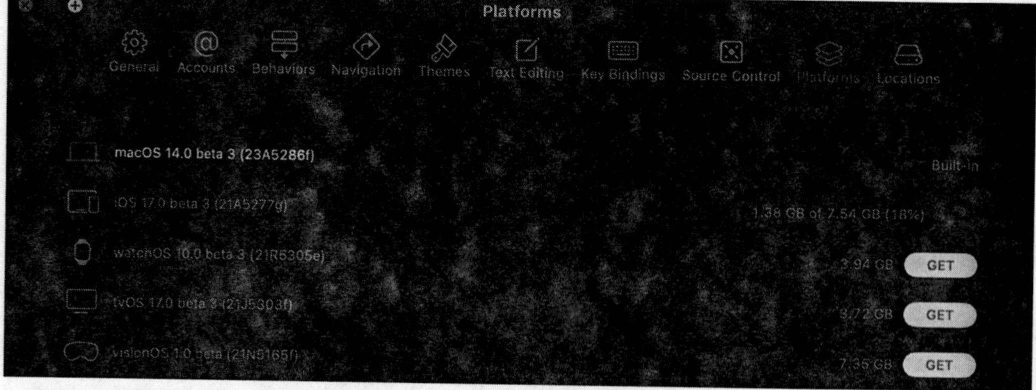

***Figure 1.10**: Platform Install Window*

The simulator runtimes for watchOS and tvOS are not included in Xcode versions 14 and later in order to reduce download size. To generate projects and run the simulator on those platforms, you require the most recent version of the simulator runtimes. When you initially start Xcode, or later from the Xcode run destination, from Xcode Preferences, or from the command line, you can download and install these files as shown in *Figure 1.11* as follows:

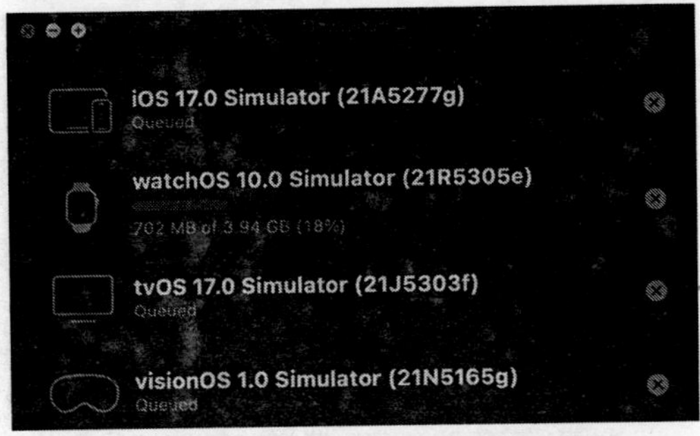

Figure 1.11*: Xcode Download Window*

Installing and managing simulator

You can select **Xcode | Preferences | Platforms** to view a list of simulator runtimes that are already on your Xcode system and those that you can download. Xcode displays the built-in simulator runtime that Xcode needs and the amount of storage you can reclaim if you uninstall a simulator runtime.

Select a simulator runtime, click the **Delete** button (-) in the lower left corner, and then click **Delete** in the confirmation window to free up storage space from unused simulator runtimes. Select the **Get** button on a simulator runtime to install the most recent version. To browse a list of available earlier versions for a platform, click the **Add** button (+) in the lower left corner and then choose a platform. After making your choice, click **Download and Install**. Projects can be built on older versions of the simulator runtime, but you must install the most recent one to run them:

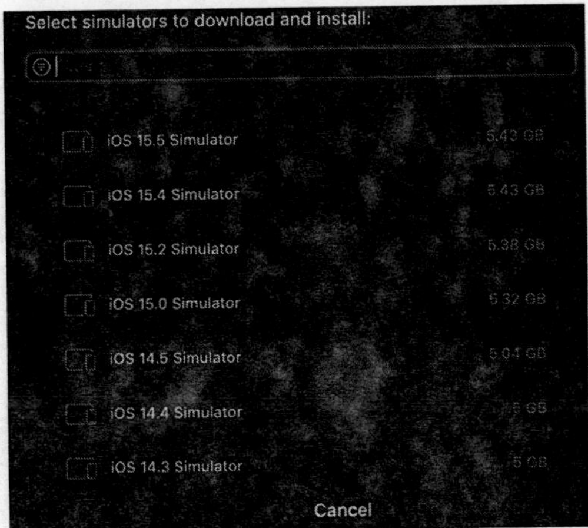

Figure 1.12*: Simulator Download*

Running and building Xcode iOS project

We already discussed some of the buttons at the beginning of this chapter. Now, we will see how these can be used to run and build your app or simulator. Before moving further, let's discuss simulators.

Simulator

In general, we can define a simulator as a machine designed to provide a realistic imitation of the controls and operations of complex systems. In our case, we are developing the apps that will run on the iPhone, iPad, and other Apple devices. It's good to have an Apple device to test, but it is not required to have one; instead, the Xcode toolset provides Simulators of all the Apple devices with Xcode, which we can choose while running your app and test the app in almost the same way as on the real device. Refer to *Figure 1.13* as follows:

***Figure 1.13**: iOS App in Simulator*

Limitations of simulator

There is a limitation to the simulator: it won't support the features which can be supported by mobiles, such as network calling, network messages, Bluetooth communication, and so on.

To run your app in the simulator, you need to complete the following steps:

1. Click on the **Scheme** menu in the upper toolbar of Xcode, and you will see the list of simulators. Choose the **iPhone 15** from the list of simulators.

2. Click on the **Run** button in the same toolbar to run your app in the currently selected simulator. You can also use the *command* + *R* shortcut on the keyboard for this same function.
3. If your **Developer Tool Access** dialog box appears, then you need to enter the username and password of the Mac machine admin account.
4. The simulator application will launch in some time, which will replicate the iPhone 15, and then your app will launch in that iPhone simulator.
5. To stop the running of the app again, switch back to Xcode and click on the Stop button in the toolbar to stop your currently running app.

Simulations in simulator

Rather than just running a simple app, you can simulate some other action in the simulator to check the impact of these actions on the real devices. These actions are given as follows:

- **Device rotation**: If you are developing your app for both portrait and landscape modes, then you need to check your app by switching to these two modes with the help of the device rotation feature on the simulator.
- **Simulating GPS**: From the menu in the **Debug** option, select **Location**. By choosing a custom location, you can set the latitude and longitude of any location to test the GPS features with the Simulator.
- **Device shake**: If you add an action that will happen only if the user of the app shakes the device, then you can test it by selecting the device shake option in the simulator, and your code will trigger those actions that are attached to the shaking of the phone.

Run app on device

If you have an Apple device such as iPhone, iPad, and so on, you can run the developed app from Xcode directly. The step-by-step guide is given as follows:

1. First plug the Apple device into the Mac machine via USB.
2. When you try to run the app after selecting a device in the menu, it will give you an `Error: "Signing for <App Name> requires a development team"`.
3. A valid Apple digital certificate is required to run the app on the Apple devices. You can use either the Apple ID or the Apple developer account to add a team in the section **Signing and Certificates** which will generate the digital certificates.
4. Login with your Apple ID which you used for the Xcode download as well.
5. You will see a dialog box asking to trust this computer on the phone; to continue, click on **Yes**.
6. Xcode will ask you to confirm if you want to use this device for development purposes; to continue, click on **Yes**.
7. Now, you will be able to see your device in the list of devices, above the simulator list.

Almost all the instructions in this book won't require you to have an Apple device to learn and practice iOS 17 app development with Swift. Not setting up a device with Xcode will not affect your learning path. If you are not able to set up your device with Xcode (which could have many reasons, such as an old device, not having an active Apple account, and so on; discussing all these cases here is out of the scope of this book), then please refer to the following Apple support link:

https://developer.apple.com/documentation/Xcode/running_your_app_in_the_simulator_or_on_a_device

Code with Xcode Playground

Playground in Xcode can be used to quickly write Swift code and experiment on that code to see the results without creating any new Xcode projects. It's not a full-fledged project and is not intended for complete app development; rather, it is to practice or experience the Swift code on it. Playgrounds are a great learning, teaching, and practice tool for beginners. Refer to *Figure 1.14* as follows:

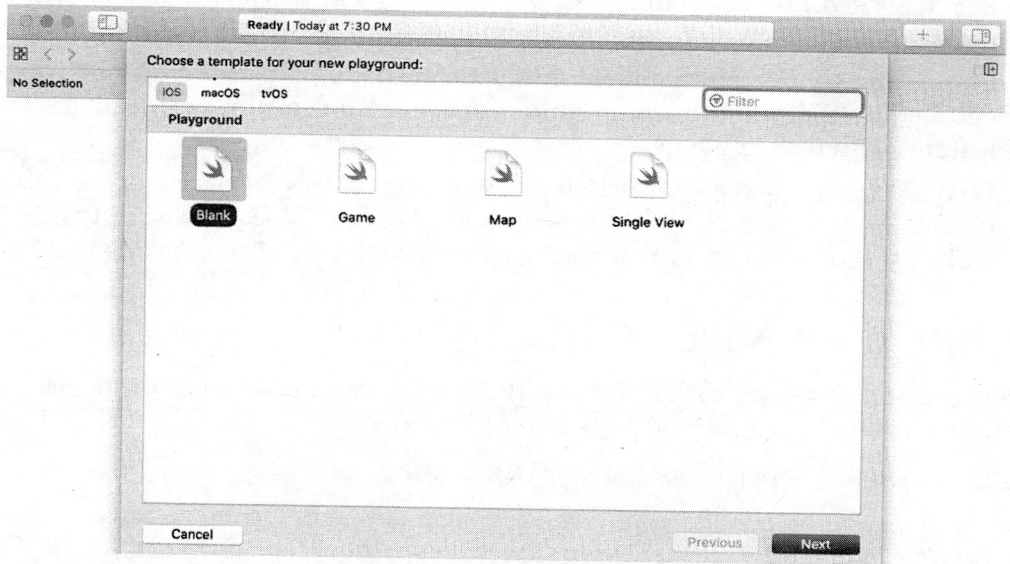

***Figure 1.14**: Choose Playground Template*

To create a new playground setup, go to **File | New**, and then select **Playground**. This will open up the setup of a playground for Swift coding. If you just started Xcode, then on the Xcode welcome page, you would find the option to get a **Playground**. Let's do a quick tour of the Playground functions in Xcode, as follows:

- **Editor**: At the top left of the **Playground** window, you can write the Swift code in the editor. This is an area where you will do most of the work as coding practice.
- **Console**: At the bottom left of the **Playground** window, you will see a console where you can see the output of your code. On the top of the console, there are two buttons from which you can close and open the console area.

- **Output**: When your code runs, you can see your intermediate results on the side output bar. These outputs are faster than the iOS project run results. You can also inspect the values of the variables in your code.
- **Status bar**: On top of the **Playground**, you can see a status bar that shows whether your code runs **OK** or if it might contain some errors.

Refer to *Figure 1.15* as follows:

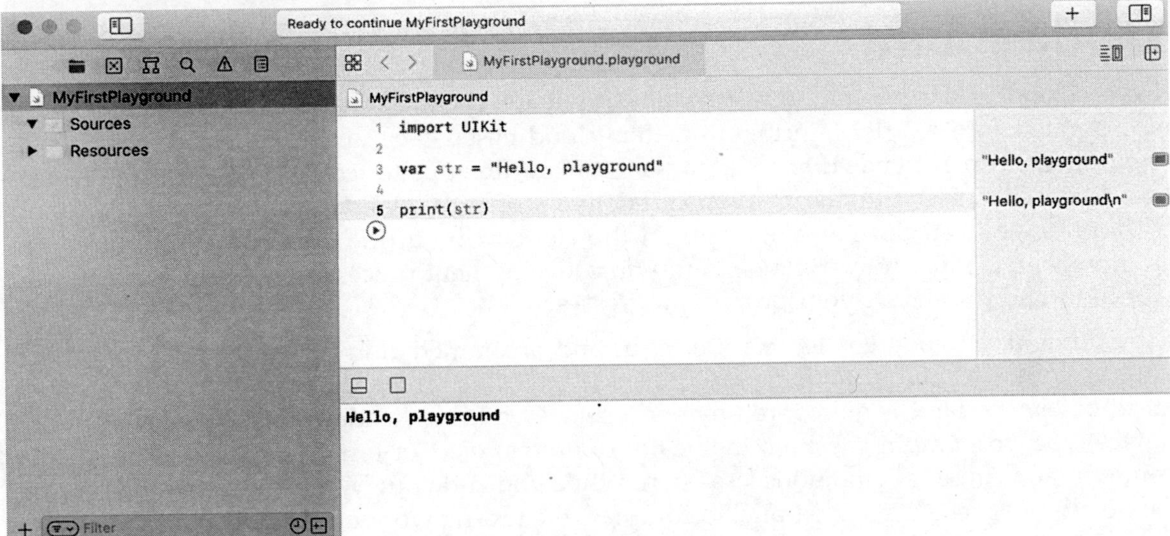

Figure 1.15: Playground Test

Now, run the Swift code in the editor. Click on the button **Run** at the bottom right of the playing area and wait for the execution to finish. Xcode will compile your code and show you the results. The default code doesn't return anything to the console, but you should be able to see the value of the variable on the sidebar to the right of Xcode.

Xcode Organizer

Xcode Organizer is a place that enables supportive components of Apple software development. There are mainly four components in Xcode Organizer, which are explained in detail as follows:

- **Archives**: The Archives section has a list of projects that you developed recently or in the past, and every project has Xcode build the archives with the file format `xcarchives`. From this `xcarchives` file, you can create a `.ipa` file, which is the final executable of the apps for the devices to run. (We will study about app distribution in detail in *Chapter 20: Publish Apps on the App Store*.)
- **Crashes**: Whenever there is any crash in your device for your app, you can just plug in your device via USB and see this section of crashes. This will give you a file that includes the crash's technical details, which will help you resolve the crash.

- **Energy**: When your app consumes 80% CPU energy for more than three minutes in the foreground mode of the app and one minute in the background mode of the app, then this section shows the energy logs.
- **Metrics**: When you release a build on the App Store, you can see the app metrics in this section. You need to sign in with the same Apple ID from which you uploaded the app to the App Store.

Xcode Cloud

Xcode Cloud is a continuous integration and delivery tool for Apple developers that is incorporated into Xcode. It brings together cloud-based technologies that let you design applications, run automated tests in parallel, distribute apps to testers, and see and manage user feedback to speed up the creation and delivery of high-quality apps. Using Xcode Cloud workflows, you can develop your app on the cloud without the need for a separate build environment. Configure workflows to fit your development process or start with the built-in workflow and tweak it as your process progresses.

Every committed code change can be built, and an immediate notification will be sent to your entire team if any problems are caused by the change, potentially saving days of lost effort before the fault is discovered by end users. Configure Xcode Cloud to test one or two device types for a rapid check on the health of your project or test a wider variety of device configurations for edge situations less often. While you and your Mac continue to code, Xcode Cloud allocates resources in parallel to complete the testing work quickly.

Automated building

When you are setting up an automated application, your approach can include running `XCTest` created unit tests as well as integration, performance, and user interface tests to locally check changes. Even though Xcode can speed up these processes, it still takes a lot of your time to complete them. This is particularly true for intricate frameworks or apps that support a variety of hardware and operating systems. However, you can create, run, and test your project on numerous emulated devices more quickly with Xcode Cloud than you can otherwise.

Continuous delivery

Although automatic building and testing are crucial for creating high-quality apps and frameworks, they cannot take the place of team members' and testers' hands-on testing. A new version of your app can be instantly delivered (CD) to internal testers using TestFlight when Xcode Cloud confirms a modification to your code (CI). For TestFlight external testing and submission for app review, Xcode Cloud can sign your program. The resulting app archive or framework can alternatively be uploaded to a server of your own.

Conclusion

In this chapter, you learned about downloading and installing the Apple Software Development **Integrated Development Environment (IDE)**, Xcode. Then you became familiar with the different parts of the Xcode user interface. Further, you created your first iOS app with Xcode and learned about it. Some of the key takeaways from this chapter are given as follows:

- While creating a new app, especially, when for the first time you are selecting the **Single View App** option, you can choose other options such as master-detail or tab, but it is better to embed these controllers in a single view app.
- Apple will initially provide a default file setup for the creation of new projects. You can select the Swift file to code in the editor area and the main storyboard file to design your app interface.
- We studied assistant editors, which can help you when you want to connect your code to the user interface components so that at run time, you can control the interface actions via code.
- We discussed the new multiplatform, single target support given in Xcode 15 to enable code sharing while developing apps for iOS, macOS, iPadOS, tvOS, and visionOS.
- While developing the user interface components, we used the utility area for file inspection as well as for changing the properties and size of the UI elements.
- We studied simulators and their use while testing your newly developed app.
- We played with the Xcode Playground for development and experimentation with coding in Swift.

Whatever we used in this chapter is just for introductory purposes and will be used again and again in the upcoming chapters in detail. For example, when we learn any new concept in Swift, we will experience our code on the playground rather than on the Xcode project, because initially it's not required. But when we come to the design section, we will start working on a full-fledged iOS project.

In the next chapter, we will start learning the Swift language, the core of all the new Apple Software development, and experience it on Xcode Playgrounds.

Multiple choice questions

1. **Xcode Playground is used for _______________.**
    a. Performance Analysis
    b. Swift Code Practice
    c. Command line tool
    d. App Building
2. **Which feature cannot we test on a Simulator?**
    a. Device Shake
    b. Device Rotation
    c. Network Phone Calling
    d. GPS Simulation

3. **Assets Components used to have ______________________.**
    a. Font files
    b. Large video files
    c. Swift files
    d. 1x, 2x, and 3x Image files
4. **Attribute Inspector is used by __________________.**
    a. To change the size of the UI element.
    b. To change the properties of the UI element.
    c. To inspect the file.
    d. To run the simulator.
5. **Archives is part of which section of Xcode?**
    a. Simulator
    b. Xcode Organizer
    c. Xcode Playground
    d. Xcode Navigator

Answers

1. b
2. c
3. d
4. b
5. b

Join our book's Discord space

Join the book's Discord Workspace for Latest updates, Offers, Tech happenings around the world, New Release and Sessions with the Authors:

https://discord.bpbonline.com

Chapter 2
Swift Fundamentals

Introduction

Swift is a fairly new programming language made by Apple. Most apps for iOS, macOS, watchOS, and tvOS are written in Swift. Apple has made Swift and its related resources available as an open-source project, which has helped the language's capabilities grow in big ways. As a result of the ongoing open-source developments, the Swift language continues to evolve and improve with each passing day.

Structure

In this chapter, we will cover the following topics:

- Swift features
- Types, constant and variable
- Swift operators
- String and characters
- Collection types
- Control flow
- Conditional statements
- Control Transfer Statements

- Functions
- Closures

Objectives

The chapter will teach you everything you need to know about how to use types, variables, and constants well in Swift. You will also gain a solid foundation in coding with Swift's conditional paradigm, and an in-depth knowledge of working with strings and characters. In addition, you will learn how to effectively utilize Collection Types, Functions, and Closures in your coding projects. By the end of this course, you will possess a strong skill set and a deep understanding of Swift programming that will enable you to tackle even the most complex coding challenges with confidence.

Swift features

Swift, like most other programming languages, uses variables to store and refer to values, while constant values are set once and stay the same. Additionally, Swift provides a mechanism for variables to be designated as optional, indicating the presence or absence of a value. This feature makes sure that accessing variables is safe because it makes it impossible to return a null value. This is a significant improvement over Objective C, which was plagued by the problem of null pointer exception and frequently caused code to crash when attempting to access a pointer with a null value.

Some of the features of modern language Swift includes are as follows:

- **Clean syntax**: Syntax of Swift makes code more readable and cleaner, which helps developers to program efficiently.
- **Type safe**: Swift is a type safe language which means the language itself is clear about types of values. Let us consider an example, if you require **`String`** type values, language will stop you from passing an int value.
- **Type inference**: When you do not specify the type of a value, Swift uses the Type inference to enable the compiler to detect the type of value by itself.

Types, constant and variable

In Swift, it is necessary to declare constants and variables before their use in the code structure. To this end, Apple has provided two keywords, one for each constant and variable. The **`let`** keyword is used for constants, while the **`var`** keyword is used for variables. By adhering to these conventions, developers can ensure that their code is structured effectively and operates smoothly. Let us have a look on code as follows:

```
let numberOfCounts = 10

var levelOfGame = 0
```

Let us understand the code variable **`numberOfCounts`** has assigned value as **`10`** with **`let`** keyword which means we want that value to be unchanged but **`levelOfGame`** has assigned value `0` with keyword **`var`**, which means that value could be changed during further code.

You can also declare comma separated variables or constants in single line:

```
var a = 90, b = 20, c = 178
```

NOTE: In Swift, it is recommended that stored values in code which will not change be declared as constants using the `let` keyword. Variables should only be used for storing values that are expected to change over time. Adhering to this convention helps ensure code clarity and maintainability by clearly indicating the intended use of each stored value.

You can declare variables and constants with type annotations to give more clarity about the type of values:

```
var apple, orange, grapes: String
apple = "Apple"
var cube, cone, rhombus: Double
cube = 3.4
```

As we can see in examples that we declared three variables with type of **`String`**, you can save string values to these variables. In the next code statements. variables of type **`Double`** declared where we assigned the double value **`3.4`** in one of the declared variables.

Swift 5.8 supports following basic type annotation:

- **Int Or UInt**: This can be used in the form of **`Int32`** and **`Int64`** more specifically for 32- and 64-bit signed Integers. For example, 67, -87.
- **Float**: This represents a 32-bit floating point number and holds only small decimal type values. For example: 9.3, 8.34.
- **Double**: Double is used to represent a 64-bit floating-point number and used when floating-point values must be very large. For example - 78.908, 98.23445.
- **Bool**: **`Bool`** type a Boolean value which is either true or false.
- **String**: String is an ordered collection of characters. For example, **`Hello World`**.
- **Character**: This is a single-character string literal. For example, **`T`**.
- **Tuples**: Tuples is used to group multiple values in a single Compound Value.

Swift operators

Operators are a set of special symbols that enable developers to manipulate and combine values in Swift. Generally, there are three types of operator terminologies in Swift, which we will discuss in further detail:

- **Unary**: Operators operate on a single target, apply prefix just before their target (**`-c`**) and postfix just after the target (**`x-`**).
- **Binary**: Operates on two targets and applied or infixed in between the target.
- **Tinary**: Operates on three targets. Swift only have single ternary conditional operator, such as (**`x ? y : z`**).

Assignment operator

Assignment operators serve the purpose of initializing and updating the value of one variable from another in Swift. For example, in the assignment expression **x = y**, the equal sign **=** serves as the assignment operator, initializing the value of **x** with the value of **y**. This operator plays a fundamental role in Swift programming, enabling developers to efficiently manage and manipulate values in their code:

```
let x = 90

var y = 20

y  = x
```

Arithmetic operator

Swift Supports four types of arithmetic operators for math number types:

- Addition (+)
- Subtraction (-)
- Multiplication (*)
- Division (/)

In Swift above operators perform their respective math in the programming language. Addition can be applied on the *String* type too.

```
var classString = "My" + "Class" // will print as My Class
```

Compound assignment operator

Compound assignment operator combines the assignment (=) with another type of operation such as addition assignment operator (+=):

```
var x = 5

x  += 3

// Now x value will become 8
```

Comparison operator

Swift language supports the following type of comparison operators:

- Equal to (**x == y**)
- Not equal to (**x != y**)
- Greater than (**x > y**)
- Less than (**x < y**)
- Greater than or equal to (**x >= y**)
- Less than or equal to (**x <= y**)

```
let x = "Class"
        if x == "Class" {
            print("My Class")
        } else {
            print("I'm sorry \(x), but I don't recognize you")
        }
        // Prints "My Class", because the name is indeed equal to "Class".
```

You can also compare two tuples if they have the same type. Tuples are formed in **(1, j)** manner where **i** and **j** are values which could have different types from each other. Let us look into this with code example:

```
(3, "Bird")  < (9, "Animal")
// return TRUE only first element of tuples matched with
// operator less than so Bird and Animal are not checked
(6, "Turtle") == (6, "Turtle")
// return TRUE for the first and second element too.
```

Ternary conditional operator

The ternary conditional operator is a type of operator in Swift that consists of three parts, resembling a query with two possible answers. The syntax of this operator is as follows: **query ? answer1 : answer2**. In this case, if the query evaluates to true, the operator returns **answer1**; otherwise, it returns **answer2**. This operator is particularly useful in streamlining code and reducing the need for small **if-else** structures:

```
heightCell1 = 50
heightOtherCell = 30
var height = cellIndix == 0 ? heightCell1 : heightOtherCell
```

In the above example we want to set height different for cell index **0** and different height for others. If we try to write this code with **if…else** then it will look like this:

```
heightCell1 = 50
heightOtherCell = 30
var height = 0
if (cellIndix == 0)
{
    height = heightCell1
}
```

```
else
{
    height = heightOtherCell
}
```

The ternary conditional operator has the advantage of simplifying code and making it more readable. However, it is important to exercise caution when using this operator, as overuse in a single sentence or line of code can lead to reduced code readability and comprehension. It is therefore recommended that developers use the ternary operator judiciously and appropriately, striking a balance between code conciseness and clarity.

Nil-coalescing operator

To avoid program crashes caused by the presence of nil values, Swift features the nil-coalescing operator, which can be used in conjunction with optional values. The operator, represented as `x ?? y`, is designed to simplify the syntax of the ternary operation by handling nil values more effectively. This operator is a useful tool for Swift developers seeking to streamline their codes and ensure that their programs execute smoothly and reliably.

```
x  !=  nil ? x! : y
```

The nil-coalescing operator is a valuable tool for Swift developers, as it simplifies the process of checking for the presence of nil values in a variable. This operator is used to evaluate the value of `x` and determine whether or not it is `nil`. If `x` has a value, the operator unwraps the optional value and returns it. If `x` is nil, the operator returns the value of `y`. By using the nil-coalescing operator, represented as `x ?? y`, developers can write more concise and readable codes, as demonstrated by the given example code:

```
var safeValue = x ?? y
```

NOTE: If the value of `x` is non-nil, the value of `y` is not evaluated. This is called a short-circuit evaluation.

Range operator

Swift uses several types of range operators, which are shortcuts for expressing a range of values.

Closed range operator

Closed range operators in Swift are defined using the syntax (`x...y`) and define a range that includes all values between `x` and `y`, inclusive. It is important to note that the value of `x` must be greater than or equal to `y` for the closed range operator to work correctly. One of the primary use cases of the closed range operator is for iterating over all the values within the specified range. It provides a convenient shorthand for writing loops that need to iterate over a range of values:

```
for index in 1...3 {
    print("\(index) times 3 is \(index * 3)")
}
// 1 times 3 is 3
// 2 times 3 is 6
// 3 times 3 is 9
```

Half open range operator

The half range operator (**x..< y**) defines a range that runs from **x** to **y**, but unlike the closed range operator, the value of **y** is excluded from the range. If the value of **x** is equal to **y**, the resulting range will be empty. When working with zero-based lists, the half-open range operator is especially useful because it lets you go through all the elements without including the last one in the loop:

```
let names = ["Ram", "Ajay", "Vijay", "Rubi"]
let countNumber = names.count
for i in 0..< countNumber {
    print("Person \(i + 1) is called \(names[i])")
}
// Person 1 is called Ram
// Person 2 is called Ajay
// Person 3 is called Vijay
// Person 4 is called Rubi
```

One-sided ranges

One of the variations of the closed range operator found in Swift is one in which the range extends in just one direction. For example, a range that contains all of the items in an array falls under this category. In circumstances like this, the value on one side of the range operator might be omitted from the expression. It is referred to as a one-sided range because the range only has a value on one side of the operator. This sort of range is called a **one-sided range**:

```
for name in names[2...] {
    print(name)
}
// Vijay
// Rubi
for name in names[...2] {
```

```
    print(name)
}
// Ram
// Ajay
// Vijay
```

The half-open range operator also has a one-sided form that uses only the final value to show what it means. Furthermore, when including a value on both sides, the final value is not considered part of the range.

Logical operator

Logical operators modify or combine Boolean logic values (**`true`** and **`false`**). The language supports three logical operators:

- Logical NOT (**`!x`**)
- Logical AND (**`x && y`**)
- Logical OR (**`x || y`**)

Logical NOT operator

The logical **`Not`** operator inverts the Boolean value. If the value is true after applying this operator, then true will become false and false will become true. This **`NOT`** operator is a prefix operator and appears just before the value, on which it is required to apply. It can be read as **`Not x`**:

```
let gateEntry = false
if !gateEntry {
    print("No Access")
}
// No Access
```

Logical AND operator

For an expression to be evaluated as true, both of its values need to be accurate in order to employ the logical **`AND`** operator (**`x && y`**), which is used to generate the expression. If one of the values being evaluated is not true, then the whole phrase is evaluated as having the value false. It is important to keep in mind that if the first value is untrue, there is no use in attempting to determine the truth of the second value since the whole expression would be invalid in that case:

```
let enterCodeToUnlock = true
let fingerPrintToMatch = false
```

```
if enterCodeToUnlock && fingerPrintToMatch {
    print("Welcome To Office")
} else {
    print("NO ACCESS")
}
// Prints - NO ACCESS
```

Logical OR operator

The logical **OR** operator (**x || y**) is an infix operator that allows you to create logical expressions where only one of the two values needs to be true for the entire expression to evaluate as true. Logical **OR** operators employ short-circuit evaluation for expressions. If the left side of a logical **OR** expression is true, the right side is not evaluated, as it cannot alter the overall outcome of the expression.

```
let haveOfficeKey = false
let knowDigitalDoorPassword = true
if hasDoorKey || knowsOverridePassword {
    print("Welcome To Office")
} else {
    print("NO ACCESS")
}
// Output - Welcome To Office
```

Combining logical operators

Longer compound expressions can be formed by combining multiple logical operators:

```
if enterCodeToUnlock && fingerPrintToMatch || haveOfficeKey || knowDigitalDoorPassword
{
    print("Welcome To Office!")
} else {
    print("NO ACCESS")
}
 Output - Welcome To Office!
```

In the above example, multiple operators are used to form a compound expression. But it is important to remember that both operators only work on two values, so the result is a chain of smaller expressions put together. For example, we can get into the office if we enter the correct door code and our fingerprints match, or if we have an office key or know the digital password. If not, we cannot get in.

NOTE: In Swift, the logical AND operator (&&) and the logical OR operator (||) are left-associative. This means that when there are multiple logical operators in an expression, the leftmost subexpression is evaluated first.

Strings and characters

When working with user input or formatting a language, you may need to work with strings and do operations on them to get the result you want. Swift has many ways to work with strings, such as character operations, which allow for more advanced string handling. In the following discussion, we will delve into detail on how to perform these string operations in the Swift language.

String literals

String literals are used to include a set of characters in the code, for this you can pass this set in the form of the sentence, words or just a list of some characters in double quotation marks ("). Let us see the example:

```
let makeSenetence = "This is an example sentence."
```

Similarly, multi-line string quotation can be used but that would have a little different syntax to use in Swift. The string begins on the first line after the opening quotation marks """ and ends on the line before the closing quotation marks:

```
let makeSenetence = """This is an example sentence.
As well as multiline example for string lateral
"""
```

Special characters

String literals use the below table of special characters:

`\0`	null character
`\\`	backslash
`\t`	horizontal tab
`\n`	line feed
`\r`	carriage return
`\"`	double quotation mark
`\'`	single quotation mark
`\u{n}`	Unicode char

***Table 2.1:** Special characters*

Empty strings

In Swift, you can easily create an empty string by assigning an empty string literal ("" in double quotes) to a variable or by using the appropriate initializer syntax to create a new String instance with no value. This is extremely useful when you need to represent a blank or empty value in a string:

```
var empty = "" // Empty String
var initEmpty = String() // initialize String
```

String mutability

The approach of string mutability in Swift is different from Objective C. In objective C **NSString** and **NSMutableString** are used for mutable and non-mutable string types respectively. But Swift *String* can be modified by assigning to a variable when you want to modify and constant when you do not want to modify.

```
var mutableString = "This String is"
mutableString += "Mutable"
// mutableString Prints "This String is Mutable"
let immutableString = "This String is not"
immutableString += "Mutable"
// this reports a compile time error
```

Characters

You can get individual character values for a **String** by iterating in the loop over the string with a **for-in** loop or while:

```
for character in "CHARACTER" {
    print(character)
}
// Will print every character of string "CHARACTER"
```

Similar to **String** type you can initialize a character by providing it to a **Character** type annotation.

```
let questionMark : Character = "?"
```

Concatenated strings and characters

You can concatenate string values using the addition operator (+), just like how we use it with numbers in arithmetic operations. It is a handy feature that allows you to join different string literals or string values together to create a new combined string. So, you can apply the addition operator to strings, just like we learned about in the *Arithmetic operator* section:

```
let string1 = "Hello"
let string2 = " World"
var firstLine = string1 + string2
// firstLine will print "Hello World"
```

You can append a character to a string variable as with method **`append()`**:

```
var question = "What is the capital of India "
let questionMark : Character = "?"
question.append(questionMark)
// question print as "What is the capital of India ?"
```

String interpolation

String interpolation is a way to make a new string in Swift by combining variables, constant literals, and expressions into a single string literal. Each item that is incorporated into the string literal is enclosed in parentheses, preceded by a **`backslash ()`**. This facilitates the dynamic and versatile generation of strings, with values that are assessed and inserted during runtime:

```
let addition = 3
let sentence = "\(addition) plus 10 is \(addition + 10)"
// sentence is "3 plus 10 is 13"
```

Collection types

In Swift, there are primary collection types that can hold collections of data, namely Array, Set, and Dictionary, for storing values. These collection types are implemented as generics, allowing for flexible and type-safe collections. Generics will be covered in detail in later chapters, providing a deeper understanding of their usage and benefits in Swift programming.

Mutability of collections

In Swift, it is generally a good idea to make Arrays, Sets, and Dictionaries into immutable collections whenever possible. By using immutable collections, you can improve the performance of your collections and make sure they use memory and run more efficiently and predictably.

Arrays

An array represents and maintains values of the same kind as an ordered list in which the same item may appear several times. In Swift, the syntax for an array is **`ArrayElement>`**, where **`Element`** is the type of the array list. Array initializer may construct an empty array list of a certain kind:

```
var listOfString = [String]()
var listOfInt   = [Int]()
```

The method **count()** on array variables gives you a count of items in the list so you can check if there are any modifications and changes in the array.

```
let countList = "\(listOfString.count) string items"
// countList prints 0 items
```

When you to initialize array and not sure of the type of array list you can simply create it by blank list without type information provided:

```
var array = []
```

Method of **append()** is used to add a data value to array list :

```
listOfInt.append(5)
listOfInt.append(9)
print("\(listOfString.count) string items") \\ ountList prints 2 items
print(listOfInt) \\ [5, 9]
```

The **remove(at:)** method is used to delete or remove using the index of a data value item from an array list. This operation on arrays decreases the count and removes items permanently:

```
listOfInt.remove(at: 1) // [5]
```

Deleting an element based on specific search or condition can be applied through closures with **removeAll { where:}**:

```
var numbers = [2, 3, 4, 8, 2, 7, 3, 2]
numbers.removeAll {$0 == 2} \\ [3, 4, 8, 7, 3]
```

Similarly, to remove all methods, **filter()** method works the difference is it will return a modified array after filter operation.

```
Numbers.filter { $0 != 3 } \\ [4, 8, 7]
```

Sets

A set stores distinct values which are of the same type of collection with no ordering. You can use set instead of Array if you want distinct values in the collection. The type of set values must be hashable in order to be stored in a set. All of Swift's basic types such as **String**, **Int**, **Double** and **Bool** are hashable by default. The syntax of set in Swift is written as **Set<Element>**, where **Element** is the type of elements that is allowed to store:

```
var characters = Set<Character>()
characters.insert("c")
characters.count()        // Prints - 1
```

```
characters = []
characters.count()          // Prints - 0
```

In the above example, we created a variable with a set of characters and inserted a new character in the set. A set type cannot be inferred from an array literal, so in such cases the type **Set** must be explicitly declared. Although, because of Swift's type inference, you do not have to write the type of the set's elements if you are initializing it with an array literal.

Swift gives you access to a set's methods and properties, which you can use to change it. To check, is set empty or not, **isEmpty** can be used to check. Similarly, **remove** can be used to remove value in a **set** and **contains** can be used to check the existence of value in a set.

```
characters.isEmpty  // returns true or false depending on the set Elements.
characters.remove("c") // remove an element
characters.contains("c") // to check if set contains a value
```

Dictionaries

In Swift, a Dictionary stores associations between keys of the same type and values of the same type in a collection with no defined ordering. A dictionary key can be either int or string, but it should be unique within the dictionary.

Syntax of Swift dictionary is written in full as **Dictionary<Key, Value>** where **Key** is the type of value that is used as a dictionary key and **Value** is the type of value that is used to store the values in a dictionary. As with arrays, you can create an empty dictionary of a certain type by below syntax:

```
var friendsName = [Int: String]()
```

You can also initialize a dictionary with its literal, which has a similar syntax to the array literals. A key-value pair is a combination of a key and a value, the key and value in each value pair are separated by a colon. The key-value pairs are written as a list, separated by commas, surrounded by a pair of square brackets:

```
[<key 1>: <value 1>, <key 2>: <value 2>, <key 3>: <value 3>]
var roads: [String: String] = ["ABC": "Grand Trunk Road", "BCE": "Delhi"]
```

This dictionary literal contains two String: **String** pairs. This key value type matches the type of the **roads** variable. You can also access and modify a dictionary via its methods and properties. Similar to array, you can find out the number of items in a **Dictionary** by checking its **count** property:

```
print(roads.count)  // prints - 2
```

You can also add a new key-value pair item to a dictionary with subscript syntax. For this you can use a new key of the correct type and assign a new value.

```
roads ["PVC"] = "MJ Road"
print(roads.count)  // Now prints - 3
```

You can also iterate over the key-value pairs in the dictionary with a for-in loop. Each item in the dictionary is returned as a (key, value) tuple, and you can decompose the tuple into constants and variables.

```
for (roadsCode, roadsName) in roads {
    print("\(roadsCode): \(roadsName))
}
// "ABC": "Grand Trunk Road"
// "BCE": "Delhi"
```

Control flow

Swift language encompasses various types of control flow statements that can be employed for either iteration or transfer of code control. For-in loop and while loop facilitate repetitive execution of operations with varying data. Also, control flow statements like if-guard and switch are used to run different branches of code based on certain conditions. break and continue are used to move the flow of execution to different points in the code.

For-in loops

You can use the **for-in** loop to iterate over a sequence, like items of the array, some range of number or list of characters in string sentences. The following example code will iterate the list of the array:

```
let names = ["Ram", "Shaym", "Ajay", "Sunita"]
for name in names {
    print("Hey, \(name)!")
}
// Hello, Ram!
// Hello, Shaym!
// Hello, Ajay!
// Hello, Sunita!
```

You can use **for-in** with numerical range. The following example will do this iteration to explain further:

```
for index in 1...4 {
    print("\(index) times 4 is \(index * 4)")
}
// 1 times 4 is 4
```

```
// 2 times 4 is 8
// 3 times 5 is 12
// 4 times 5 is 16
```

The above sequence iterated over a range of numbers from `1...4`, with the use of a closed range operator (`...`) The value of index sets the first number as (`1`) and then statements in the loop start execution. In this case, we have only one statement inside the loop to be executed.

While loops

The **`while`** loop is a control flow construct in Swift that executes a set of statements as long as a given condition remains true. This type of loop is particularly useful when the exact number of iterations cannot be determined before the first iteration commences. Swift provides two kinds of loops:

- While evaluating its condition at the start of each pass through the loop.
- Repeat while evaluating its condition at the end of each pass through the loop.

While

The **`while`** loop starts by evaluating a single condition. If the condition is **`true`**, a set of statements under the loop will execute until the condition becomes **`false`**:

Here is the basic form of **`while`** loop:

```
while <condition> {
    <statements>
}
```

Repeat - While

The other variation of the **`while`** loop, the **`repeat…while`** loop, performs a single pass through the loop block first, before considering the loop conditions. Then it continues the loop until the condition is false.

Here is the basic form of **`repeat…while`** loop:

```
repeat {
    <statements>
} while <condition>
```

NOTE: The `repeat…while` loop in Swift is a control flow construct that shares similarities with a `do…while` loop found in other programming languages.

Conditional statements

In certain cases, it may be necessary to incorporate conditional logic in your code. In Swift, there are two ways to implement conditional code branches - through if statements and switch statements. If the code structure is complex and entails multiple possible outcomes, where pattern matching is required to determine which set of instructions should be executed, switch statements are often preferred.

If...else

The **`if`** statements have only a single **`if`** condition and it executes a single or multiple set of program statements only if that condition is true.

```
var bookprice = 400
if bookprice < 450 {
    print("I can buy this book.")
}
// prints - I can buy this book.
```

In the example above, we are checking if the price of a book is less than **`450`**, and if it is, we print a statement about the buying decision. However, if the book price is greater than **`450`**, no message will be printed based on the given code block.

The **`if`** statements in Swift also provide an alternative way to handle cases when the condition is false, which is called the **`else`** clause. You can use the **`else`** keyword to indicate the statements that should be executed in such cases.

```
var bookprice = 500
if bookprice < 450 {
    print("I can buy this book.")
}
else {
    print("I cannot buy this book.")
}
// prints else clause - I cannot buy this book.
```

In such a case one of the two branches of code will execute for sure. You can chain multiple **`if...else`** clause statements to form more complex code execution decision branching:

```
var bookprice = 245
if bookprice > 450 {
    print("I cannot buy this book.")
}
```

```
else if bookprice < 250 {
    print("It's too cheap, I can easily buy this book.")
}
else {
    print("It's in my budget, I can buy this book.")
}
// prints - It's too cheap, I can easily buy this book.
```

The final else in this example can be optional and excluded if there is no need for it.

Switch

The **switch** statements in Swift involve the consideration of a value to be compared against multiple matching patterns. When a match is found, the corresponding block of code is executed based on the matched expression. Switch statements offer an alternative to complex **else...if** structures when dealing with multiple potential states.

The simplest form of a switch structure in Swift involves the comparison of a value against one or more values of the same type:

```
switch <some value to consider> {
    case <value 1>:
        <respond to value 1>
    case <value 2>,
         <value 3>:
        <respond to value 2 or 3>
    default:
        <otherwise, do something else>
}
```

In such cases, every **switch** statement consists of multiple possible cases and each of which starts with a **case** keyword.

Control transfer statements

Control transfer statements in Swift facilitate the alteration of the order of code execution by transferring control from one segment of code to another. The Swift language encompasses five control transfer statements for this purpose:

- Continue
- Break
- Fallthrough

- Return
- Throw

We will **study, continue, break** and **fallthrough** in this section, the return statements in the next section of this chapter - *Functions and the throw-in error handling* section of further chapters.

Continue

The **continue** statement in Swift is used to instruct a loop to immediately move on to the next iteration, bypassing any remaining statements within the current iteration. This can be useful when you want to skip certain characters or elements within a loop and continue with the next iteration. The following example illustrates the usage of continue in skipping specific characters from an English statement:

```
let inputStatement = "Welcome to this University !"

var outputStatement = ""

let characterRemove: [Character] = ["a", "e", "i", "o", "u", " "]

for character in inputStatement {

    if characterRemove.contains(character) {

        continue

    }

    outputStatement.append(character)

}
print(outputStatement)
// Prints "WlcmtthsUnvrsty!"
```

The provided code in the example includes the use of the **continue** keyword, which is employed when a match is found with a vowel or space character. This results in the immediate termination of the current iteration of the loop, and the control is transferred to the beginning of the next iteration, skipping any remaining statements within the current iteration.

Break

The **break** statement in Swift is utilized to prematurely terminate the execution of an entire control flow statement. It can be used within a switch or a loop when it is necessary to abruptly end the ongoing execution. If used within a loop, the break statement will halt the execution of the loop entirely, and the control flow of the program will exit from the loop.

Fallthrough

In Swift, switch statements do not fall through to the bottom of each case, meaning that the execution of the entire switch case is completed when the first matching case is encountered.

Therefore, it is not necessary to explicitly include a break statement at the end of each case block. However, if you want to enable the flow of execution to continue into the next case block without terminating, you can use the **fallthrough** keyword. The following example demonstrates the use of **fallthrough** to create a statement:

```
let integerToCheck = 5

var sentence = "The number \(integerToCheck) is"

switch integerToDescribe {

    case 2, 3, 5, 7:

        sentence += " a prime number, and also"

        fallthrough

    default:

        sentence += " an integer"

}

print(sentence)

// Prints - The number 5 is a prime number, and also an integer
```

Early exit

In Swift, **guard** statements are similar to **if** statements in that they execute based on the Boolean value of an expression. However, unlike **if** statements, **guard** statements always include an **else** clause. The **else** clause is used to specify the code that should be executed if the condition of the **guard** statement is not met:

```
var number = - 2

guard number >= 0 else {

    return nil

}

// code block will return nil
```

Functions

In Swift, functions are encapsulated blocks of code that are defined by a specific function name. These functions can be called by their name to perform specific tasks and may return a value during the execution of the program code.

Each function in Swift has a type, which includes the parameter types and return type of the function. Function types can be passed as parameters to other functions and functions can also return other functions. Additionally, functions can be written within other functions, allowing for encapsulation of functionality within a nested function scope.

Defining and calling functions

Each function in Swift is defined by a unique function name that reflects the task it performs. You can invoke a function by its name and provide input values, known as **arguments**, which must match the type of the function's parameters as specified in its definition:

```
func meetToFriends(friendName: String) -> String {
    let meetMessage = "Hey, " + friendName + "!"
    return meetMessage
}
```

The block of code that begins with the keyword **func** and contains the function name, parameters, return type, and function body is known as the **function definition**. The return value of the function is specified using the **return** keyword followed by the desired return value, and the return type is indicated by an arrow **->** followed by the type. The function definition provides a detailed description of the tasks performed by the function.

```
print(meetToFriends(friendName:"Ashok"))
    // Prints - Hey, Ashok!
print(meetToFriends(friendName:"Mohan"))
    // Prints - Hey, Mohan!
```

Parameters and return values

Function parameters in Swift are highly flexible and versatile. You can define simple string parameters or complex functions with expressive parameter names and various parameter options. Functions can have zero parameters or multiple parameters, which are enclosed in a single set of parentheses and separated by commas, as demonstrated in the following example:

```
func meetToFriends(friendName: String, isGreeted: Bool) -> String {
    if isGreeted {
        return meetAgain(friendName: person)
    } else {
        return meetToFriends(friendName: person)
    }
}
print(meetToFriends(friendName: "Ram", isGreeted: true))
    // Prints - Hello again, Ram!
```

Nested functions

All the functions discussed so far are examples of global functions, which are defined at the global scope in Swift. However, you can also define functions inside the bodies of other functions, known as **nested functions**. Nested functions are by default hidden from the outside world, but they can be accessed and used by their enclosing function. In addition, an enclosing function can also return one of its nested functions to be used in another scope of the program. The basic structure or syntax of a nested function is shown below:

```
func funcname() {
    //statements of outer function
    func anotherFuncname() {
        //statements of inner function
    }
}
```

Variadic function

In Swift, a *variadic function* is a function that can accept a variable number of arguments of any type. It uses the ellipsis (`...`) notation in the function parameter list to indicate that it can accept multiple values.

Here is an example of a variadic function in Swift:

```
func printSum(_ numbers: Double...) {
    var sum: Double = 0
    for number in numbers {
        sum += number
    }
    print("Sum: \(sum)")
}
printSum(1.0, 2.0, 3.0) // Sum: 6.0
printSum(10.5, 20.25, 30.75, 40.1) // Sum: 101.6
```

In the preceding example, the **`printSum`** function accepts a variable number of **`Double`** values. The function body calculates the sum of all the numbers passed as arguments and prints the result.

Variadic functions are useful when you need to accept an unknown number of arguments or when the number of arguments may vary at runtime. They provide flexibility and convenience in certain situations where the number of arguments is not fixed. However, it is important to note that variadic functions should be used judiciously, as they can make code harder to read and maintain if used excessively.

Closures

Closures in Swift are self-contained blocks of code or programs that can be passed as arguments and used in your code. Closures have the ability to capture and retain references to constants and variables from the context in which they are defined. Swift takes care of all memory management tasks related to capturing contexts, ensuring proper handling of memory references.

Global and nested functions are special cases of closures. Closures usually take one of three forms:

- Global functions are closures that have a name but do not capture a value.
- Nested functions are closures that have a name and can capture values for their enclosing function.
- Closure expressions are unnamed closures written in a lightweight syntax that can capture values from their surrounding context.

Closures syntax optimizations include:

- Inferring parameter and return value types from context
- Implicit returns from single expression closures.
- Shorthand arguments name
- Trailing closures syntax

Closure expression

Closure expressions in Swift provide a concise and focused syntax for writing inline closures. They offer syntax optimizations for shorthand without sacrificing clarity. The following examples demonstrate the use of closure expressions with the **sorted(by:)** method to sort an array of **String** values in reverse alphabetical order:

```
let friendsName = ["Suraj", "Vijay", "Pratibha", "Nirav", "Vishal"]
```

Here, one way to provide the sorting closure is to write a normal function of the correct type and pass it in as an argument to the sorted(by:) method:

```
func back(_ s1: String, _ s2: String) -> Bool {
    return s1 > s2
}
var reverseNames = friendsName.sorted(by: back)
// reverseNames - ["Vishal", "Vijay", "Suraj", "Pratibha", "Nirav"]
```

Closures expression syntax is given below:

```
{ (parameters) -> return type in
    statements
}
```

```
    reverseNames = names.sorted(by: { (s1: String, s2: String) -> Bool in
            return s1 > s2
})
```

The body of a closure in Swift is introduced by the keyword **in**. This indicates that the definition of the closure's parameters and return type has concluded, and the actual body of the closure is about to commence.

Escaping closures

An escaping closure is a closure that outlives the scope it was defined in and can be executed after the enclosing function has completed. Here is an example of an escaping closure in Swift:

```
func delayedPrint(message: String, delay: TimeInterval, completion: @escaping
() -> Void) {
    DispatchQueue.main.asyncAfter(deadline: .now() + delay) {
        print(message)
        completion()
    }
}
// Call the function with an escaping closure
delayedPrint(message: "Hello, World!", delay: 2.0) {
    print("Printed after delay")
}
```

In the above example, the **delayedPrint** function takes a message parameter to be printed, a **delay** parameter to specify the time delay, and an escaping closure completion that will be called after the delay. The closure is marked with **@escaping** to indicate that it will be stored and executed outside the scope of the **delayedPrint** function. The closure is executed asynchronously after the specified delay using **DispatchQueue.main.asyncAfter**, which dispatches the closure to run on the main queue after the specified time interval. This allows the function to return immediately, and the closure will be executed later when the delay expires.

Escaping closures are commonly used in asynchronous programming scenarios, such as when dealing with network requests, animations, or other time-delayed operations, where the closure needs to be executed after the function has completed and returned. However, it is important to handle potential memory management issues, such as retaining cycles, when working with escaping closures to avoid memory leaks.

Non-escaping closures

A non-escaping closure is one that must be executed within the scope of the **enclosing** function and cannot be stored for later use. Here is an example of a non-escaping closure in Swift:

```
func performOperation(_ operation: () -> Void) {
    print("Performing operation...")
    operation()
    print("Operation completed.")
}
// Call the function with a non-escaping closure
performOperation {
    print("Executing closure")
}
```

In the above example, the **performOperation** function takes a closure as an argument, which represents an operation to be performed. The closure is not marked with @escaping, indicating that it must be executed within the scope of the **performOperation** function. The closure is executed synchronously within the function, meaning the function will not complete until the closure has finished executing. This allows the closure to access local variables and other resources within the function's scope.

Non-escaping closures are useful when you need to pass a closure as an argument to a function, but you want to ensure that the closure is executed immediately and does not outlive the function's scope. Non-escaping closures can provide performance optimizations and simplify memory management compared to escaping closures, as they do not require the same level of consideration for potential memory leaks or retaining cycles.

Trailing closures

When you need to pass a closure expression to a function as the function's **final** argument and the expression is long enough that it can be useful to write it as a trailing closure instead. A function call can include multiple trailing closures, but the first few examples use a single trailing closure:

```
func aFuntionThatTakesClosure(closure: () -> Void) {
        // function body goes here
    }
    // Here's how you call this function without using a trailing closure:
    aFunctionThatTakesClosure(closure: {
        // closure's body goes here
    })
    // Here's how you call this function with a trailing closure instead:
    aFunctionThatTakesClosure() {
        // trailing closure's body goes here
    }
```

The string-sorting closure can be written outside of the **sorted(by:)** method's parentheses as a trailing closure:

```
reverseNames = friendsName.sorted() { $0 > $1 }
```

Autoclosures

In Swift, an **autoclosure** is a special type of closure that is automatically created when passed as an argument to a function. It is used to delay the evaluation of an expression until it is actually needed, and it is automatically invoked when the function is called. Here is an example of an **autoclosure** in Swift:

```
func printIfTrue(_ condition: @autoclosure () -> Bool) {
    if condition() {
        print("Condition is true")
    } else {
        print("Condition is false")
    }
}
// Call the function with an autoclosure
printIfTrue(2 + 2 == 4) // Condition is true
```

In the preceding example, the **printIfTrue** function takes an **autoclosure** condition as an argument, which represents a Boolean expression. The **@autoclosure** attribute indicates that the argument is an **autoclosure**, allowing the caller to pass a simple expression that will be automatically converted into a closure. When the function is called, the condition **autoclosure** is automatically evaluated to obtain the result of the Boolean expression. The result is then used within the function to determine which message to print.

Auto closures are useful when you want to delay the evaluation of an expression until it is actually needed, such as in situations where the expression is expensive to compute or when you want to provide a more concise syntax for passing Boolean conditions or other simple expressions to a function. In certain scenarios, autoclosures can provide performance optimizations and improve code readability.

Conclusion

In this chapter, we have delved into the fundamentals of Swift programming, with a focus on the behavior of variables and constants. We have covered various operations involving strings and characters and explored the collection types provided by Apple, including arrays, sets, and dictionaries, which allow for efficient management of data within the program code. Our understanding of control flow has enabled us to make informed decisions, both conditional and unconditional, during coding. Additionally, we have explored the concept of functions and nested functions, which promote code modularity and readability by encapsulating tasks into separate functions. Closures, with their ability to capture and store references to variables and constants from the surrounding context, have been discussed, with an emphasis on Swift's robust memory management. In the next chapter, we will delve into advanced Swift topics, such as classes, structures, and enumerations.

Multiple choice questions

1. **Which of the following is the correct Data Type in Swift ?**
    a. Double
    b. UInt
    c. Optional
    d. Char
2. **What are / is the control transfer statements used in swift?**
    a. Continue
    b. Break
    c. Fallthrough
    d. All of the Above
3. **What is the collection type in Swift?**
    a. Dictionary
    b. Optional
    c. Fallthrough
    d. Closure
4. **Swift is an _____ language, which means anyone can take the code , build it and share it with a greater community?**
    a. Loose
    b. Open Source
    c. Optional
    d. Protected
5. **In Swift, what is similar to do-while?**
    a. while
    b. for-in
    c. repeat-while
    d. None of the above

6. **In Swift, which keyword is used for function?**
   a. function
   b. @function
   c. func
   d. @objc
7. **Which of the following correctly declares a mutable array?**
   a. let array = [Int]()
   b. var array = [Int]()
   c. let array = [Int]
   d. var array = [Int]
8. **What is the type of Conditional Statements?**
   a. Break
   b. Switch
   c. Optional
   d. Closures

Answers

1. d
2. d
3. a
4. b
5. c
6. c
7. b
8. b

Join our book's Discord space

Join the book's Discord Workspace for Latest updates, Offers, Tech happenings around the world, New Release and Sessions with the Authors:

https://discord.bpbonline.com

CHAPTER 3
Class, Structure, and Enumerations

Introduction

In our previous discussions on Swift fundamentals, we covered basic Swift syntax coding and the use of operators. In this session, we will delve into the implementation of classes, structures, and enumerations using the knowledge we have gained so far. Classes are used for encapsulation and inheritance when organizing features or properties within a single entity. Structures, on the other hand, are useful for binding data together as data models. Enumerations provide multiple options of the same type. Let us explore these concepts further.

Structure

In this chapter, we will cover the following topics:

- Enumerations
- Structures and classes
- Properties
- Methods
- Inheritance
- Initialization
- Deinitialization

Objectives

Upon completing this chapter, you will gain the ability to create classes, structures, and enumerations in Swift programming, complete with their instances, properties, and methods for performing desired tasks and operations. Furthermore, you will be equipped with the knowledge to perform advanced operations on classes, structures, and enumerations, utilizing the capabilities of inheritance, subclasses, and customized initializations.

Enumerations

An enumeration, commonly referred to as an **enum**, is a symbolic name representing a set of values of the same type. Enums in Swift are considered data types that can be utilized as variables and properties. One of the notable advantages of enums in Swift is their flexibility, as they do not necessarily require associated values for every case. Associated values can be of various types, such as string, character, integer, or floating-point.

Furthermore, **enum** cases in Swift can specify associated values of any type, allowing for storage of different values along with each case. Enumerations in Swift also adopt many features commonly used with classes, such as computed properties that provide information about the current value. Additionally, enums can define initializers to provide initial associated values for cases and extend their functionality beyond their original implementations. Enums can also conform to protocols, allowing them to provide standard functionalities in accordance with protocol requirements.

Swift enumerations use the **enum** keyword:

```
    enum nameOfEnum {
        // Definition of Enumeration
}
```

Following is an example of storing points on the compass:

```
enum PointOfCompass {
    case north
    case south
    case east
    case west
}
```

Like any other data type in Swift, enumeration's name starts with a capital letter. Let us see how we can access the value of **enum** in a variable.

```
    var mainDirection = PointOfCompass.south
```

Recursive enumeration

In Swift, recursive enumeration, when another instance of enumeration forms as an associated value for one or more enumeration cases. This way enumeration cases become recursive by writing keywords indirectly before it. Following is the example of recursive **enum**:

```
enum ArithmeticExp {
    case number(Int)
    indirect case addition(ArithmeticExp, ArithmeticExp)
    indirect case multiplication(ArithmeticExp, ArithmeticExp)
}
```

The given enumeration can save three kinds of arithmetic expression: a number, addition of expressions, and multiplication of expressions. In this **enum**, addition and multiplication cases have values that are also arithmetic expressions, three associated values make it possible to nest expressions.

Structures and classes

Structures and classes are fundamental components that provide a framework for organizing and encapsulating code. They allow for the definition of properties and methods, which enable the addition of desired functionalities. In the Swift programming language, it is not mandatory to separate interfaces and implementations into distinct entities or files, both can be defined within the same building block or file.

Comparison of classes and structure

Classes and structure both:

- Have properties to store values
- Have methods to provide functionalities
- Have subscripts to provide access to values
- Have initializers to set up their initial state values
- Are available for extend to expand functionality beyond a default implementation
- Confirm to protocol which provide standard functionality

Classes have some extra features that structures would not have as listed in *Table 3.1*:

Feature	Class	Structure
Inheritance	Where one class inherits the features of another class	Here one structure cannot inherit another structure.
Type casting	Check and interpret the type of class instance at runtime.	Check and interpret the type of struct at compile time
Deinitialization	Free up resources from the instance of the class.	Deinit not allowed in structure due non reference type.
Reference	Reference counting allows more than one reference to a class instance.	Reference counting is not allowed.

Table 3.1: *Classes vs. Structure*

Classes come with more complexities compared to structures. In general, most of the data types defined by you will be structures and enumerations.

Reference type classes

Reference types are not copied when they are assigned to a variable or passed to function. But a copy to the same instance is used. Following is the example explanation of reference types:

```
let video = VideoPlayer()

video.resolution = hd

video.name = "10089"

video.frameRate = 25.0
```

Identity operator

Swift classes are classified as reference types, meaning that multiple constants and variables have the potential to reference the same instance of a class. However, this behavior does not apply to structures and enumerations, as they are considered value types and always perform a copy when assigned to another variable or constant. To identify or verify if two constants or variables refer to the same instance of a class, Swift offers two operators:

- Identical To (===)
- Not Identical To (!==)

We can use these operators to check whether two constants or variables refer to the same single instance:

```
if bigXObject === alsoBigXObject {

     print("bigXObject and alsoBigXObject referring to the same instance of class")

          }

// prints "bigXObject and alsoBigXObject referring to the same instance of class"
```

Properties

Properties are used to associate values with classes, structures, and enumerations. These properties can either be constants or variables and may be used for computation as part of instances. In addition, computed values can also be stored as type properties. These properties are associated with the type itself and are known as type properties.

In Swift, property wrappers provide a mechanism for reusing code in the getter and setter of multiple properties. They allow for encapsulation of custom behavior and logic, making it easier to manage properties with similar functionality in a concise and modular way. Property wrappers offer a flexible and powerful means of adding additional functionality to properties, while promoting code reuse and maintainability.

Stored properties

A stored property is a constant or variable that is stored as part of an instance of class or structure. You can also provide a default value to a stored property as well as modify the value.

Computed properties

In computed property classes, structure and enumerations can define properties in such a manner that it actually does not store the values but instead they provide a getter and an optional setter to retrieve and set the properties and values indirectly.

Read-only computed property

A computed property with a getter but no setter is known as a read-only computed property. Such a read-only computed property always returns a value and can be accessed by dot syntax, but it cannot be set to a value:

```
struct Cuboid {
        var width = 0.0, height = 0.0, depth = 0.0
        var volume: Double {
            return width * height * depth
        }
    }
    let fourByFiveByTwo = Cuboid(width: 4.0, height: 5.0, depth: 2.0)
    print("the volume of fourByFiveByTwo is \(fourByFiveByTwo.volume)")
    // Prints "the volume of fourByFiveByTwo is 40.0
```

Property observers

Property observers observe the changes in value of a property. Property observers are called every time when a change value is set to property which is being observed. You can add property observers in the following mentioned cases:

- Stored properties defined by you
- Stored properties inherit by you
- Computed properties inherit by you

In case of inherited properties, you can add property observers via overriding that property in a subclass. There are options to define either or both of these below observers on a property:

- **willSet** observer method is called just before the value is stored in case, if you want to perform any operation before change of value on property.
- **didSet** is called just after the new value is stored into the property which is observed.

When implementing a **willSet** observer in Swift, the new property value is passed as a constant parameter. If you do not explicitly specify a parameter name and parentheses in your implementation, the default parameter name **newValue** will be used.

Similarly, when implementing a **didSet** observer, a constant parameter containing the old property value is passed. You have the option to specify a parameter name or use the default parameter name **oldValue**. It is important to note that if you assign a value to the property within its own **didSet** observer, the newly assigned value will replace the one that was just set. This behavior allows for further customization and control over the property's value and behavior in response to changes:

```
class TapCounter {
        var totalTaps: Int = 0 {
            willSet(newTotalTaps) {
                print("About to set totalTaps to \(newTotalTaps)")
            }
            didSet {
                if totalTaps > oldValue  {
                    print("Added \(totalTaps - oldValue) Taps")
                }
            }
        }
    }
    let tapCounter = TapCounter()
    tapCounter.totalTaps = 200
    // About to set totaltaps to 200
    // Added 200 taps
    tapCounter.totaltaps = 360
    // About to set totalSteps to 360
    // Added 160 taps
    tapCounter.totaltaps = 896
    // About to set totaltaps to 896
    // Added 536 taps
```

Property wrappers

Property wrappers in Swift provide an additional layer of separation in code, allowing for management of how properties are stored and defined. For instance, if you need to add thread safety to multiple properties in your code, you do not need to implement thread safety measures separately for each property. Instead, property wrappers allow you to encapsulate the necessary code within the wrapper itself. Once defined, this code can be easily reused for other properties by simply applying the property wrapper.

To create a property wrapper, you can use a structure, enumeration, or class that defines a **wrapperValue** property. This property serves as the underlying storage for the wrapped property and allows for customization of the behavior and management of the property's value. By using property wrappers, you can achieve more concise and modular code that promotes reusability and maintainability.

```
@propertyWrapper
        struct FifteenOrLess {
            private var number: Int
            init() { self.number = 0 }
            var wrappedValue: Int {
                get { return number }
                set { number = min(newValue, 15) }
            }
        }
```

To apply the wrapper to a property, you can write the wrapper's name before the property as an attribute:

```
struct Rectangle {
            @FifteenOrLess var height: Int
            @FifteenOrLess var width: Int
        }
        var rectangle = Rectangle()
        print(rectangle.height)
        // Prints "0"
        rectangle.height = 10
        print(rectangle.height)
        // Prints "10"
        rectangle.height = 24
        print(rectangle.height)
        // Prints "15"
```

Global and local variables

In Swift, global variables refer to variables that are defined outside of any function, closure, or method, and are accessible from any part of the program. On the other hand, local variables are defined within a function, method, or closure, and are only accessible within their scope.

Similar to stored properties in Swift classes, both global and local variables provide storage for values of a certain type. Additionally, computed variables can also be defined in both global and local variables, allowing for custom computation of values. Furthermore, observers, such as **`willSet`** and **`didSet`**, can be implemented for stored values in global and local variables, enabling further customization and logic to be applied to variable changes.

Type properties

In Swift, instance type properties are properties that belong to instances of a specific type. Each instance of that type has its own set of values for these properties, which are distinct from the values of other instances of the same type. These properties are stored in a single copy, regardless of how many instances of the type are created and are commonly referred to as type properties.

Type properties are particularly useful for defining properties that are universal to all instances of a particular type. For instance, type properties can be defined as constant properties that apply to all instances of the type. This concept is similar to static variables in the C programming language, where there is only one copy of the variable shared across all instances of the class.

Stored type properties can be declared as either constants or variables, depending on whether their values are intended to be mutable or immutable. On the other hand, computed type properties are always declared as variable properties, as their values are computed at runtime and can be changed during the lifetime of the program.

NOTE: The following example is for read-only computed type properties, but you can also define read-write computed type properties with the same syntax as for computed instance properties.

```
struct SampleStructure {
        static var storedTypeProperty = "Sample value."
        static var computedTypeProperty: Int {
            return 1
        }
    }
    enum SampleEnumeration {
        static var storedTypeProperty = "Sample value."
        static var computedTypeProperty: Int {
            return 6
```

```
    }
}
class SampleClass {
    static var storedTypeProperty = "Sample value."
    static var computedTypeProperty: Int {
        return 27
    }
    class var overrideComputedTypeProperty: Int {
        return 107
    }
}
```

Querying and setting type property

The following code represents an example of querying and setting type properties:

```
print(SampleStructure.storedTypeProperty)
// Prints "Sample value."
SampleStructure.storedTypeProperty = "Another value."
print(SampleStructure.storedTypeProperty)
// Prints "Another value."
print(SampleEnumeration.computedTypeProperty)
// Prints "6"
print(SampleClass.computedTypeProperty)
// Prints "27"
```

Methods

Methods are functions which are associated with a particular type. Classes, structure and enumeration all define instance methods which can encapsulate some task and functionalities for the instances. Swift has a major difference from C and Objective C languages that structure and enumeration too have methods in Swift.

Instance methods

Instance methods are functions that belong to instances of particular classes, structure or enumerations. You write an instance method within the opening and closing braces of the type it belongs to. Instance methods have implicit access to all other instance methods and properties of that type. An instance method can be called on a specific instance of the type it belongs to. It cannot be called in isolation without an existing instance.

```
class IncreaseCounter {
    var count = 0
    func increment() {
        count += 1
    }
    func increment(by amount: Int) {
        count += amount
    }
    func reset() {
        count = 0
    }
}
```

Type methods

You can also define methods that are called on the type itself. Such methods are called type methods. You can syntax it by writing the **`static`** keyword before the methods keyword **`func`**. Although classes can use the class keyword instead, to allow subclasses to override the superclass implementation of that method:

```
class AnyClass {
    class func anyTypeMethod() {
        // type method implementation
    }
}
AnyClass.anyTypeMethod()
```

Within the body of a type method, the implicit **`self`** property refers to type itself. A **`type`** method can call another **`type`** method with the other method name without any prefix of its type name.

Inheritance

A Class can inherit properties, methods and other features from another class. When one class inherits from another, the inheriting class is known as its superclass. Classes in swift can call its methods and properties belonging to their superclass and can provide. In such cases, Swift ensures that your overrides are correct by checking it from superclass method definitions.

Base class

Any class which does not inherit from another class is known as a base class. Swift classes do not inherit from the universal base class. Classes you define without mention of superclass automatically become base classes to build upon.

Subclassing

Subclassing is used to form a new class on an existing class as base. The subclass inherits all features from the existing class, which can be redefined in the subclass. To form a subclass which has a super class, you need to write the subclass name before the superclass name, separated by a colon (**:**):

```
class SampleSubclass: SampleSuperclass {
    // subclass definition goes here
}
```

Other than a simple syntax given above we can understand it better by the following example:

```
class Vehicle {
    var currentSpeed = 0.0
    var description: String {
        return "traveling at \(currentSpeed) miles per hour"
    }
    func makeNoise() {
        // do nothing - an arbitrary vehicle doesn't necessarily make a noise
    }
}
class Car: Vehicle {
    var hasBreak = true
}
```

The new **Car** class inherits all the features of **Vehicle** class, such as its **currentSpeed**, **description** properties and **makenoise** method. From the instance of **class Car**, you can change stored property values of subclass as well as superclass:

```
let car = Car()
car.hasBreak = false
car.currentSpeed = 50.0
print("Car: \(car.description)")
// Car: traveling at 50.0 miles per hour
```

Overriding

A subclass can provide its own custom implementation of an instance method, type method, instance property, type property which inherits from a superclass. This is known as **overriding**. The **override** keyword uses a swift compiler to check that your overriding class's superclass has a declaration that matches with the one you provided.

You can use **super** prefix to access the property and methods of superclass from the instance of subclass. Let us see where it is appropriate to do so:

- An overridden method named **sampleMethod()** can call the superclass version of **sampleMethod()** by calling **super.sampleMethod()** within the overriding method implementation.
- An overridden property called **sampleProperty** can access the superclass version of **sampleProperty** as **super.sampleProperty** within the overriding getter or setter implementation.
- An overridden subscript for **someIndex** can access the superclass version of the same subscript as **super[someIndex]** from within the overriding subscript implementation.

Initialization

Initialization is the process of preparing an instance of a class, structure or enumeration for use. This process includes setting up of initial values of stored properties and performing any other setup or initialization which is required for that instance. You can set an initial value for a stored property either within an initializer or by assigning a default property value as part of property definition.

Initializers

Initializers are called to create new instances of a particular type. An initializer is like a method without parameters:

```
    init() {
        // perform some initialization process
}
```

The following example defines a new structure to store temperature expressed in **Celsius** scale. The **Celsius** structure has one stored property of type **Double**:

```
struct Celsius {
    var temperature: Double
    init() {
        temperature = 35.0
    }
}
```

```
var c = Celsius()
print("The default temperature is \(c.temperature)° Celcius")
// Prints "The default temperature is 35.0° Celsius"
```

Customizing initialization

You can also customize the initialization via adding input parameters that entail values of stored property type. You can provide initialization parameters as part of a definition of initializer as follows:

```
struct Celsius {
    var temperatureInCelsius: Double
    init(fromFahrenheit fahrenheit: Double) {
        temperatureInCelsius = (fahrenheit - 32.0) / 1.8
    }
}
let boilingPointOfWater = Celsius(fromFahrenheit: 212.0)
// boilingPointOfWater.temperatureInCelsius is 100.0
```

In the preceding example, the initializer has a single initialization parameter with an argument label of **fromFarenheit** and a parameter name of **fahrenheit**.

Deinitialization

In Swift, deinitializers are special methods that are called automatically before a class instance is deallocated. The keyword **deinit** is used for deinitialization, similar to **init** which is used for initialization. It is important to note that deinitializers are only available in classes and not in structures or enumerations.

A class definition in Swift can have at most one deinitializer per class. Deinitializers do not take any parameters and are written without parentheses, as shown in the following example:

```
deinit    {
    // Here You can perform Deinit Operation
}
```

You cannot call a deinitializer yourself, instead, the system calls them automatically before deallocating an instance. In addition, superclass deinitializers are inherited by their subclasses and are called automatically at the end of a subclass's deinitializer implementation. Superclass deinitializers are also invoked.

While it is not always necessary to use deinitializers, they can be useful when you need to perform cleanup operations before an object is deallocated. For example, if your class manages a file or another resource, you can close the file handle in the deinitializer to ensure that it doesn't persist after the object has been deallocated.

Conclusion

The explanation provided in this chapter will help you gain a clear understanding of the differences between classes and structures in Swift. While using structures should be the default choice in Swift programming, as recommended, it may not always be feasible or practical, and using classes instead will not necessarily cause any harm. With more practice and familiarity, you will likely become accustomed to using structures more frequently.

However, there are cases where **object-oriented programming (OOP)** features are required, and classes become the obvious choice. In this chapter, we discussed inheritance with subclassing and overriding methods, which make classes more powerful than structures in certain scenarios. Additionally, instances of the same class or structure can access enumerations declared within those classes and structures.

In the next chapter, you will further delve into topics such as extensions, protocols, and error handling in Swift, which will expand your understanding of advanced Swift programming concepts.

Multiple choice questions

1. **Which feature is part of classes only?**
    a. Property
    b. Method
    c. Subscripts
    d. Inheritance
2. **The class which does not inherit from another class is called as -**
    a. SubClass
    b. Superclass
    c. Base class
    d. Main Class
3. **Which operator is used to check if two variable or constant refer to same instance of class**
    a. (==)
    b. (!==)
    c. (!=)
    d. (===)
4. **If you want to perform action when a stored property value changed, Which feature you will use:**
    a. Computed Property
    b. Read-Write Property

    c. Property Observer
    d. Override

5. **A subclass provides custom implementation of type method which inherits from superclass, is called as:**
    a. Property Observer
    b. Initialization
    c. Override
    d. Inheritance

Answers

1. d
2. c
3. d
4. c
5. c

CHAPTER 4

Protocols, Extensions, and Error Handling

Introduction

In this chapter, we will delve into some advanced topics of Swift programming, including optional chaining, optional binding, error handling, type casting, extension, protocols, and nested types. These concepts are crucial to master as they can help you write efficient and robust code. Optional chaining is a powerful feature of Swift that allows you to chain multiple optional values together in a single expression, reducing the need for forced unwrapping. Optional binding is another essential feature that helps you safely unwrap optional values by checking if they are nil or not. Error handling is a mechanism in Swift that enables you to gracefully handle errors and exceptions that occur during runtime. With error handling, you can write code that is more resilient to unexpected conditions and errors.

Type casting is a feature in Swift that allows you to check and convert the type of an object to another type. It is useful when working with polymorphic code or when you need to downcast a superclass to a subclass. The extension is another important concept in Swift that enables you to add new functionality to an existing type without modifying its source code. You can use extensions to extend classes, structs, enums, and protocols with new methods, properties, and subscripts. Protocols are a fundamental feature of Swift that allows you to define a blueprint of methods, properties, and other requirements that a conforming type must implement. Protocols are useful when you want to define a set of behaviors that different types can conform to. Nested types are types that are defined inside other types, such as classes, structs, or enums. They can be used to organize related code and encapsulate implementation details.

Structure

In this chapter, we will cover the following topics:

- Optional binding
- Optional chaining
- Error handling
- Type casting
- Nested types
- Extension
- Protocols

Objectives

By studying this chapter, you will acquire the ability to master optional chaining and error-handling techniques while developing intricate coding solutions for various tasks. Additionally, you will gain proficiency in the Swift programming language, which is characterized as a protocol-oriented language that facilitates protocol-based communication between multiple code blocks and components. This language also features extensions that offer enhanced flexibility, reusability, and extensibility.

Protocol oriented programming

Protocol-oriented programming (POP) is a modern approach to software development that emphasizes the use of protocols, rather than classes or objects, as the building blocks for designing and implementing software systems. The Swift programming language is one of the most prominent examples of a language that has embraced the principles of POP. At its core, POP is all about using protocols to define a set of rules and guidelines that software components must follow in order to communicate and interact with each other. By using protocols, developers can create flexible, reusable, and composable code that can be easily adapted and extended over time.

Swift's support for POP is built into its core language features. In Swift, protocols are treated as first-class citizens, which means that they can be used just like any other data type, such as integers, strings, or arrays. This makes it easy to create and define protocols that can be used throughout an application or system. One of the key advantages of using Swift as a POP language is that it encourages developers to think about software design in a modular and composable way. By breaking down complex software systems into smaller, independent components that communicate with each other via well-defined protocols, developers can create software that is easier to understand, test, and maintain over time. Here are some reasons why Swift is considered a POP language:

- **Emphasis on protocols:** Swift places a strong emphasis on protocols, which are used to define a set of rules and guidelines that software components must follow in order to communicate and interact with each other.

- **First-class citizen:** In Swift, protocols are treated as first-class citizens, which means they can be used just like any other data type, such as integers, strings, or arrays.
- **Protocol extensions:** Swift supports protocol extensions, which allows developers to add new functionality to existing protocols without modifying the original source code.
- **Protocol inheritance:** Swift supports protocol inheritance, which allows developers to define new protocols that build on the functionality of existing protocols.
- **Composability:** The emphasis on protocols in Swift makes it easy to create modular, composable, and reusable code that can be easily adapted and extended over time.
- **Flexibility:** Swift's support for POP provides developers with the flexibility to create software systems that can adapt and evolve over time while still maintaining a high degree of functionality and reliability.
- **Testability:** The modular and composable nature of code written in Swift using POP principles makes it easier to test individual components and ensure that they work correctly within the larger system.

Optional binding

The optional binding feature in Swift allows developers to safely unwrap optional values and use them in their code. Optional binding helps to avoid runtime errors and improves 31 (**?**), indicating that the value may be nil. If you try to use an optional value without unwrapping it first, your code will result in a runtime error. The optional binding provides a safe way to unwrap optional values and use them in your code. Here's an example of optional binding in Swift:

```
let optionalValue: Int? = 42
if let unwrappedValue = optionalValue {
    print("The unwrapped value is \(unwrappedValue)")
} else {
    print("The optional value is nil")
}
```

In this code example, we declare an optional value named **optionalValue** and assign it the value **42**. We then use an **if…let** statement to check if the value is nil. If the value is not nil, the optional value is unwrapped and assigned to a new constant called **unwrappedValue**. We can then safely use **unwrappedValue** in our code without worrying about runtime errors. Here's another example of optional binding in Swift:

```
func printGreeting(name: String?) {
    if let name = name {
        print("Hello, \(name)!")
    } else {
```

```
        print("Hello, world!")
    }
}
printGreeting(name: "Alice") // Output: Hello, Alice!
printGreeting(name: nil) // Output: Hello, world!
```

In this code example, we define a function called **printGreeting** that takes an optional parameter name. We then use optional binding to safely unwrap the name and print a personalized greeting if the name is not nil. If the name is **nil**, we print a generic greeting. Optional binding is a great feature in Swift that can help to improve the stability and reliability of your code. By using **if…let** statements to safely unwrap optional values, you can avoid runtime errors and write code that is more robust and error-resistant.

Optional chaining

In Swift programming language, optional chaining refers to the process of querying and calling properties, methods, and subscripts on an optional value to check whether it might be nil or not. The properties, methods, and subscripts are called successfully only if they have non-nil values; otherwise, they return **nil**. Optional chaining allows for the possibility of querying multiple properties, methods, and subscripts successively, and if any of the values in between are nil, the entire chain will return **nil**.

Importance of optional chaining

In programming, forced unwrapping occurs regardless of the presence or absence of a nil value, and it can result in abrupt failures or crashes. In contrast, optional chaining fails gracefully when the optional value is **nil**. The expected return value of an optional chaining call is a value of the same type as the original but wrapped in an optional value. For instance, a property that would normally return an Int value will return an **Int** value with optional wrapping whenever accessed through optional chaining.

Optional chaining can be used by placing a question mark (**?**) after the optional value on which in programming you wish to call property, methods or subscripts. The following code snippets can give us a better understanding.

```
Class Letter {
    var address: Address?
}
Class Address {
    var houseNumber = 201,
}
```

Letter instances have a single **Int** property called **houseNumber**, with a default value of **201**.

Error handling

Error handling refers to the process of handling error conditions in a program gracefully, ensuring that the user flow continues, and the system and application are not negatively affected. The Swift language offers built-in support for throwing, catching, propagating, and manipulating errors at runtime.

In some cases, certain operations may not always complete execution and produce meaningful results, resulting in failed operations. In such cases, it is essential to inform or notify the user of the reasons for the failure, so that they can take appropriate actions.

Throwing errors

Values of types that adhere to the **`Error`** protocol serve as errors' representations in the Swift programming language. Swift enumerations are well-suited for modeling error conditions with associated values, which communicate the types of errors as shown here. Later in this chapter, we will discuss protocols in detail:

```
enum CoffeeMachineError: Error {
    case invalidSelection
    case insufficientWater(waterNeedediInml: Int)
    case outOfStock
}
```

Throwing an error from the program indicates that something unexpected happened and normal flow of execution cannot be continued in such a case. You can use the **`throw`** keyword statement to throw an error from the program code as shown here:

```
throw CoffeeMachineError.insufficientWater(waterNeedediInml: 5)
```

Handling errors

When an error is thrown by a program code, it is important to handle it gracefully and notify the user of the type and reason for the error. In Swift, there are primarily four ways to handle errors:

- Errors using throwing function
- Handling error using **`do…catch`**
- Errors as optional values
- Disabling error propagation

Errors using throwing function

After the parameters of a function, method, or initializer, you write the **`throws`** keyword in the function's declaration to indicate that it can throw an error. A throwing function is a function that is marked with throws. You write the **`throws`** keyword before the return arrow (**`->`**) if the function specifies a return type as shown here:

```
func canThrowErrors() throws -> String

func cannotThrowErrors() -> String
```

Only throwing functions can propagate errors, and any errors thrown inside a non-throwing function must be handled inside the function.

Handling errors using do...catch

By running a block of code or a code clause, you can use a **do...catch** statement to handle errors. If the code in the **do** clause throws an error, it is compared to the **catch** clauses to see which one can handle the condition, as shown here.

Here we can see the general form of a **do...catch** statement:

```
do {
    try <expression>
    <statements>
} catch <pattern > {
    <statements>
} catch <pattern 2> where <condition> {
    <statements>
} catch <pattern 3>, <pattern 4> where <condition> {
    <statements>
} catch {
    <statements>
}
```

After you catch, you add a pattern to identify which mistakes that clause may handle. If a **catch** clause doesn't have a pattern, it matches any error and assigns it to a local variable named **error**.

Errors as optional values

You use **try?** to handle an error by converting it to an optional value. If an error is thrown while evaluating the **try?** expression, the value of the expression is **nil**. When you use **try?** then you write concise error handling code when you want to handle all errors in the same way. For example, the following code uses several approaches to fetch data, or returns **nil** if all of the approaches fail:

```
func loadData() -> Data? {
    if let data = try? loadDataFromDisk() { return data }
    if let data = try? loadDataFromServer() { return data }
    return nil
}
```

Disabling error propagation

If you are certain that a throwing function or method will not throw an error at runtime, you can disable error propagation by using the **`try!`** keyword before the expression and wrapping the call in a runtime assertion that no error will be thrown. However, if an error is truly thrown, a runtime error will occur. For instance, consider the **`loadImage(atPath:)`** function in the following code example, which loads an image resource at a specified path or throws an exception if the picture cannot be loaded. Since the image is provided with the application, no error will be thrown at runtime, making it reasonable to disable error propagation as shown below:

```
let photo = try! loadImage(atPath: "./Resources/Mango.jpg")
```

Type casting

Type casting is a technique used to determine the type of an instance in Swift. The **`is`** and **`as`** operators are used to implement type casting in a simple and expressive manner. These two operators make it easy to check the type of a value or cast a value to a different type. When dealing with a hierarchy of classes and subclasses, you can use type casting to check the type of a specific instance. An example of this is as follows:

```
class Media {
    var name: String
    init(name: String) {
        self.name = name
    }
}
```

The preceding class **`Media`** provides the basic functionality of digital goods and declares a **`name`** property of type **`string`** and an **`init`** name initializer. We can define two subclasses of the **`Media`** superclass in the first **`Movie`** class, which encapsulates movie name and director name information as shown here:

```
class Movie: Media {
    var director: String
    init(name: String, director: String) {
        self.director = director
        super.init(name: name)
    }
}
class Song: Media {
    var artist: String
```

```
    init(name: String, artist: String) {
        self.artist = artist
        super.init(name: name)
    }
}
```

Checking types

Type casting involves using the type checker operator **is** to determine if an instance is of a subclass type. The type checker operator returns a Boolean value of true if the instance is of the subclass type, and false if it is not of the subclass type.

Downcasting

A constant or variable of a class type may refer to an instance of a subclass that is hidden from the user. In such cases, you can attempt to downcast to the subclass type using a type cast operator (**as?** or **as!**). However, since downcasting can sometimes fail, type cast operators are available in two forms.

- The conditional form (**as?**) returns a value of the type you want to downcast to.
- The forced form (**as!**), attempts the downcast and force unwraps the results.

When there is uncertainty about the success of downcasting, it is advisable to use the conditional form of the downcast operator. This form of the operator always returns an optional value, and the value will be **nil** if the downcast is not possible. This allows for proper checking of downcasting. On the other hand, the forced form of the type cast operator (**as!**) should be used when one is confident that the downcast will always succeed. However, attempting to downcast to an improper class type with this type of operator will result in a runtime error.

Casting for Any and AnyObject

Swift provides two special types for two non-specific types:

Any, including function types, can represent an instance of any type. The **Any** type can represent values of any type, including optional types. Swift warns you if you use an optional value in a place where a value of type **Any** is required. If you use an optional value as an **Any** value, you can use the as operator to cast the optional to **Any**.

Any object can be used to represent an instance member of any class type. When you specifically require the behavior and capabilities that **Any** and **AnyObject** provide, you can utilize them. It is always preferable to be as clear as possible about the types you plan to work with in your code.

Nested types

In Swift, it is possible to define a type within another type. This concept is known as nested types, and it can be useful for organizing and encapsulating related functionality within a larger type. To declare a nested type in Swift, you simply define the type within the braces of the outer type. For example, consider a struct called **Outer** that represents a person, with properties for their **name**, **age**, and **address**:

```
struct Outer {
    var name: String
    var age: Int
    var address: String

    // Nested type
    struct Inner {
        var phoneNumber: String
        var email: String
    }
}
```

In this example, we have defined a nested type called **Inner** within the **Outer** struct. **Inner** represents contact information for the person, with properties for their phone number and email address. To access the nested type from outside the outer type, you simply use the dot syntax, as you would for any other property or method. For example:

```
let person = Outer(name: "John Smith", age: 30, address: "123 Main St")
let contactInfo = Outer.Inner(phoneNumber: "555-1234", email: "john.smith@
example.com")
print(contactInfo.phoneNumber) // Output: "555-1234"
print(contactInfo.email) // Output: "john.smith@example.com"
```

In this example, we have created an instance of the **Outer** struct and an instance of the nested **Inner** struct. We can access the properties of the nested struct using dot syntax, just as we would for the outer struct, as shown above. Nested types can be useful for organizing related functionality within a larger type, and for encapsulating implementation details. They can also make code easier to read and understand by grouping related code together.

Extensions

In Swift, Extensions add new functionality to an existing class, structure, enumerations or protocol type. Extension includes the ability to extend the types on which you do not have access in actual class or structure.

Extensions can:

- Add computed instance properties and computed type properties
- Define instance method and type methods
- Provide new initializer
- Define subscripts
- Define and user new nested type
- Make an existing type conform to a protocol

But there is one thing you need to understand that extensions in Swift can add new functionalities to a type and they cannot override existing functionalities. You can declare the Extension with **`extension`** keyword:

```
extension sampleExtension {
    // new functionalities can be added here
}
```

An **`Extension`** can extend an existing type and adapt with one or more protocols as shown in the followingg code. To add protocol for extending Extension, you write the protocol names as you write for classes and structures:

```
extension sampleExtension: SampleProtocol, AnotherProtocol {
    // implementation of protocol requirements goes here
}
```

Computed properties

Extension can add computed instances properties and computed type properties to existing types. But we need to understand clearly that Extensions can add new computed property but they cannot add stored properties or add property observers to existing property types.

Initializers

Extensions can introduce new initializers to the existing types. In such a case, you can add new convenience initializers to a class, but new designated initializers cannot be added by extensions. You can call the default initializer and member wise initializer for that value type if you apply an extension to add an initializer to it that offers default values for all of its stored attributes and doesn't define any custom initializers. Furthermore, if you use an extension to add an initializer to a structure declared in another module, the new initializer will not be able to access **`self`** until it calls an initializer from the defining module as shown here:

```
struct Size {
    var width = 0.0, height = 0.0
}
```

```
struct Point {
    var x = 0.0, y = 0.0
}
struct Rect {
    var origin = Point()
    var size = Size()
}
```

Now you can add the **Rect** structure to provide an additional initializer that takes specific points and size as shown here:

```
extension Rect {
    init(center: Point, size: Size) {
        let originX = center.x - (size.width / 2)
        let originY = center.y - (size.height / 2)
        self.init(origin: Point(x: originX, y: originY), size: size)
    }
}
```

If you provide a new initializer with an expansion, you are still responsible for making sure that each instance is fully initialized once the initializer completes.

Methods

Extensions can add new instance methods and type methods to existing class or structure types:

```
extension Int {
    func repeat(task: () -> Void) {
        for _ in 0..<self {
            task()
        }
    }
}
```

After defining the Extension you can call the **repeat(task:)** method on any integer to perform a task as shown here:

```
4.repeat {
    print("Hello World !")
}
```

```
// Hello World
// Hello World
// Hello World
// Hello World
```

Protocols

In Swift, Protocol defines a blueprint of methods, properties and other requirements and functionality performed by the class or structure which will perform this protocol. **Any** type that satisfies the requirements of a **protocol** is said to confirm that protocol. You can define **protocol** simply similar to class and structure as shown here:

```
protocol SampleProtocol {
    // protocol definition
}
```

While implementing Protocols to class and structure, multiple protocols can be listed, and are separated by commas:

```
struct SampleProtocol: FirstProtocol, AnotherProtocol {
    // structure definition
}
```

Property requirement

Swift Protocols can require any confirming type to provide an instance with a particular name and type. Each property must be gettable or gettable and settable, according to the protocol. Property needs are always preceded with the **var** keyword and specified as variable properties. After their type definition, gettable and settable properties are expressed by writing get, set, and gettable properties are denoted by writing **{get}** as shown here:

```
protocol SampleProtocol {
    var aSettable: Int { get set }
    var notNeedToBeSettable: Int { get }
}
```

You must always prefix **type** property requirements with the **static** keyword when you define them in a protocol:

```
protocol LiveProtocol {
    static var liveTypeProperty: Int { get set }
}
```

Method requirement

Protocols which are implemented by confirming types require instance methods and type methods. These methods are written in the definition of protocol similar to normal instance and **type** methods. You are required to prefix always type methods with **static** keywords when they are defined in protocol definition:

```
Protocol SampleProtocol {
    static func sampleTypeMethod()
}
```

Sometimes methods need to modify (or mutate) the instance it belongs to. When you construct a protocol instance method requirement that is meant to mutate instances of any type that uses the protocols, you must include the **mutating** keyword in the protocol specifications. You don't need to write a **mutating** keyword while implementing a mutating method type. The **mutating** keyword is only used by structures and enumerations as shown here:

```
protocol ToggleProtocol {
    mutating func toggle()
}
enum OnOffSwitch: ToggleProtocol {
    case off, on
    mutating func toggle() {
        switch self {
        case .off:
            self = .on
        case .on:
            self = .off
        }
    }
}
var lightSwitch = OnOffSwitch.off
lightSwitch.toggle()
// lightSwitch is now equal to .on
```

Initializer requirements

You can write initializers as part of the protocol's definition in exactly the same way as for normal initializers, but without curly braces or an initializer body:

```
protocol SampleProtocol {
    init(someParameter: Int)
}
```

Protocols as types

Protocols do not implement any functionalities themselves and should be considered as types in your code. Using protocol as a type is called an **existential type**. You can use protocol at many places, where others price is allowed:

- As a parameter type or return type in a function, method, or initializer.
- As the type of a constant, variable, or property.
- As the type of items in an array, dictionary, or other container.

Delegations

Delegation is a design pattern in Swift that enables a class or structure to delegate (or hand off) some of its responsibilities to an instance of another type. Delegation design pattern implemented by defining a protocol that delegated the responsibilities which is known as delegate and guaranteed to provide the functionality that has been delegated. Delegating objects keeps a reference to another object and when required or at appropriate time sends the message to it. And delegation makes it possible for one object to alter the behavior of another object without the need to inherit from it.

```
protocol ImageImporterDelegate: AnyObject {
    func imageImporter(_ importer: ImageImporter,
                       shouldImportImage image: Image) -> Bool
    func imageImporter(_ importer: ImageImporter,
                       didAbortWithError error: Error)
    func imageImporterDidFinish(_ importer: ImageImporter)
}
class ImageImporter {
    weak var delegate: ImageImporterDelegate?
    private func processFileIfNeeded(_ file: File) {
        guard let delegate = delegate else {
            return
        }
```

```
        let shouldImport = delegate.imageImporter(self, shouldImportImage: file)
        guard shouldImport else {
            return
        }
        process(file)
    }
}
```

In the preceding code **`ImageImporterDelegate`** is protocol, and we declare this protocol type object named delegate in the class in which we want to implement this protocol.

Protocols inheritance

Similar to class and struct, a Protocols can also inherit from one or more other protocols, and they can add to the criteria they inherit. Protocol inheritance uses the same syntax as class inheritance, with the addition of the ability to list several inherited protocols., separated by commas as shown here:

```
protocol InheritingProtocol: SampleProtocol, AnotherProtocol {
    // protocol definition goes here
}
```

Here's an example of a protocol that inherits the **`TextRepresentable`** protocol:

```
protocol PrettyTextRepresentable: TextRepresentable {
    var prettyTextualDescription: String { get }
}
```

Class only Protocols

In Swift, it is possible to specify a protocol that is specific to a class and not for structures and enumerations. You can do this by including the **`AnyObject`** protocol in the protocol's inheritance list. When defining a class-only protocol, it is important to consider the behavior that is defined by the protocol's requirements. If the behavior assumes or requires that the type conforming to the protocol has reference semantics, rather than value semantics, then a class-only protocol should be used.

Reference semantics refers to the way objects are managed in memory. With reference semantics, multiple variables can refer to the same instance of an object. This means that changes made to the object are visible to all variables that refer to it. In contrast, with value semantics, each variable has its own copy of an object, so changes made to one variable are not visible to others. To define a class-only protocol, you can use the class keyword before the protocol's name:

```
protocol MyClassOnlyProtocol: class {
    // Protocol requirements
}
```

Structures and enumerations are unable to adopt this protocol; only classes can. Using class-only protocols can help ensure that the behavior defined by the protocol is implemented correctly, by enforcing reference semantics. It can also make code more readable and easier to understand by clearly indicating the intent of the protocol. When defining a protocol that assumes or requires reference semantics, a class-only protocol should be used. This can be achieved by adding the **`AnyObject`** protocol to the protocol's inheritance list and using the class keyword before the protocol's name.

Conclusion

This chapter illustrates how one can improve the efficiency of their code through the implementation of error handling mechanisms, which can enhance code proactivity and provide protection against unhandled cases. Additionally, utilizing protocols as a communication mechanism between classes and structures during complex tasks can contribute to making one's code more robust and diligent. The delegate pattern remains a critical component of both Apple's frameworks and our own codebases. The utilization of generics plays a vital role in achieving reusability and flexibility while developing Swift programs.

In the next chapter, we will delve into the intricacies of user interface building with various UI components and navigating through the application flow with **`UINavigationcontroller`**.

Multiple choice questions

1. **Which of these keywords is not a part of exception handling?**
    a. try
    b. throw
    c. thrown
    d. catch
2. **If there is a direct communication between two objects then which concepts we are talking about?**
    a. Error handling
    b. Generics
    c. Delegate
    d. Optional Chaining
3. **You can achieve reusability of code from -**
    a. Protocols
    b. Error handling
    c. Generics
    d. Delegate

4. **In case you want to add Features to an existing class, you will use -**
   a. Protocol
   b. Extension
   c. Generics
   d. Optional Chaining
5. **Which Swift concepts are used heavily in Swift Standard Libraries?**
   a. Protocol
   b. Extension
   c. Generics
   d. Optional Chaining

Answers

1. c
2. c
3. c
4. b
5. c

Join our book's Discord space

Join the book's Discord Workspace for Latest updates, Offers, Tech happenings around the world, New Release and Sessions with the Authors:

https://discord.bpbonline.com

CHAPTER 5
Automatic Reference Counting and Memory Safety

Introduction

When you write code in Swift for iOS app development, **Automatic Reference Counting** (**ARC**) takes care of memory allocation and deallocation on its own. It is not a garbage collector but works similarly to a garbage collector in any other language. But due to the ARC architecture, there may be possibilities for issues, especially in the case of object-to-object reference, closures, and creating custom delegates. In this chapter, we will learn what caused these problems and how developers can fix them quickly. If read and write permissions on properties differ in a single-thread or multiple-thread environment, there could be a conflict when accessing memory.

Structure

In this chapter, we will cover the following topics:

- Automatic Reference Counting
- Memory safety

Objectives

By learning this chapter, you will be able to learn and understand how ARC works. Also, you will be able to learn more about how to handle memory safety in Swift when handling in-out parameters and properties.

Automatic Reference Counting

Automatic Reference Counting (**ARC**) is a feature of Swift that keeps track of and manages how much memory your app uses. Most of the time, this means that memory management in Swift works automatically, so you do not have to think about it. When class instances are no longer needed, ARC automatically frees up the memory they used.

In a few situations, ARC needs more information about how different parts of your code work together to manage memory for you. Only instances of classes are counted when reference counting is used. Structures and enumerations are value types, not reference types, so they cannot be stored and passed by reference.

Managing ARC in Swift

ARC allocates a part of its internal memory to keep information about each new instance of a class that is created. The values of any stored attributes linked to the instance and information about the instance's type are saved in this memory.

Also, when an instance is no longer needed, ARC releases the memory it was using to be used for something else. By doing this, class instances that are no longer needed won't keep taking up memory. The access to those instance attributes and method calls would be lost if ARC were to deallocate an instance while it was still in use. Indeed, your app would probably break if you tried to access the instance. To better understand it, consider the following example:

```
class Student {
    let name: String
    init(name: String) {
        self.name = name
        print("\(name) is initialised")
    }
    deinit {
        print("\(name) is deinitialised")
    }
}
```

The initializer for the **Student** class sets the instance's name property and produces a message to show that initialization is taking place. The following code snippet creates four variables of type **Student?** used in the following code fragments to make several references to a new **Student** instance. Since these variables are of the optional type (**Student?**, not **Student**), and they do not currently belong to a **Student** instance, they start with nil.

```
var ref1: Student?
var ref2: Student?
```

```
var ref3: Student?
var ref4: Student?
```

Now we will make a new instance of the **Student** class and connect it to the **ref1** we already have.

```
ref1 = Student(name: "David Warner")
```

When you call the initializer for the **Student** class, you should take note that the message **Davin Warner is initialized** is printed. This is evidence that initialization has occurred.

There is now a strong reference from **reference1** to the new **Student** instance since the new **Student** instance has been set to the **reference1** variable. The ARC ensures that this student is retained in memory and is not deallocated because there is at least one solid reference to them. If we assign this **ref1** to the other three student references, the following three strong references are linked to it:

```
ref2 = ref1
ref3 = ref1
ref4 = ref1
```

There are now four distinct references to the **Student** class in the same instance. If we want to break three of these references including which we initialized initially via assigning nil even then **Student** class instance will not be deallocated completely as follows:

```
ref1 = nil
ref2 = nil
ref3 = nil
```

Here, ARC will not deallocate the **Student** instance, which we initialized on **ref1**, until the final **ref4** is not broken and assigned to nil. If we assign nil to the 4th reference, then it will print the deallocation message as follows:

```
    ref3 = nil
// Prints "David Warner is deinitialized"
```

ARC keeps track of how many attributes, constants, and variables are now referring to each class instance to make sure that instances do not disappear when they are still needed. As long as there is still at least one active reference to an instance, ARC will not deallocate it.

<Image>

Strong reference cycle class problem

It is possible to develop code so that a class instance never reaches the state of having no strong references. This can happen if two different instances of the same class keep a strong reference to each other, which keeps the other instance alive. Strong reference cycles can be fixed by changing some of the links between classes from strong to weak or unowned references, which we will go over in greater depth in the next section. Still, first we must understand how this strong reference cycle is produced when coding:

```
class Student {
    let name: String
    init(name: String) { self.name = name }
    var apartment: Department?
    deinit { print("\(name) is deinitialized") }
}
class Scholarship {
    let amount: Int32
    init(amount: String) { self.amount = amount }
    var awardedTo: Student?
    deinit { print("Scholarship \(amount) is deinitialized") }
}
```

Each **Student** instance contains a **String** type **name** property and an optional, initially nil **Scholarship** property. Given that not everyone has been awarded a **Scholarship**, the scholarship is optional. Similar to this, each **Scholarship** instance has an optional **awardedTo** property that starts out nil and an amount property of type **Int32**. Because a **Scholarship** may not always have a **Student** to grant it to, the **awardedTo** parameter is optional.

Both of these classes have a deinitializer that sends a message when an instance of the class is being thrown away. You may then check to verify if instances of **Student** and **Scholarship** are being dealt with in the manner you anticipate.

Strong reference cycle class solution

When working with properties of a class type, Swift offers two solutions to strong reference cycles: weak references and unowned references. With weak and unowned references, one instance in a reference cycle can point to the other instance while still only having a weak hold on it. Instances may then make references to one another without establishing a stable reference cycle. Use a weak reference when the other instance can be freed before the current one and has a shorter life than the current one.

Weak reference

A weak reference is one that does not hold on tightly to the instance it points to. This lets ARC get rid of the object it points to without being stopped. Due to this behavior, the reference cannot join a powerful reference cycle. You can show that a property or variable is a weak reference by putting the keyword **weak** in front of the declaration.

A weak reference does not have a firm hold on the object it points to, so it is possible for an instance to be freed up even though it still points to it. So, when the instance it points to is freed, ARC sets the weak reference right away to nil. Also, weak references are usually written as variables instead of constants of an optional type because their value must be able to change to **nil** at runtime.

Like any other optional value, the **weak** reference may be checked for values, and you will not ever get a reference to an incorrect instance that no longer exists:

```
class Customer {
    let name: String
    var card: CreditCard?

    init(name: String) {
        self.name = name
    }

    deinit {
        print("\(name) is being deinitialized")
    }
}
class CreditCard {
    let number: String
    weak var customer: Customer?

    init(number: String, customer: Customer) {
        self.number = number
        self.customer = customer
    }

    deinit {
        print("Card #\(number) is being deinitialized")
    }
}
// Create a customer and credit card
var john: Customer? = Customer(name: "John")
var johnsCard: CreditCard? = CreditCard(number: "1234-5678-9101-1121", customer:
john!)
// Assign the credit card to the customer
john?.card = johnsCard
```

```
// Destroy the original references to the objects
john = nil
johnsCard = nil
```

In the given example, the **CreditCard** class has a weak reference to a **Customer** object. This means that the **CreditCard** object does not have a strong reference to the **Customer** object, and therefore will not prevent the **Customer** object from being deallocated. However, the **CreditCard** object will still be able to access the **Customer** object as long as it is not nil.

Unowned reference

An unowned reference has a weaker hold on the instance it refers to than a weak reference does. An unowned reference is used, as opposed to a weak reference, when the other instance has the same or a longer lifespan. The **unowned** keyword should come before the declaration of a property or variable to show that the reference is not owned by anything. As opposed to a weak reference, a reference that is not owned is expected to always have value. Since ARC never sets an unowned reference's value to nil, designating a value as unowned does not make it optional.

It is important to do that; use an unowned reference only if you are certain that it always links to a non-deallocated instance. If you try to access the value of an unowned reference after that instance has been freed, you will get a runtime error.

Unowned optional reference

An optional reference to a class can be designated as unowned. The ARC ownership model says that a **weak** reference and an optional reference that is not owned can be used in the same ways. The difference is that when you use an unowned optional reference, it is up to you to make sure it always points to a valid object or is set to nil:

```
class CreditCard {
    let number: String
    unowned let customer: Customer

    init(number: String, customer: Customer) {
        self.number = number
        self.customer = customer
    }

    deinit {
        print("Card #\(number) is being deinitialized")
    }
}
```

```
// Create a customer and credit card
var peter: Customer? = Customer(name: "Peter")
var peterCard: CreditCard? = CreditCard(number: "1234-5678-9101-1121", customer:
peter!)
// Assign the credit card to the customer
peter?.card = peterCard
// Destroy the original references to the objects
peter = nil
peterCard = nil
```

In the example, the **CreditCard** class has a reference to a **Customer** object that it does not own. This means that the **CreditCard** object does not have a strong reference to the **Customer** object, and therefore will not prevent the **Customer** object from being deallocated. However, the **CreditCard** object can still access the **Customer** object as long as it is not nil.

Strong reference cycle problem - closures

As we have seen before, a strong reference cycle can happen when two class instance properties keep strong references to each other. You also learned how to break these powerful reference cycles by using weak references and references that are not yours.

If you set a closure to a class instance's property and the closure's body captures the instance, a strong reference cycle may also result. This capture may happen when the closure calls a method on the instance, such as **self.someMethod**, or when the closure's body accesses a property of the instance, such as **self.anyProperty**. Because of both of these accesses, the closure *captures* itself, which makes the reference cycle stronger.

Closures, like classes, are reference types, which leads to the existence of this strong reference cycle. When you give a property a closure, you give it a reference to the closure. When you give a property a closure, you give it a reference to the closure. In essence, it is the same issue as before—two powerful references are maintaining one another. However, instead of two class instances, this time a class instance and a closure are the ones who keep each other alive:

```
class MyClass {
    var closure: (() -> Void)?
    init() {
        closure = {
            guard let strongRef = self else { return }
            // Use strongRef to do something.
    }
}
```

In the given code example, the closure grabs a reference to **self** (the object it is defined in) and holds on to it, causing a strong reference cycle.

Strong reference cycle solution - closures

By including a capture list in the definition of the closure, you can prevent a strong reference cycle from happening between the closure and a class instance. A capture list tells you how to handle capturing one or more reference types in the body of the closure. You declare each captured reference to be a weak or unowned reference instead of a strong reference, just like you do when two class instances are in a strong reference cycle. Whether you should use weak or unowned depends on how the different parts of your code work together.

```
closure = { [weak self] in
            guard let strongRef = self else { return }
            // Do something with strongRef
        }
```

To avoid this, we can use the **weak** keyword to create a weak reference to **self** in the closure. This breaks the cycle and lets the object be freed up when it is no longer needed.

Capture list

With closure capture lists, the problem of a strong reference cycle in Swift can be solved in a very elegant way. But it helps to know how a cycle like this could start before learning how to break it with a closing capture list. In each item of a capture list, the **weak** or **unowned** keyword is paired with a reference to a class instance, like self, or a variable that has been set to a value, like **delegate = self.delegate**. These pairs are shown by a pair of square brackets with a comma in between.

```
var value = 10
let incrementer = { [value] in
    value += 1
    print(value)
}
incrementer() // prints 11
incrementer() // prints 12
```

In the example, the value variable is sent to the closure via the capture **list [value]**. This lets the closure access the value of the value and change it, even though the value is defined outside of the scope of the closure.

If we did not include value in the capture list, the closure would not have access to the variable, and we would get a compile-time error.

Memory safety

Swift automatically stops dangerous behavior from occurring in your code. Swift, for instance, makes sure that memory is not accessed after it has been deallocated and that array indices are checked for out-of-bounds errors. Swift also stops memory access conflicts by making sure that the code that changes a part of memory has exclusive access to that part of memory. Most of the time, you do not even have to think about accessing memory because Swift handles memory automatically. It is important to be aware of potential conflict points, so you do not write code that accesses memory at the same time. Conflicts in your code will result in a compile-time or run-time error.

Conflict in accessing memory

Access to memory happens when you do things in your code, like change the value of a variable or pass an argument to a function. When separate sections of your code attempt to access the same region in memory at the same time, a conflicting memory access might happen. Multiple simultaneous visits to the same part of memory could lead to behavior that is unexpected or doesn't make sense. In Swift, you can change a value over several lines of code, so it is possible to try to access a variable while it is still being changed. Sometimes there are several solutions to the issue, each of which yields a different result, and it is not always clear which solution is right.

Main characteristic of accessing memory

In the case of conflicting access, three aspects of memory access should be taken into consideration: the length of the access, the location in memory being accessed, and whether the access is a read or a write. A conflict happens specifically if you have two accesses that satisfy each of the requirements listed as follows:

- A write access or a nonatomic access is present in at least one.
- They make use of the same memory address.
- Their time frames intersect together.

A write access modifies the address in memory, but a read access does not. This distinction between the two operations is generally clear-cut. What is being accessed, like a variable, constant, or property, is shown by where it is in memory. Memory accesses can be short-term or long-term in duration.

Instantaneous memory access

An access is said to be instantaneous if no more code can be run after it starts but before it ends. Two simultaneous instantaneous accesses are inherently impossible. Instantaneous memory access is the norm. For instance, all read and write accesses in the following code listing happen instantly:

```
func addOneNumber(than num: Int) -> Int {
    return number + 1
}
var numone = 1
```

```
myOne = addOneNumber(than: numone)
print(myOne)
// Prints "2"
```

Long-term accesses, or ways to get to memory that do not depend on the execution of other code, come in many different forms. Long-term access is different from instantaneous access because other code can run before a long-term access starts but after it ends. This is called **overlap**. A long-term access may cross paths with both short-term and long-term accesses.

Conflicting access

There are mainly three ways that can cause conflicting access while doing code in Swift. And we have to handle those memory conflict accesses so that they will not cause any issues. Those three code patterns and sequences are as follows:

- In-Out parameters
- Self - In methods
- Properties

In- Out parameters

All of a function's in-out parameters are permanently accessible for writing. The write access for an in-out parameter starts after all non-in-out arguments have been evaluated and continues for the whole function call. If there are several in-out parameters, the write accesses begin with the first one.

Because of this long-term write access, you cannot access the original variable that was given as in-out, even if access control and scoping constraints would normally let you. This is because any access to the original causes a conflict:

```
func modifyArray(array: inout [Int]) {
    // Modify the array
    array[0] = 100
    array[1] = 200
    array[2] = 300

    DispatchQueue.global(qos: .background).async {
        print(array[0]) // This will cause a conflicting access error
    }
}
var numbers = [1, 2, 3]
modifyArray(array: &numbers)
```

```
// Output: "fatal error: conflicting accesses to In-Out parameter 'array'"
```

Self - In methods

During the method call, a mutating method on a structure has write access to self. Consider a report where each student has a certain quantity of energy and a certain amount of grade score, which both diminish when they are damaged or when they use special skills.

```
struct Student {
    var name: String
    var health: Int
    var gradeScore: Int

    static let maxHealth = 10
    mutating func restoreHealth() {
        health = Student.maxHealth
    }
}
func balance(_ x: inout Int, _ y: inout Int) {
    let sum = x + y
    x = sum / 2
    y = sum - x
}
extension Student {
    mutating func shareHealth(with classmate: inout Student) {
        balance(&classmate.health, &health)
    }
}
var jane = Student(name: "Jane", health: 10, gradeScore: 10)
var john = Student(name: "John", health: 5, gradeScore: 10)
jane.shareHealth(with: &john)
jane.shareHealth(with: &jane) // This will cause a runtime error due to conflicting
access to self in the changeName method.
```

Properties

Individual constituent values, such as the characteristics of a structure or the members of a tuple, makeup types like structures, tuples, and enumerations. Since they are value types, any change to any part of the value changes the whole value. This means that you need access to the whole value to read or write to any of the attributes. For example, there is a conflict when two writers have access to the same part of a struct's properties at the same time:

```
struct Person {
        var name: String
        var age: Int
    }
var person1 = Person(name: "John", age: 30)
```

Here it will show a conflicting access error because we are trying to access the **age** property of **person1**. while another thread is changing it:

```
DispatchQueue.global().async {
        person1.age = 35
    }
print(person1.age)
```

We can fix the conflicting access error by using a dispatch group to synchronize access to the **age** and **name** properties. Since **DispatchGroup** is part of iOS's idea of *multithreading*, we will talk about it in the chapter about multithreading.

Conclusion

iOS's Automatic Reference Counting tool for managing memory keeps track of and controls how long application objects live. So, resources are freed up when they are no longer needed. This keeps memory leaks from happening. Memory safety, on the other hand, means that a program can access memory in a safe and reliable way. When developers use ARC and other safe programming techniques, they can make iOS apps that work well and do not have the usual bugs when working with memory.

In this chapter, we learned how ARC and memory safety are important concepts in iOS development. ARC takes care of your app's memory by keeping and releasing objects as needed. This helps stop memory leaks and other problems. Memory safety makes sure that your app accesses memory safely and predictably. This can keep your app from crashing or making other mistakes. By understanding ARC and memory safety and using them correctly, you can make iOS apps that work better and are more stable.

In the next chapter, we will start learning about implementing iOS 17 architecture in iOS app development with the Swift language.

Multiple choice questions

1. **What is the full form of ARC _____________.**
    a. Automatic Retain Count
    b. Automatic Reference Count
    c. Automatic Refine Count
    d. Automatic Reframe Count
2. **When does the retain count increase with +1 ___________ ?**
    a. For strong reference
    b. For weak reference
    c. For unowned reference
    d. None of the above
3. **Which one is the main characteristic of accessing memory?**
    a. Weak and unowned references are just type aliases.
    b. A property makes use of the same memory address.
    c. Strong references are never deallocated.
    d. None of the above
4. **Which one is the type of conflicting access?**
    a. Strong, weak, or unowned
    b. In-Out parameters, Self - In Methods, Properties
    c. Strong Reference Cycle, Weak Reference Cycle
    d. None of the above
5. **What is instantaneous memory access?**
    a. Creating a new collection type and access its element
    b. Creating a new strong and one weak reference
    c. No more code can be run after it starts but before it ends
    d. None of the above
6. **How Strong Reference Cycle occurs?**
    a. When two struct reference points to each other
    b. When two Strong reference of class instance part of each other
    c. Creating a new strong and one weak reference
    d. None of the above

7. **What is correct with respect to capture list?**
    a. When two Strong reference of class instance part of each other
    b. The weak or unowned keyword is paired with a reference to a class instance
    c. When two struct reference points to each other
    d. None of the above
8. **What is correct with respect to Weak and Unowned?**
    a. Unowned reference will not be nil whenever accessed
    b. Weak reference will not be nil whenever accessed
    c. Strong reference will not be nil whenever accessed
    d. All of the above
9. **Strong reference cycle can occur:-**
    a. In Between Class and Closure
    b. In Between Struct and Closure
    c. In Between Struct and Enum
    d. None of the above
10. **Why does the capture list have a weak or unowned self:**
    a. To avoid a strong reference cycle in closures
    b. To avoid a strong reference cycle in classes
    c. To avoid a strong reference cycle in structure
    d. None of the above

Answers

1. b
2. a
3. b
4. b
5. c
6. b
7. b
8. a
9. a
10. a

Chapter 6
Implementing iOS 17 Architecture

Introduction

iOS 17 is the latest version of Apple's operating system for its line of mobile devices, such as the iPhone and iPad. It adds a lot of new features and improvements to the platform, like tweaks to the user interface, better performance, and new versions of core apps and frameworks. One of the key aspects of developing apps for iOS is the use of architecture patterns. These patterns give a structured way to design and build software, which helps make sure it is easy to understand, maintain, and grow.

In this chapter, we will talk about some of the most important things to think about when building an iOS 17 architecture, such as picking the right pattern, organizing your codebase, and following best practices for performance and ease of maintenance. We will also talk about some common tools and technologies used in iOS development.

Structure

In this chapter, we will cover the following topics:

- Architecture of iOS 17 OS
- Implementation of iOS 17 architecture

Objectives

By reading this chapter, you will be able to learn how to put the iOS 17 architecture into action. Also, you will be able to learn more about iOS features, advantages, disadvantages, patterns, and anti-patterns.

iOS 17 architecture

The architecture of iOS 17 is a complex and highly sophisticated system that was made so that users can use their devices in a way that is smooth and easy to understand. The architecture is made up of several layers, each of which is important to how the operating system works as a whole; refer to the following figure:

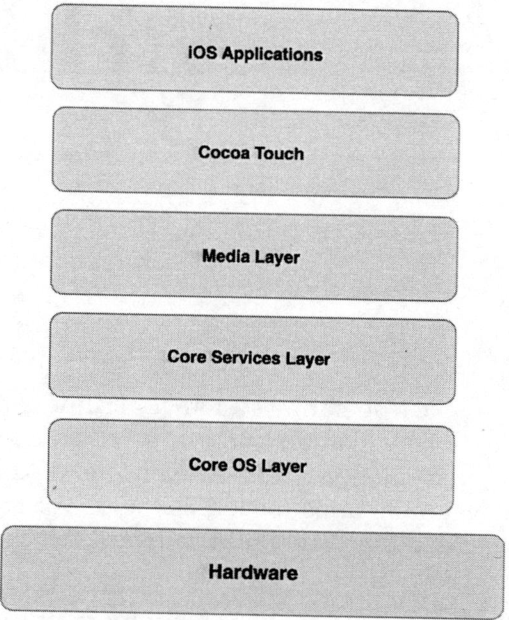

Figure 6.1: *iOS 17 architecture*

At the core of the iOS 17 architecture is the kernel, which is responsible for managing the hardware resources of the device and providing a platform for the other layers of the operating system to run on. The kernel does a lot of different things, such as managing memory, processes, and device drivers, among other things. It also talks to the device's hardware, letting applications use the camera, microphone, and sensors, among other hardware features.

Let us discuss all the layers and components of architecture:

- **Hardware**: This is the physical device, including the processor, memory, storage, and other hardware components.
- **Core OS**: This layer includes low-level system services, such as the kernel, drivers, and firmware. It is in charge of managing the device's hardware resources and giving the other parts of the system basic services.

- **Core services:** This layer is made up of the basic system services that the higher levels of the system need. Examples of core services include the Core Foundation and Core Location frameworks.
- **Media**: This layer includes the frameworks and technologies that are used to support audio, video, and graphics on the device.
- **Cocoa Touch:** This is the top layer of the iOS architecture, and it is in charge of the user interface and how apps work. It has the UIKit framework and other frameworks that support multitasking, touch-based input, and other features.
- **Apps**: This layer includes the individual apps that are installed on the device. These apps were made with the help of the Cocoa Touch layer's frameworks and technologies.

The core services layer provides a range of APIs and frameworks for developers to use when building their applications. These core services include things like networking, database management, and location services, among others. They provide the building blocks that developers need to create complex and feature-rich applications that can take advantage of the capabilities of the device. The media layer sits on top of the core services layer. It is in charge of all the audio and video needs of the operating system and applications. This layer supports a wide range of media formats and codecs and has hardware acceleration to make sure that playback is smooth and quick.

Finally, at the top of the iOS 17 architecture is the Cocoa Touch layer, which is the layer that users interact with when using their devices. This layer has the user interface frameworks and controls that are used to build an application's user interface. It also includes support for touch gestures and other input methods, as well as features like accessibility and localization. Overall, iOS 17's architecture is a highly optimized and efficient system that was made so that users can use their devices in a way that is smooth and easy to understand. It shows how good Apple is at engineering and design, and it has been a key part of the success of the iOS platform.

Features of iOS 17

There are many features available in the iOS operating system, which is used on Apple's iPhone, iPad, and iPod touch devices. Some of the main features include:

- **User interface:** iOS has a user-friendly interface with a home screen that displays app icons, a dock at the bottom of the screen for accessing frequently used apps, and a control center for quick access to settings and features.
- **Multitasking:** iOS allows users to multitask, meaning they can switch between apps or run multiple apps at the same time.
- **Siri:** Siri is a voice-activated personal assistant that allows users to perform tasks, get information, and make recommendations using natural language commands.
- **Apple Pay:** Apple Pay is a mobile payment and digital wallet service that allows users to make payments and purchases using their iPhone or other compatible device.
- **iCloud:** iCloud is a cloud-based storage and synchronization service that allows users to store and access their documents, photos, and other data from any device.

- **App Store:** The App Store is a digital marketplace for downloading and purchasing apps for iOS devices. It has a wide range of apps available, including productivity tools, games, and social media apps.
- **Face ID and Touch ID:** Face ID and Touch ID are facial recognition and fingerprint recognition technologies that allow users to securely unlock their devices and make payments using biometric authentication.
- **Camera and Photos:** The iOS camera and photos app includes a variety of features and filters for taking and editing photos, as well as organizing and sharing them.
- **iMessage:** iMessage is a messaging app that allows users to send text, photos, and other media to other iOS users over the internet.
- **ARKit:** ARKit is a framework for creating augmented reality (AR) experiences on iOS devices. It allows developers to create interactive AR apps and games.

Advantages of iOS 17

iOS 17 is the latest version of the operating system for Apple's iPhone and iPad devices. Some of the main advantages of iOS 17 include:

- **Improved performance**: Apple has made a number of improvements to the operating system to make it faster and more efficient, which should lead to better performance on devices running iOS 17.
- **New features**: iOS 17 adds a number of new features and improvements to the operating system, such as a redesigned App Library, a new App Clips feature for quickly accessing small parts of app functionality, and changes to the Photos app.
- **Enhanced privacy and security**: Apple have made a number of enhancements to the privacy and security features of iOS 17, including a new **App Privacy Report** feature that shows users which apps are accessing their data and how they are using it.
- **Widgets have been made better**: iOS 17 has a new widget feature that lets users add information and functions from their favorite apps to their home screen.
- **Improved notifications**: iOS 17 includes a number of improvements to the notification system, including the ability to group notifications by app and the ability to hide or silence notifications from specific apps.

Disadvantages of iOS 17

There are a few things that you might not like about iOS 17, depending on how you use and value the features and functions on your device. Some possible disadvantages of iOS 17 include:

- **Compatibility issues**: Some older devices may not be able to run the latest version of iOS, which means they will not be able to take advantage of the new features and improvements.
- **Battery life concerns**: Some users have reported that upgrading to a new version of iOS can negatively impact their device's battery life.

- **Performance issues**: In some cases, installing a new version of iOS can lead to performance issues such as slower performance or app crashes.
- **Changes to user interface**: Some users may not like the changes to the user interface or other aspects of the operating system that come with a new version of iOS.
- **Loss of features**: While new versions of iOS typically add new features, they can also remove or change existing ones that some users may rely on or prefer.

Overall, it is important to carefully weigh the pros and cons of upgrading to a new version of iOS, as well as the pros and cons for your own needs and preferences.

Implementation of iOS 17 architecture

iOS 17 is the current version of the operating system that runs on Apple's mobile devices, such as the iPhone and iPad. It is built on top of Apple's proprietary Darwin operating system and uses a number of technologies, frameworks, and libraries to provide a wide range of features and functionality.

The architecture of iOS 17 is based on the **model-view-controller** (**MVC**) design pattern, which is a software architecture that separates the representation of information from the user's interaction with it. In the MVC pattern, the model is the application's data and business logic. The view is the user interface, and the controller is the link between the model and the view.

The Cocoa Touch framework is a key part of the iOS architecture. It gives developers the basic tools they need to make iOS apps. It includes a set of libraries, APIs, and tools that are used to create the user interface, manage the app's lifecycle, and handle device-specific features such as multitouch and the accelerometer. Now, we will talk in detail about the most important technologies and frameworks used in the iOS 17 architecture:

Foundation

Foundation is a framework for iOS that gives apps and other frameworks a basic layer of functionality. It has classes for working with data, strings, dates, file management, and other things. Foundation includes classes for dealing with basic data types, including integers, strings, and collections. In the Foundation framework, there are classes for working with dates, times, and time zones. It also has classes that teach how to read, write, and work with files and the file system. The Foundation framework has classes that let you talk to network sockets and send HTTP requests. It provides classes for interacting with threads and queues from a concurrency viewpoint, making it easier to design concurrent applications.

UIKit

The UIKit framework is a core framework in iOS that provides a set of classes and functions for building and managing user interfaces in iOS applications. It can create and manage views and view hierarchies, handle touch and gesture input, handle user input and selection, display text and images, and interact with other system frameworks and services. The UIKit framework is a key part of many common iOS user interface patterns and features. It is used a lot in iOS development.

Core animation

The Core Animation framework is a high-level framework that allows developers to create and manipulate 2D and 3D visual effects and animations in iOS apps. It provides a set of classes that can be used to create and manipulate layers, transform and animate those layers, and create complex visual effects. One of the best things about the Core Animation framework is that it can run animations smoothly and quickly, even on devices that do not have a lot of resources. It does this by using hardware acceleration whenever possible, and by using techniques such as compositing and caching to minimize the impact on the device's CPU and memory.

The Core Animation framework also provides a wide range of pre-built animations and effects, such as basic fade and slide animations, as well as more complex effects such as particle systems and physics-based animations. It also allows developers to create custom animations using keyframes and timing functions.

Core data

Core data is a framework in iOS that provides an object-oriented interface for managing data in an application. It allows developers to store, retrieve, and manipulate data in a structured and efficient manner. Core data works by creating a database schema, which defines the entities and their relationships within the data model. The framework then provides methods for interacting with this data, such as creating, updating, and deleting records. Core data also supports data validation and concurrency, making it a powerful tool for managing data in iOS applications. We will discuss its practical implementation in *Chapter 11: Storing Data in SQLite and Core Data* of this book.

Core graphics

Core graphics is a framework in iOS that allows developers to create and manipulate graphics and images. It is commonly used for creating custom views, drawing shapes and lines, and creating complex graphics such as charts and diagrams. It provides a set of APIs and classes for working with 2D graphics, including support for affine transformations, color management, and path-based drawing. It also allows developers to create and modify PDF documents, create and work with images, and use Quartz 2D to draw to the screen. We will discuss its practical implementation in *Chapter 13: App Gestures and Animation in iOS* of this book.

Core ML

Core ML is a framework in iOS that allows developers to integrate machine learning models into their apps. It allows developers to take advantage of the advanced artificial intelligence and machine learning capabilities of Apple's devices, without needing to have extensive knowledge in the field. With Core ML, developers can easily import pre-trained machine learning models and use them to make predictions or classify data in their app. The framework also provides tools for training and fine-tuning machine learning models, so developers can customize the models to their specific needs.

Core ML is optimized for on-device performance, so it can be used to make predictions and classify data even when the device is offline. This makes it a useful tool for building apps that need to work in low-connectivity or offline environments. The Core ML framework makes it easy for developers to add the power of machine learning to their iOS apps. This lets them make apps that are smarter and more complex for their users. We will discuss its practical implementation in *Chapter 16: Machine Learning with Core ML* of this book.

ARKit

Apple made ARKit, which is a framework for **augmented reality** (**AR**) apps on iOS devices. It lets developers make AR experiences that can be layered on top of the real world using the camera and sensors of the device. The ARKit framework consists of several different components, including:

- **ARSession**: This is the main class that manages the AR experience. It is in charge of tracking the device's position and orientation in the real world and figuring out what the device's sensors are telling it.
- **ARConfiguration:** This class defines the settings and parameters that the **`ARSession`** uses to give a good AR experience. It includes options such as the type of tracking used (for example, image tracking, face tracking, and so on), the level of detail in the AR scene, and the minimum and maximum tracking distances.
- **ARAnchor**: This class represents a fixed point in the real world that is used to anchor AR content to a specific location.
- **ARSCNView** is a subclass of **`UIView`** that displays AR content using **`SceneKit`**, Apple's 3D graphics framework. This is a subclass of **`UIView`** that uses **`SceneKit`**, Apple's 3D graphics framework, to show AR content. It allows developers to create 3D models and animations that can be placed in the AR world.
- **ARSKView** is a subclass of **`UIView`** that uses Apple's 2D graphics framework, **`SpriteKit`**, to show AR content. It allows developers to create 2D graphics and animations that can be overlaid on the AR world.

Core Bluetooth

With iOS's Core Bluetooth framework, developers can make apps that talk to **Bluetooth Low Energy** (**BLE**) devices. It gives you classes that you can use to find, connect, and talk to BLE devices, as well as handle BLE data and events.

Some key features of the Core Bluetooth framework include:

- **Scanning for and discovering BLE devices:** Developers can use the framework to scan for nearby BLE devices, and then connect to and communicate with them.
- **Establishing and maintaining connections**: The framework provides classes for establishing and maintaining connections with BLE devices, including handling disconnections and reconnections.
- **Communicating with BLE devices:** The framework provides classes for sending and receiving data to and from BLE devices, as well as handling BLE data and events.
- **Handling BLE data and events:** The framework has classes for handling BLE data and events, like getting notified when the characteristic value of a BLE device changes.

Core NFC

The Core NFC Framework in iOS is a framework that allows developers to create apps that can read NFC tags and interact with NFC devices. This framework can be used to create a variety of apps, such as payment apps, access control apps, and loyalty programs.

For developers to use the Core NFC framework, they must first add it to their project and then set up an NFC reader session. This session can then be used to scan NFC tags and interact with NFC devices. The Core NFC framework also enables developers to write data to NFC tags that other NFC-enabled devices can read. The Core NFC framework in iOS gives developers a powerful tool for making apps that can interact with NFC tags and devices. This opens up a wide range of options for applications that use NFC.

WidgetKit

`WidgetKit` is a powerful new framework in iOS 17 that allows developers to easily build attractive, useful widgets for the iPhone lock screen and Apple Watch. Developers may use **`WidgetKit`** to build widgets that show the most recent information from their applications, such as the weather, calendar events, sports scores, and more. Widgets may be customized to show various information based on the user's requirements, and they can be added in a number of sizes on the lock screen or Apple Watch.

`WidgetKit` is a big upgrade over iOS's prior widget creation framework. Previously, developers had to write individual code for each widget, which took time and was difficult to maintain. Developers may use **`WidgetKit`** to construct widgets using **`SwiftUI`**, a powerful new declarative framework that makes it simple to design attractive, responsive user interfaces.

`WidgetKit` is a significant new feature in iOS 17, and it has the potential to transform how we interact with our smartphones. Developers may use **`WidgetKit`** to construct widgets that offer us the information we need at a glance without having to launch our applications. This may help us save time and remain productive throughout the day.

Here are some of WidgetKit's important features in iOS 17:

- Widget support for the iPhone Lock Screen and Apple Watch
- Ability to customize widgets to show various information based on the requirements of the user
- Ability to add widgets of various sizes to the Lock Screen or Apple Watch
- SwiftUI, a strong new declarative framework, is used to create widgets.
- WidgetKit is a powerful new tool for developers that may assist them in creating attractive, useful widgets for the iPhone Lock Screen and Apple Watch.

Developers may use **`WidgetKit`** to give consumers the information they need at a glance without having to launch their applications. This may help users save time and remain productive throughout the day.

WeatherKit

WeatherKit is a new framework in iOS 17 that allows developers to easily include weather data into their applications. **WeatherKit** gives you access to a variety of weather data, such as current conditions, predictions, and alarms. Developers can create weather-aware applications using **WeatherKit** that provide users with the information they require to stay safe and informed. One of WeatherKit's primary characteristics is its ability to provide real-time weather data. **WeatherKit** allows developers to receive the most up-to-date weather conditions for any area on the planet. This information may be used to construct applications that give users current weather information such as temperature, precipitation, and wind speed.

WeatherKit now gives predictions for up to ten days. This information may be used to develop applications that assist users in planning their days and activities, such as packing for a vacation or determining the optimum time to go for a walk.

Finally, **WeatherKit** gives you access to severe weather warnings. This information may be utilized to develop applications that assist users in remaining safe during extreme weather events such as hurricanes, tornadoes, and floods.

WeatherKit is a powerful new tool that may assist developers in developing weather-aware applications. Developers may use **WeatherKit** to provide users with the information they need to be safe and informed.

Here are some of WeatherKit's important features:

- Real-time weather data is available.
- Forecasts for up to 10 days are available.
- Availability of severe weather warnings
- API that is simple to use
- Supports a variety of platforms

WeatherKit is an excellent alternative for developers looking to incorporate weather data into their products. It is simple to use and gives you access to a broad variety of meteorological data. If you are working on an app that requires weather data, we suggest taking a look at **WeatherKit**.

RoomPlan

The **RoomPlan** API is a new framework in iOS 16 that makes it easy for developers to create 3D models of rooms using the LiDAR scanner on the iPhone and iPad Pro. The API can be used to create accurate and detailed models of rooms, which can be used for a variety of purposes, such as interior design, real estate, and augmented reality. To use the **RoomPlan** API, developers first need to create a **RoomCaptureSession** object. This object represents a single scan of a room. Once the **RoomCaptureSession** object is created, developers can use the API to add objects to the scan, such as walls, doors, and furniture. The API can also be used to track the user's movement as they scan the room, which can be used to create more accurate models.

Once the scan is complete, developers can export the model to a variety of formats, such as USDZ and OBJ. These formats can then be used in other applications, such as 3D modeling software or augmented reality apps.

The `RoomPlan` API is a powerful new tool that can be used to create accurate and detailed 3D models of rooms. The API is easy to use and can be used for a variety of purposes. If you are developing an app that needs to create 3D models of rooms, we recommend checking out the `RoomPlan` API.

Activitykit

Activitykit has seamless integration with other apps. For instance, an e-commerce app can utilize an Activitykit to allow users to share their favorite products on social media platforms like Facebook or Instagram directly from within the app. This integration not only enhances the user experience but also promotes organic marketing for the e-commerce brand as users' friends and followers can easily discover and engage with the shared products. A document editing app can use Activitykit to allow users to easily share and collaborate on documents with their colleagues or friends. This integration enables real-time collaboration, where multiple users can simultaneously edit and make changes to the same document, enhancing productivity and streamlining communication within teams or groups.

TipKit

TipKit is a comprehensive database of tipping guidelines for various industries, such as restaurants, hotels, and salons. This database provides users with specific information on how much to tip based on the quality of service received and the location. For instance, if a person dines at a restaurant in New York City, TipKit can provide them with the recommended tipping percentage for that specific area. A customer can use TipKit to leave a detailed review and tip amount for a hair salon, allowing future customers to make informed decisions based on previous experiences. Additionally, TipKit allows service providers to track their performance and receive feedback in real-time, enabling them to improve their services and earn higher tips.

WorkoutKit

A fitness app could allow users to create a customized workout plan that includes a mix of cardio, strength training, and yoga exercises. The app would then track the user's progress for each exercise, providing analytics and data on sets, reps, and duration. Additionally, the app could integrate with other fitness apps and wearables to provide a comprehensive overview of the user's health and fitness journey. A user could input their desired fitness goals, such as weight loss or muscle gain, and the app would generate a personalized workout plan that takes into account their current fitness level, time availability, and preferred exercise types. The app would then provide detailed instructions and videos for each exercise, allowing the user to easily follow along and track their progress. Additionally, the app could sync with popular fitness trackers and apps like Fitbit or MyFitnessPal to provide a complete picture of the user's daily activity.

Conclusion

In this chapter, we talked in detail about how implementing the architecture of iOS 17 can be both hard and rewarding for developers. It is important to consider the various patterns and anti-patterns that can impact the design and functionality of an app. By following best practices carefully and avoiding common mistakes, developers can make an iOS app that works well and meets users' needs. Developers can ensure that their apps are optimized for performance and user experience by staying up to date with the latest iOS architecture and patterns. We will learn about a few of the above frameworks in detail in *Chapter 22: Advance iOS with New Frameworks* of this book.

In the next chapter, we will start learning about user interface design with Interface Builder, which is used in iOS app development with the Swift language.

Multiple choice questions

1. **ARKit is used for _______________.**
    a. Artificial Reality Implementation
    b. Artificial Reflection Implementation
    c. Augmented Reality Implementation
    d. None of the above
2. **Core Data is used for ___________ ?**
    a. Updating Data to Network
    b. Upload Data to Server
    c. Efficiently Save data to Local
    d. None of the above
3. **In Core ML, ML referrals to ____?**
    a. Mobile Learning
    b. Machine Learning
    c. Maintaining Leaning
    d. None of the above
4. **Which layer includes audio, `video` and graphics in it?**
    a. Core Services Layer
    b. Core OS Layer
    c. Media Layer
    d. None of the above

5. **iCloud is used for _______?**
   a. To maintain data locally
   b. To Save Data and sync with Apple iCloud
   c. For Data privacy and Security only
   d. None of the above
6. **The core OS Layer has significance for _______?**
   a. High level system
   b. low level systems and drivers
   c. Developers framework
   d. None of the above

Answers

1. c
2. c
3. b
4. c
5. b
6. b

Join our book's Discord space

Join the book's Discord Workspace for Latest updates, Offers, Tech happenings around the world, New Release and Sessions with the Authors:

https://discord.bpbonline.com

CHAPTER 7

User Interface Design with UIKit

Introduction

An app that helps users to perform a serious task, can keep them focused by using robust and unobtrusive graphics, standard controls and managed behaviors, can deliver captivating appearance with encouraging discovery. To maximize the overall impact and reach, designs should follow clarity with depth where users feel like they are in control by keeping interactive elements familiar and predictable, and making it easy to cancel operations, even when they are already underway.

Structure

In this chapter, we will cover the following topics:

- Interface builder
- UI components
- UINavigationController
- Size classes and AutoLayout

Objectives

By learning this chapter, you should be able to create your first UI page with Interface builder and Storyboard with different UI controls and Navigations as well as create complex UI Components and Navigation flow of application with List and grid style components.

Interface builder

Interface builder (IB) is a software development tool that is part of Xcode IDE. IB provides a collection of user interface objects for app developers to use while designing the interface of applications. To make UI with IB developer simply drags interface objects from the palette or collection onto a window or menu.

Storyboard

A Storyboard can represent visual flow of single and multiple screen designs of an application, and it is composed of a sequence of scenes, each of which represents a view controller and its views, scenes are connected by segue objects, which represent a transition between two view controllers. On iPhone, each scene corresponds to a full screen's worth of content but on iPad, multiple scenes can appear on screen at once, using popover view controllers. Each scene has a dock, which displays icons representing the top-level objects of the scene. The dock is used primarily to make action and outlet connections between the view controller and its views.

The reason behind why it's called storyboard is, it tells the story of your app designs and flow in terms of segue and scenes which could have a little difference in view as per size of screen in which you are viewing the app.

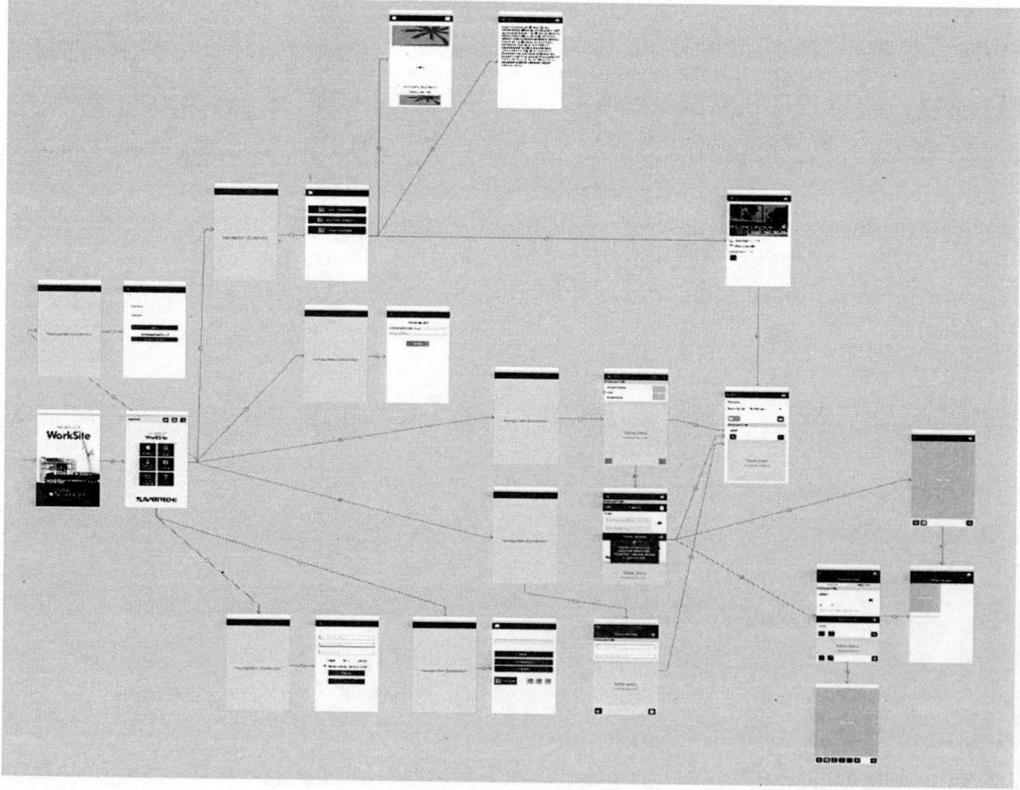

***Figure 7.1**: Storyboard*

In *Figure 7.1*, You can see a developed app with a storyboard which has 20 plus view controllers interconnected in a continuous flow either navigated from segue or with program code.

View Controller Scene

To set up a project with a storyboard initially while creating your project you need to select the interface option as **Storyboard** and **Life Cycle** option as **UIKit App Delegate** with language option **Swift**.

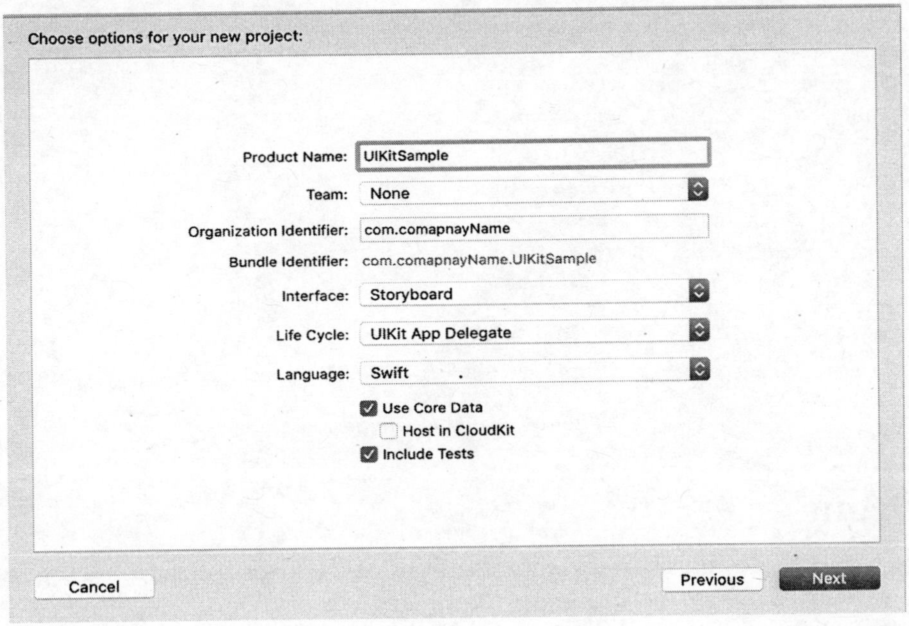

Figure 7.2: New Project

Further when Xcode window opened for project, you will find below files auto created by IDE:

- **`AppDelegate.swift`**
- **`SceneDelegate.swift`**
- **`ViewController.swift`**
- **`Main.storyboard`**
- **`Assets.xcassets`**
- **`LaunchScreen.storyboard`**

Here, **`LaunchScreen.storyboard`** is used as a launch page screen which is not part of the actual app flow and will appear till the time the app takes time to start the app to show its first screen. The **`Main.storyboard`** (by default) contains the start point of the app as well as the first screen of the app which is in general termed as **View Controller Scene**. Initial View Controller Scene represents and contains view controller, First Responder, next moving flow (in below case **Exit**), and storyboard entry point. Every Storyboard contains a single-entry point. Whichever screen pointed by the storyboard entry point will present first on the simulator of the iOS device.

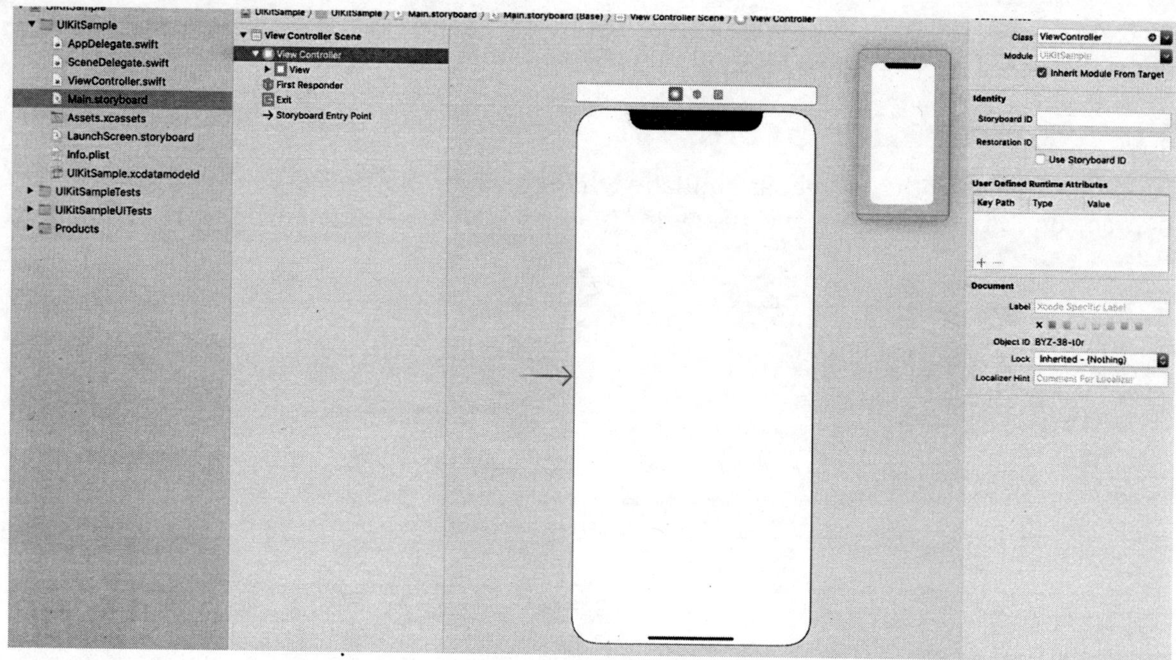

Figure 7.3: Interface Builder

Using Segue

From Segue, you can design and navigate the flow of the user interface. A segue defines a transition between two view controllers in your app's storyboard file. When selecting the relationship type for your segue, select an adaptive segue whenever possible. Adaptive segues adjust their behavior automatically based on the current environment. For example, the behavior of a show segue changes based on the presenting view controller.

App lifecycle

App lifecycle is responsible for responding to system notifications when your app is in the foreground or background and handling other significant system-related events:

- **`UISceneDelegate`** is implemented from and after iOS 13 supported apps to respond to lifecycle events in a scene-based app.
- **`UIApplicationDelegate`** is implemented till and before iOS 12 supported apps to respond to lifecycle events.

Responding to launch of app - UIApplicationDelegate

Initialize your app's data structures, prepare your app to run, and respond to any launch-time requests from the system. The following figure shows the app launch flow:

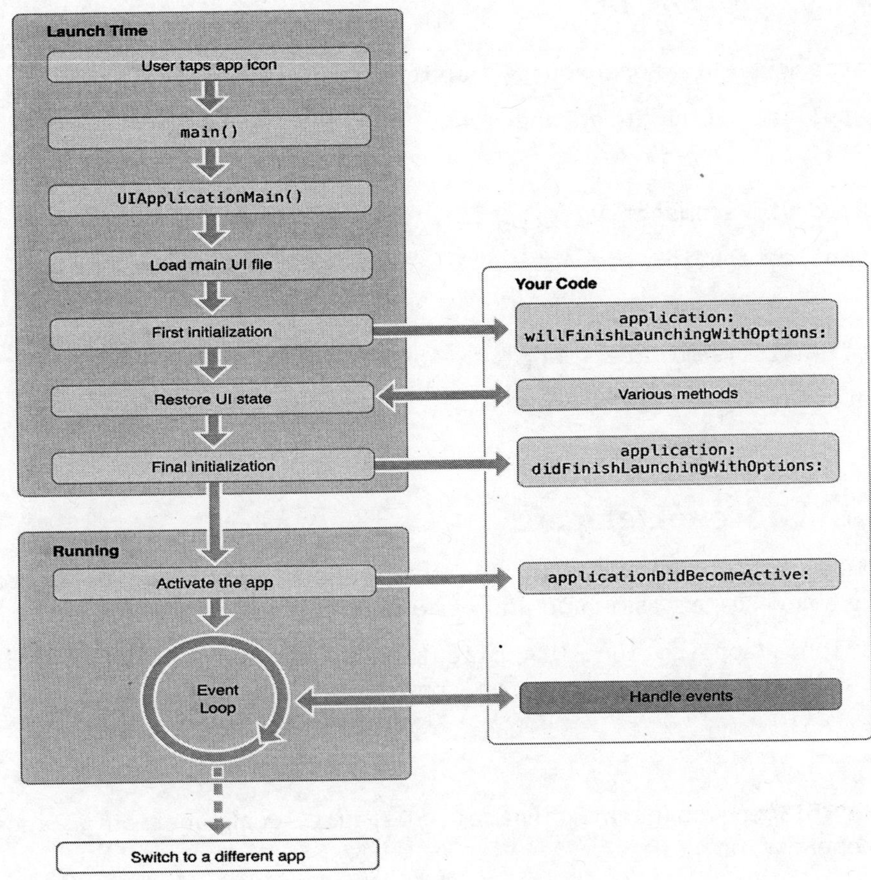

Figure 7.4: App Launch Flow

```
@UIApplicationMain
class AppDelegate: UIResponder, UIApplicationDelegate {
var window: UIWindow?
func application(_ application: UIApplication, didFinishLaunchingWithOptions
launchOptions: [UIApplication.LaunchOptionsKey: Any]?) -> Bool {
    return true
}
func applicationWillResignActive(_ application: UIApplication) {
    print("applicationWillResignActive")
}
func applicationDidEnterBackground(_ application: UIApplication) {
    print("applicationDidEnterBackground")
```

```
}
func applicationWillEnterForeground(_ application: UIApplication) {
    print("applicationWillEnterForeground")
}
func applicationDidBecomeActive(_ application: UIApplication) {
    print("applicationDidBecomeActive")
}
func applicationWillTerminate(_ application: UIApplication) {
    print("applicationWillTerminate")
}
```

Launch with UISceneDelegate

Further if you are using scene in your interface that will add two **UISceneDelegate** methods, one for starting a new scene session and another one for discarding a scene session:

```
func application(_ application: UIApplication, configurationForConnecting connectingSceneSession: UISceneSession, options: UIScene.ConnectionOptions) -> UISceneConfiguration
{
        return UISceneConfiguration(name: "Default Configuration", sessionRole: connectingSceneSession.role)
}
func application(_ application: UIApplication, didDiscardSceneSessions sceneSessions: Set<UISceneSession>) {
    // Use this method to release any resources that were specific to the discarded scenes, as they will not return.
}
```

Respond to app-based lifecycle events

When the app launches, the system puts the app in the inactive or background state, depending on whether the UI is about to appear on screen. When launching to the foreground, the system transitions the app to the active state automatically. After that, the state fluctuates between active and background until the app terminates (see *Figure 7.5*):

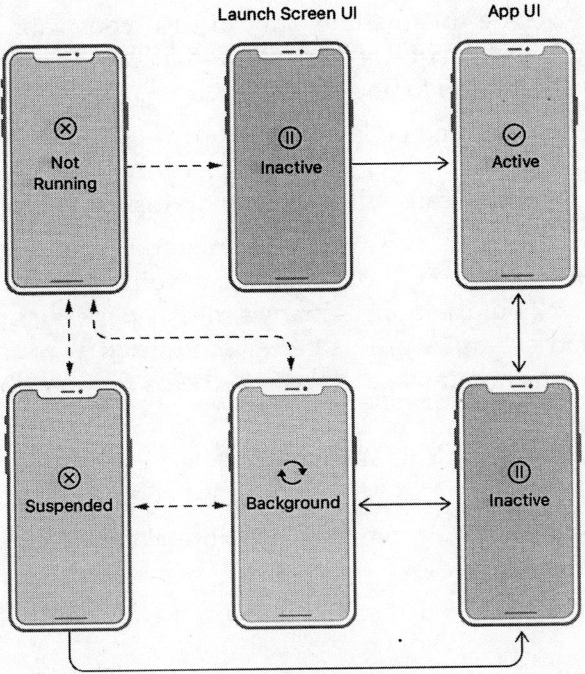

Figure 7.5: App States

View controller works as an intermediary between views of controller and data which is going to appear on view. Apple provides a class **`UIViewController`** so whenever we make a new view controller scene then we have to connect its view controller to a subclass of the **`UIViewController`**. This connection of **`UIViewcontroller`** subclass and view controller scene on the storyboard ensures that now your code can communicate with UI elements present on scenes. As you can see in *Figure 7.3* that in place of **`Content`** Class **`ViewController`** is present, which is a subclass of **`UIViewController`** auto created by Xcode IDE:

```
class ViewController: UIViewController {
    override func viewDidLoad() {
        super.viewDidLoad()
        // Do any additional setup after loading the view.
    }
}
```

View controller lifecycle

View controller life cycle discusses what stages a view controller goes and what trigger is available for you to override while it gets initialized and becomes part of the application.

- **`init`**: View controllers are initiated by storyboard usually, and internally calls **`initwithCoder()`** which you can override if required.

- **loadView**: You override this method only in case you want to make your interface completely by code instead of storyboard or nib file. And don't use this method unless there is a good valid reason to do so.
- **viewDidLoad**: When this method is called it is ensured that views of the view controller are created, and all outlets of view are in place. A good place to start background activity and start network calls when the view is loaded completely.
- **viewWillAppear**: You need to override this method when you want to repeat a task every time a view appears on screen, a view controller loads one time when pushed to the navigation stack but can appear many times as per your app flow and navigation architecture. Good examples of this case would be network calls for refresh data of some animation which you want to show to the user every time the view appears on screen.
- **viewWillLayoutSubviews**: This method is called every time the frame changes, for example when the view rotates or is marked as needing layout.
- **viewDidLayoutSubviews**: You can make additional changes here in this method after view layouts subviews.
- **viewDidAppear**: This method is called when the view controller completely appears on screen.
- **viewWillDisappear**: Before transitioning to another screen and leaving the view of the current screen this method is called.
- **viewDidDisappear**: When the current view controller is removed from the screen and another/next view controller loads on screen then this method of view controller of previous VC (not which loads recently) is called.
- **deinit**: You can override this method to clean resources that the view controller has allocated that are not freed by **Automatic retain count** (**ARC**).
- **didReceiveMemoryWarning**: When memory starts to fill up, iOS does not automatically move data from memory to its limited hard disk space. It does, however, issue this warning and as a developer you are responsible for clearing memory. Be aware that if the memory of your app goes over a certain threshold, iOS will shut down your app. And this will look similar to a crash to the end user.
- **viewWillTransition**: When the app interface orientation changes, UIKit framework calls this method to the window's root controller which sends this message to all its child view controllers just before the size is going to make changes.

```
override func viewDidLoad() {
    super.viewDidLoad()
}
override func viewWillAppear(_ animated: Bool) {
    super.viewWillAppear(animated)
}
override func viewDidAppear(_ animated: Bool) {
```

```
        super.viewDidAppear(animated)
    }
    override func viewWillLayoutSubviews() {
        super.viewWillLayoutSubviews()
    }
    override func viewDidLayoutSubviews() {
        super.viewWillLayoutSubviews()
    }
    override func viewWillDisappear(_ animated: Bool) {
        super.viewWillDisappear(animated)
    }
    override func viewDidDisappear(_ animated: Bool) {
        super.viewDidDisappear(animated)
    }
    override func didReceiveMemoryWarning() {
        super.didReceiveMemoryWarning()
        // Dispose of any resources that can be recreated.
        print("Memory Warning %@", children)
    }
```

Self vs Super keyword

If a method is overridden, then self can be used to access the method in the subclass, otherwise, for accessing the **`super`** class from a base class, the best practice is to use **`super`**.

Override keyword

When a subclass provides its custom implementation of an **`instance`** method, **`type`** method, **`instance`** property, **`type`** property, or **`subscript`** that it would otherwise inherit from a superclass. So, while customizing the implementation of the instance method, the **`override`** keyword is used in front of those functions of the **`super`** class.

UI components

An iOS app screens or pages under navigation work similar to **`Stack`** operations, the start point of this stack is window object of **`UIWindow`** class which is a singleton in **`AppDelegate.swift`** (implements **`UIApplication`** class delegate methods to achieve app initialization).

Exploring window

Window object in **AppDelegate.swift** consists of a root **viewcontroller** which starts the app screen flow. The view controller's view will automatically be set as the contents of the window and presented to the user.

How to add UI control on Storyboard view controller?

In *Figure 7.1*, from the right-side options on the upper menu you can find a **+** action on Xcode. You can add interface control objects from the window shown below which will appear after plus action. Here, you can search and read about those controls to know better what they can achieve with their inclusion on the interface.

You can add these controls via drag from this UI object pane to drop on the storyboard view controller as shown in the following figure:

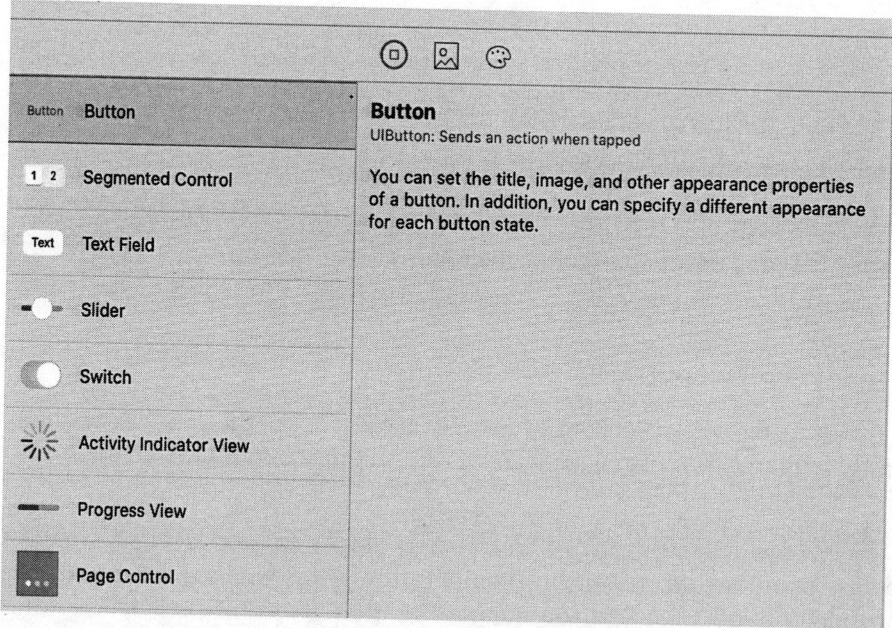

Figure 7.6: *Add UI Control*

Connect UI element to swift code

Every UI element on the storyboard or view controller required a connection representation in code which is of type **@IBOutlet** (Interface Builder Outlet). When you right select the UI element, there will be many options relevant to user interface connection. Refer to the following figure:

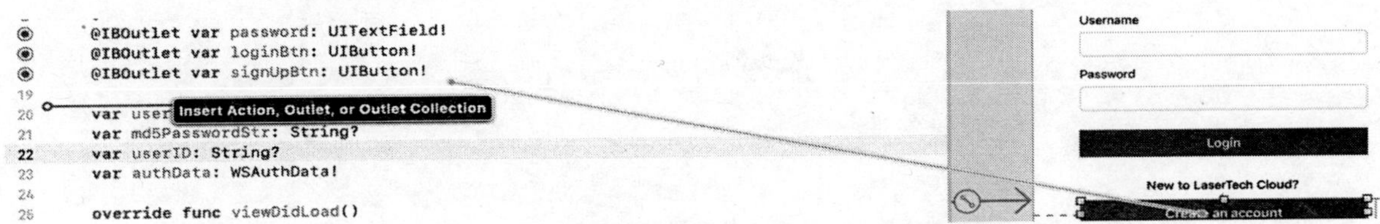

Figure 7.7: Connect UI Control

In the **Reference Outlet** section, you need to attach a new reference outlet to the **`IBOutlet`** variable in code. After that if you want to set property or text for that element, you can set it from code and that will reflect when you execute the code.

UIControl

You never create any direct instance of **`UIControl`**. **`UIControl`** is used for subclassing of other controls such that common features and target actions of all controls can be easily combined. The iOS system calls action methods when the user interacts with the control in specific ways. **`UIControl.Events`** enum has multiple events to send such as **`touchDown`**, **`touchUpInside`**, and so on. When a control-specific event occurs, the control calls any associated action methods immediately. The current **`UIApplication`** object dispatches action methods and finds an appropriate object to handle the message, following the responder chain, if necessary.

First Responder

In UI designs components hierarchy there is responder chain, which maintains the one-by-one chaining of UI elements such that when the user interacts with UI, responder chain gets the response back from related elements. So, the first responder is usually the first object in a responder chain which receives an event or action message.

UIButton

`UIButton` is the most used control in iOS designs, after iPhone 7+ changes it looks simple like a text but highly customizable component. Customizing buttons allows you to style everything from text style, drop shadow, choose fonts, text weights and color to an icon that is either prepended or centered if there is no text label, as well as fully custom backgrounds.

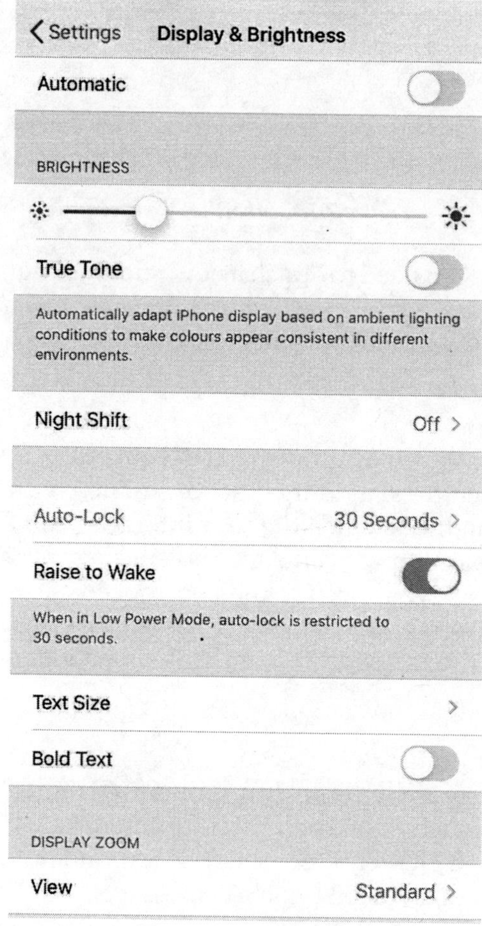

Figure 7.8: UI Controls

UILabel

A simple text which could be as much as long ↔ which could have input as a **`string`** type in **`text`** property. You can supply either a string or an attributed string that represents the content. In case If you are using a non-attributed string, you can also configure the appearance of the label. Other than text properties you can set font, font weight, color, text alignment, line break, number of lines and many more such customizable properties which can enhance overall appearance.

UITextField

`UITextField` is used for display of an editable single line text area in your UI interface. In general, you would be required to take inputs or gather text-based information from the user using an onscreen keyboard then you could use this control. The keyboard is configurable for many different types of input such as plain text, emails, phone, numbers, and so on. Text fields use the target-action mechanism and a delegate object to report changes made during the course of editing.

UITextView

`UITextView` is used for display of an editable multiline text area in the UI interface. This control has a scrollable area with text so that if there is large content then it would be visible correctly on a scrollable text field with one line. When the user taps in an editable text view, that text view becomes the first responder and automatically asks the system to display the associated keyboard. Because the appearance of the keyboard has the potential to obscure portions of your user interface, it is up to you to make sure that does not happen by repositioning any views that might be obscured. Some system views, like table views, help you by scrolling the first responder into view automatically. If the first responder is at the bottom of the scrolling region, however, you may still need to resize or reposition the scroll view itself to ensure the first responder is visible.

The appearance of the keyboard itself can be customized using the properties provided by the **`UITextInputTraits`** protocol. Text view objects implement this protocol and support the properties it defines. You can use these properties to specify the type of keyboard (ASCII, Numbers, URL, Email, and others) to display. You can also configure the basic text entry behavior of the keyboard, such as whether it supports automatic capitalization and correction of the text. When the system shows or hides the keyboard, it posts several keyboard notifications. These notifications contain information about the keyboard, including its size, which you can use for calculations that involve repositioning or resizing views. Registering for these notifications is the only way to get some types of information about the keyboard. The system delivers the following notifications for keyboard-related events:

- **`keyboardWillShowNotification`**
- **`keyboardDidShowNotification`**
- **`keyboardWillHideNotification`**
- **`keyboardDidHideNotification`**

UISlider

`UISlider` user for selecting a single complete or in fraction value from the minimum and maximum range of values as shown in the following figure:

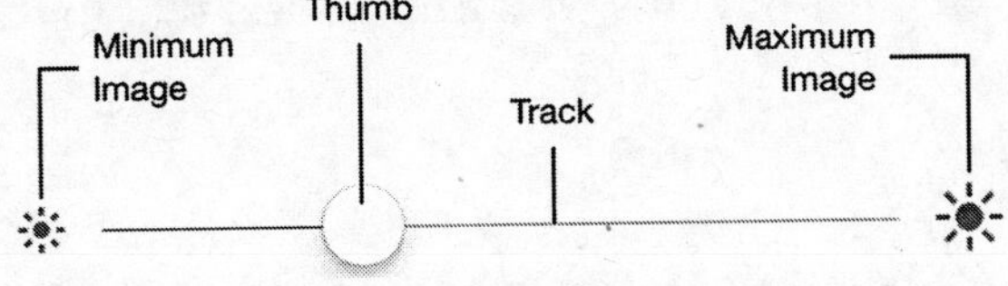

Figure 7.9: UISlider

When the thumb of the slider moves it passes the action of `UIControl.Event valueChanged` to the targeted method. By default, the slider sends value-changed events continuously as the user moves the slider's thumb control. Setting up the `isContinuous` property to false causes the slider to send an event only when the user releases the slider's thumb control, setting the final value.

Use either a custom tint color or a custom image, but not both. When customizing slider appearance with images or tint, use one option or the other, but not both. Conflicting settings for track and thumb appearance are resolved in favor of the most recently set value. The current value must be between the minimum and maximum values. If you try to programmatically set a slider's current value to be below the minimum or above the maximum, it is set to the minimum or maximum instead. However, if you set the value beyond the range of the minimum or maximum in Interface Builder, the minimum or minimum values are updated instead. Set custom images for all control states. If you use custom track and thumb images for your slider, remember to set an image for every possible `UIControl.State`. Any control state that does not have a corresponding custom image assigned to it will display the standard image instead. If you set one custom image, be sure to set them all.

UISwitch

`UISwitch` controls binary choice of option via **`On`** and **`Off`**. Similar to **`UISlider`** when a user manipulates the switch control or just flips it on and off, the target method for event action **`valueChanged`** triggers. You can also customize the appearance of the switch by changing the color used to tint the switch when it is on or off.

UIStepper

`UIStepper` is a user interaction control to increment and decrement by single value. By default, pressing and holding a stepper's button increments or decrements the stepper's value repeatedly. The rate of change depends on how long the user continues pressing the control. To turn off this behavior, set the auto repeat property to false. The maximum value must be greater than or equal to the minimum value. If you set a maximum or minimum value that would break this invariant, both values are set to the new value.

UISegment controller

`UISegmentedControl` is a horizontal control that consists of multiple segments such that each segment functions as a discrete button. You can customize the segment control with button texts, background image, title, number of segments as well as maintain index at run time via code. When you add and remove segments, you can request that the action be animated with sliding and fading effects.

UIPageControl

`UIPageControl` that displays a horizontal series of dots, each of which corresponds to a page in the app's document or other data-model entity. When a user taps a page control to move to the next or previous page, the control sends the **`valueChanged`** event for handling by the delegate. The delegate can then evaluate the **`currentPage`** property to determine the page to display. The page control advances only one page in either direction. The currently viewed page is indicated by a white dot. Depending on the device, a certain number of dots are displayed on the screen before they are clipped.

UIProgressView

A progress indicator view which depicts the progress of a task over time. The **`UIProgressView`** class provides properties for managing the style of the progress bar and for getting and setting values that are pinned to the progress of a task.

UIPickerView

`UIPickerView` which uses a spinning-wheel or slot-machine metaphor to show one or more sets of values. It displays one or more wheels that the user manipulates to select items. Each wheel has a series of indexed rows representing the selectable items. Each row displays a string or view so that the user can identify the item on that row. Users select items by rotating the wheels to the desired values, which align with a selection indicator.

UIDatePicker

`UIDatePicker` control which is used for the inputting of date and time values. You can use a date picker to allow a user to enter either a point in time (calendar date, time value, or both) and a time interval (for example, for a timer). You use a date picker only for handling the selection of times and dates. If you want to handle the selection of arbitrary items from a list, use a **`UIPickerView`** object.

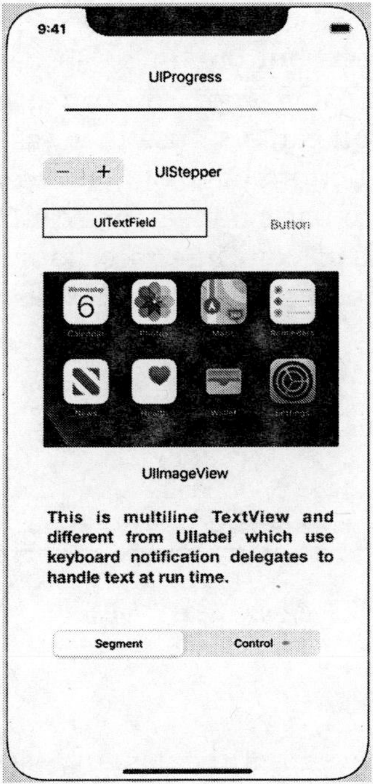

Figure 7.10: UI Elements

Date pickers use the Target-Action design pattern to notify your app when the user changes the selected date. To be notified when the date picker's value changes, register your action method with the **`valueChanged`** event. At runtime the date picker calls your methods in response to the user selecting a date or time. You connect a date picker to your action method using the **`addTarget(_:action:for:)`** method or by creating a connection in Interface Builder. The signature of an action method takes one of three forms, which are listed in **Listing 1**. Choose the form that provides the information that you need to respond to the value change in the date picker:

UIImageView

`UIImageView` is a UI container object to display an image or to show a series of images in an animated manner. Image views let you efficiently draw any image that can be specified using a **`UIImage`** object. For example, you can use the **`UIImageView`** class to display the contents of many standard image files, such as JPEG and PNG files. You can configure image views programmatically or in your storyboard file and change the images they display at runtime. Images are composited onto the image view's background and are then composited into the rest of the window. Any transparency in the image allows the image view's background to show through.

When scaling is required, the image view scales each image in the sequence separately. If the images are different sizes, scaling may not yield the results you want.

UITabBar

`UItabBar` that displays one or more buttons in a tab bar for selecting between different subtasks, views, or modes in your iOS app. You can use tab bars in conjunction with a **`UITabBarController`** object, but you can also use them as standalone controls in your app. Tab bars always appear across the bottom edge of the screen and display the contents of one or more **`UITabBarItem`** objects. A tab bar's appearance can be customized with a background image or tint color to suit the needs of your interface. Tapping an item selects and highlights that item, and you use the selection of the item to enable the corresponding mode for your app:

Figure 7.11: Tab Bar

UITableView

`UITableView` (see *Figure 7.12*) displays multiple data in a single column of customizable rows which have vertically scrolling content, divided into rows and sections. Each row of a table displays a single piece of information related to your app. Sections let you group related rows together. For example, the **Contacts** app uses a table to display the names of the user's contacts. Table view is itself not a complete element or control and built by collaboration of different control objects:

- **Cell**: Each item of `UITableView` consists of a single cell of class `UITableViewCell`. A cell provides the visual representation for your content. You can use the default cells provided by `UIKit` or define custom cells to suit the needs of your app.
- **Data source**: This data source object adopts the `UITableViewDataSource` protocol and provides the data for the table.
- **Delegate**: This delegate object adopts the `UITableViewDelegate` protocol and manages user interactions with the table's contents.

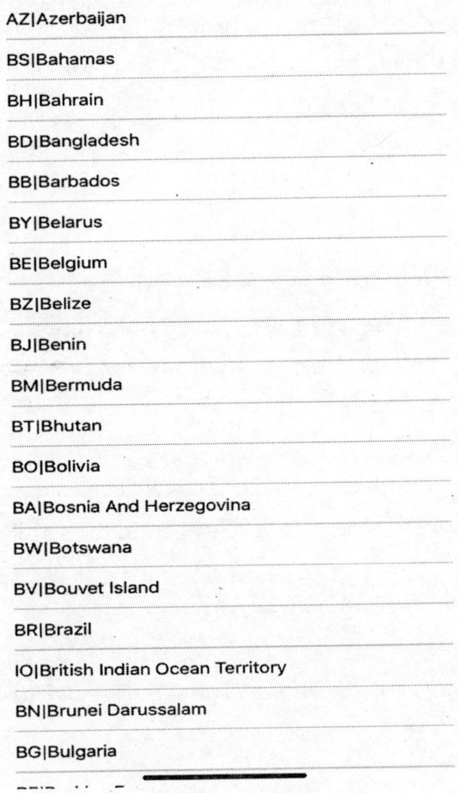

AZ|Azerbaijan
BS|Bahamas
BH|Bahrain
BD|Bangladesh
BB|Barbados
BY|Belarus
BE|Belgium
BZ|Belize
BJ|Benin
BM|Bermuda
BT|Bhutan
BO|Bolivia
BA|Bosnia And Herzegovina
BW|Botswana
BV|Bouvet Island
BR|Brazil
IO|British Indian Ocean Territory
BN|Brunei Darussalam
BG|Bulgaria

Figure 7.12: UITableView

```
import Foundation

import UIKit

class ViewController: UIViewController, UITableViewDelegate, UITableViewData-
Source

{

    var tableView: UITableView = UITableView()
```

```
    let country = ["AF|Afghanistan’’,"AL|Albania","DZ|Algeria","AS|American Samoa","AD|Andorra","AO|Angola","AI|Anguilla","AQ|Antarctica","AG|Antigua And Barbuda","AR|Argentina","AM|Armenia","AW|Aruba","AU|Australia","AT|Austria","AZ|Azerbaijan","BS|Bahamas","BH|Bahrain","BD|Bangladesh","BB|Barbados","BY|Belarus","BE|Belgium","BZ|Belize","BJ|Benin","BM|Bermuda","BT|Bhutan","BO|Bolivia","BA|Bosnia And Herzegovina","BW|Botswana","BV|Bouvet Island","BR|Brazil","IO|British Indian Ocean Territory","BN|Brunei Darussalam","BG|Bulgaria","BF|Burkina Faso","BI|Burundi","KH|Cambodia","CM|Cameroon","CA|Canada","CV|Cape Verde","KY|Cayman Islands","CF|Central African Republic","TD|Chad","CL|Chile","CN|China","CX|Christmas Island","CC|Cocos (keeling) Islands","CO|Colombia","KM|Comoros","CG|Congo","CD|Congo, The Democratic Republic Of The","CK|Cook Islands","CR|Costa Rica","CI|Côte D’ivoire","HR|Croatia","CU|Cuba","CY|Cyprus","CZ|Czech Republic","DK|Denmark","DJ|Djibouti","DM|Dominica","DO|Dominican Republic","TP|East Timor","EC|Ecuador","EG|Egypt","SV|El Salvador","GQ|Equatorial Guinea","ER|Eritrea","EE|Estonia","ET|Ethiopia"]
    let cellReuseIdentifier = "cell"
    override func viewDidLoad()
    {
        super.viewDidLoad()
        self.view.backgroundColor = UIColor.white
        tableView.frame = CGRect(x: 0, y: 50, width: UIScreen.main.bounds.size.width, height: UIScreen.main.bounds.size.height)
        tableView.delegate = self
        tableView.dataSource = self
        tableView.backgroundColor = UIColor.white
                tableView.register(UITableViewCell.self, forCellReuseIdentifier: cellReuseIdentifier)
        self.view.addSubview(tableView)
    }
    func tableView(_ tableView: UITableView, numberOfRowsInSection section: Int) -> Int
    {
        return country.count
    }
    internal func tableView(_ tableView: UITableView, cellForRowAt indexPath: IndexPath) -> UITableViewCell
    {
        let cell:UITableViewCell = (tableView.dequeueReusableCell(withIdentifier: cellReuseIdentifier) as UITableViewCell?)!
        cell.textLabel?.text = country[indexPath.row]
        cell.textLabel?.textColor = UIColor.black
```

```
        cell.backgroundColor = UIColor.white
        return cell
    }
      private func tableView(tableView: UITableView, didSelectRowAtIndexPath
indexPath: IndexPath)
    {
        print("You tapped cell number \(indexPath.row).")
    }
}
```

UICollectionView

`UICollectionView` displays nested views using a configurable and highly customizable layout. Collection view manages an ordered set of content in grid fashion, such as the grid of photos in the **`Photos`** app and presents it visually. Similar to table view, collection view is itself not a complete element or control and built by collaboration of different control objects.

- **Cell**: Each item of **`UITableView`** consists of a single cell of class **`UITableViewCell`**. A cell provides the visual representation for your content. You can use the default cells provided by **`UIKit`** or define custom cells to suit the needs of your app.
- **Data source**: This data source object adopts the **`UITableViewDataSource`** protocol and provides the data for the table.
- **Delegate**: This delegate object adopts the **`UITableViewDelegate`** protocol and manages user interactions with the table's contents.

Refer to the following figure depicting collection view:

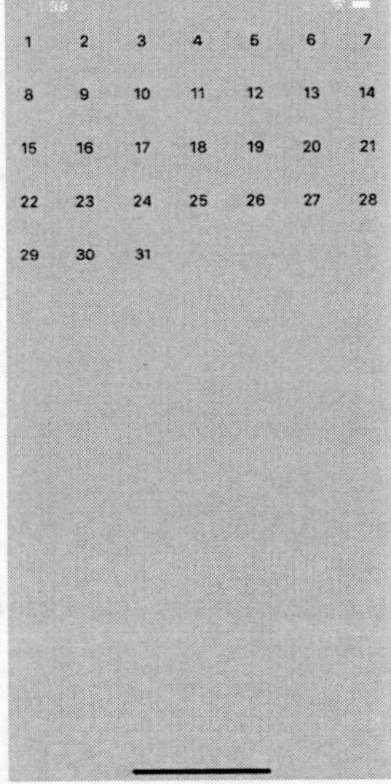

Figure 7.13: *Collection View*

```
import UIKit

class ViewController: UIViewController, UICollectionViewDataSource,
UICollectionViewDelegateFlowLayout, UICollectionViewDelegate {

    let leftAndRightPaddings: CGFloat = 80.0
    let numberOfItemsPerRow: CGFloat = 7.0
    let screenSize: CGRect = UIScreen.main.bounds
    private let cellReuseIdentifier = "collectionCell"
    var items = ["1", "2", "3", "4", "5", "6", "7", "8", "9", "10", "11", "12",
"13", "14", "15", "16", "17", "18", "19", "20", "21", "22", "23", "24", "25",
"26", "27", "28", "29", "30", "31"]
    override func viewDidLoad() {
        super.viewDidLoad()
        let flowLayout = UICollectionViewFlowLayout()
              let collectionView = UICollectionView(frame: self.view.bounds,
collectionViewLayout: flowLayout)
   collectionView.register(UICollectionViewCell.self, forCellWithReuseIdentifier:
"collectionCell")
        collectionView.delegate = self
        collectionView.dataSource = self
        collectionView.backgroundColor = UIColor.cyan
        self.view.addSubview(collectionView)
    }
     func numberOfSectionsInCollectionView(collectionView: UICollectionView) ->
Int {
        return 1
    }
   func collectionView(_ collectionView: UICollectionView, numberOfItemsInSection
section: Int) -> Int {
        return items.count
    }
       func collectionView(_ collectionView: UICollectionView, cellForItemAt
indexPath: IndexPath) -> UICollectionViewCell {
            let cell = collectionView.dequeueReusableCell(withReuseIdentifier:
"collectionCell", for: indexPath as IndexPath)
        cell.backgroundColor = UIColor.clear
```

```
        let title = UILabel(frame: CGRect(x: 0, y: 0, width: cell.bounds.size.
width, height: 40))
        title.textColor = UIColor.black
        title.textAlignment = .center
        title.text = items[indexPath.row]
        cell.contentView.addSubview(title)
        return cell     //return your cell
    }
    //MARK: UICollectionViewDelegate
  func collectionView(_collectionView: UICollectionView, didSelectItemAtIndexPath
indexPath: NSIndexPath) {
        // When user selects the cell
    }
 func collectionView(_collectionView: UICollectionView, didDeselectItemAtIndexPath
indexPath: NSIndexPath) {
        // When user deselects the cell
    }
}
```

UINavigationController

`UINavigationController` is container view controller controllers that define a stack-based scheme for navigating hierarchical content which manages one or more child view controllers in a navigation interface. In such a case only one child view controller is visible at a time:

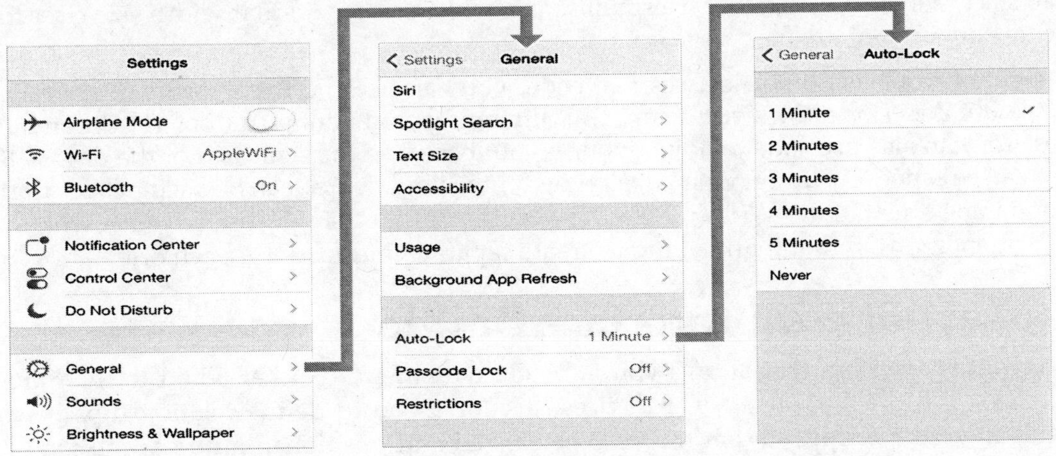

Figure 7.14: Navigation

Selecting an item in the view controller pushes a new view controller on screen using an animation, thereby hiding the previous view controller. Tapping the back button in the navigation bar at the top of the interface removes the top view controller, thereby revealing the view controller underneath.

UINavigationBar

Navigational controls that display in a bar along the top of the screen, usually in conjunction with a navigation controller. It is most commonly used within a navigation controller. The `UINavigationController` object creates, displays, and manages its associated navigation bar, and uses attributes of the view controllers you add to control the content displayed in the navigation bar. If you use a navigation controller to manage the navigation between different screens of content, the navigation controller creates a navigation bar automatically and pushes and pops navigation items when appropriate.

Size classes and AutoLayout

Size classes in iOS allow you to design a single interface that works across all of the different device sizes and orientations that your app might be used on. This helps you create a consistent user experience and avoid the need to create separate interfaces for different devices. There are three types of size classes:

- Compact
- Regular
- Any

The width and height of the screen, as well as the device orientation, determine the size class of a device. Compact size classes are used when the screen size is smaller, such as on an iPhone in portrait orientation. Regular size classes are used when the screen size is larger, such as on an iPad or an iPhone in landscape orientation. You can use size classes to design a layout that looks good on both small and large screens. For example, you might use a compact width size class to stack elements vertically on a small screen while using a regular width size class to lay elements out horizontally on a large screen.

To design a layout using size classes in Xcode, you can use the **`Size`** classes feature in the Interface Builder. This allows you to specify different layout configurations for different size classes. You can also use code to adjust your layout based on the size class of the device. **`Size`** classes can be especially useful when designing for the iPad, which can be used in both portrait and landscape orientations. With size classes, you can design a single interface that works well in both orientations, rather than having to create separate interfaces for each orientation.

AutoLayout with Interface Builder

Auto layout is a system that allows you to create user interfaces that adapt to the different screen sizes and orientations of iOS devices. It allows you to define relationships between elements in your interface so that they can be resized and positioned automatically to fit the available space. When you select a view controller screen on the storyboard, you will be able to select the device on which you want to see your UI components, as shown below:

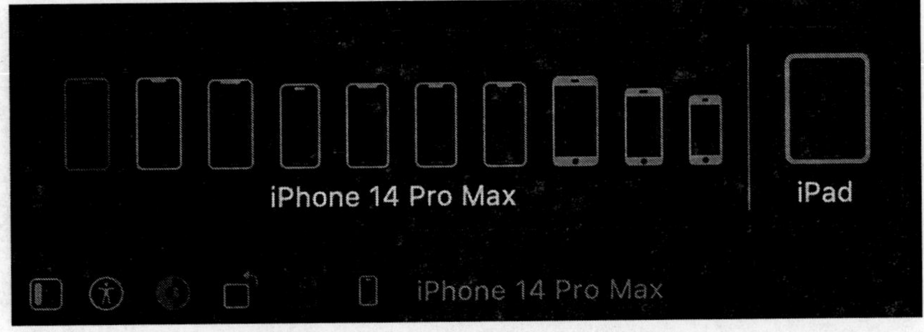

Figure 7.15: iPhone and iPad Device Configuration

If you do not apply any auto-layout constraints, then your UI component will not change or respond to size changes.

Add constraints to UI element

To use Auto Layout with Interface Builder, you first need to select the elements in your interface that you want to include in the layout. Then, you can use the Auto Layout tools in the Interface Builder editor to add constraints that specify the size, position, and relationships between these elements. In order to determine the layout of your interface at runtime, Auto Layout will use the constraints to calculate the layout of your interface at runtime. We can add layout constraints as shown below:

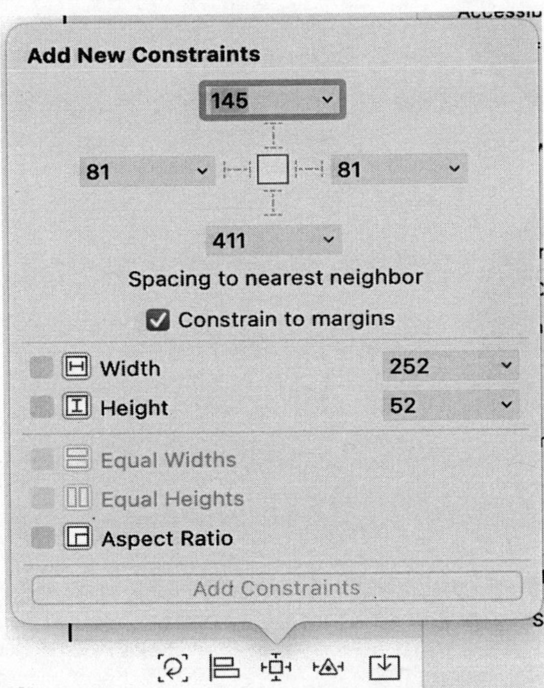

Figure 7.16: Add New Constraints

If you want to apply constraints to a single element, then you can add the below constraints in the **Add New Constraints** section.

- **Leading Constraint**
- **Trailing Constraint**
- **Top Constraint**
- **Bottom Constraint**
- **Width Constraint**
- **Height Constraint**
- **Aspect Ratio Constraint**

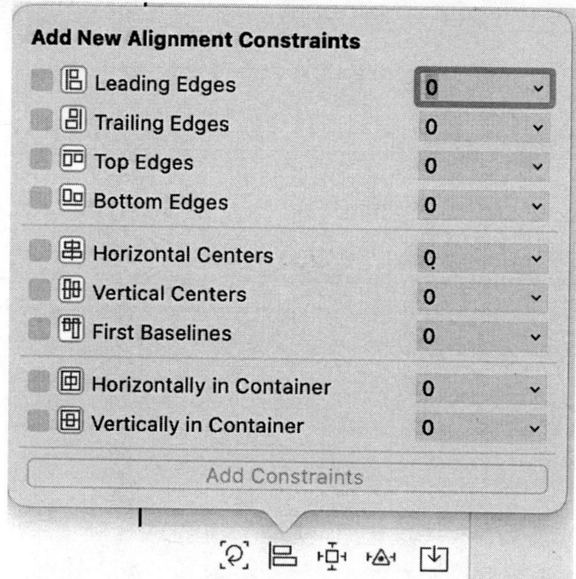

Figure 7.17: Add New Alignment Constraints

If you want to line up several UI elements, you can add constraints in the **Add New Alignment Constraints** section.

- **Leading Edges**
- **Trailing Edges**
- **Top Edges**
- **Bottom Edges**
- **Horizontal Centers**
- **Vertical Centers**
- **First Baselines**
- **Horizontally in Container**
- **Vertically in Container**

For example, you might add a constraint to specify that a label should be centered horizontally in its containing view, or that a button should be pinned to the bottom of the screen. When the app is run on a device with a different screen size or orientation, Auto Layout will automatically adjust the layout of the elements to fit the new dimensions of the screen. Run the app on different devices and in different ways to test the constraints and make sure the layout is responsive and consistent.

Customize constraints on Interface Builder

To change the constraints even more, you can change the values in the Constraints editor or use the **Size Inspector** on the right side of the screen. If you need to remove a constraint, select it in the **Constraints** editor and click the **Remove Constraint** button. Test your changes by running the app in the simulator or on a device:

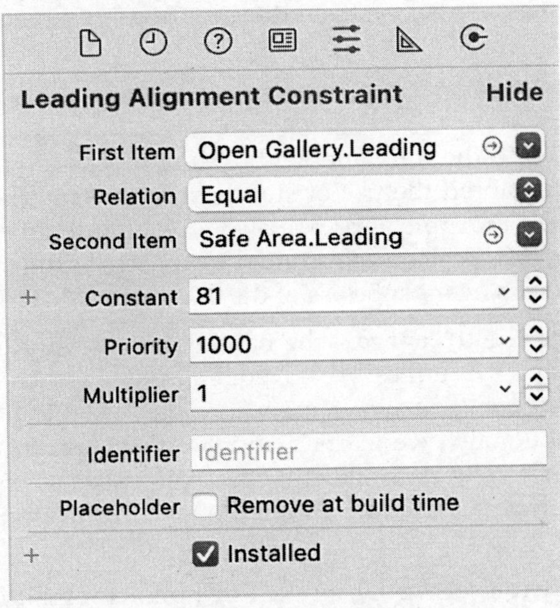

Figure 7.18: Customize Constraints

There are several types of layout constraints that you can use in your iOS app:

- **Leading and trailing:** These constraints specify the distance between the leading (left) and trailing (right) edges of the view and its nearest neighbor.
- **Top and bottom:** These constraints specify the distance between the top and bottom edges of the view and its nearest neighbor.
- **Width and height:** These constraints specify the width and height of the view.
- **CenterX and centerY:** These constraints specify the horizontal and vertical position of the view's center point.
- **Aspect Ratio:** This constraint specifies the aspect ratio (the ratio of the view's width to its height) of the view.

You can specify layout constraints in code or by using Interface Builder, a visual design tool built into Xcode. Constraints can be added to views programmatically using the `NSLayoutConstraint` class or by creating and activating constraints in Interface Builder.

- **Constraint priority**: Layout constraint priority is used to specify the priority of a particular constraint in relation to other constraints on a view. Higher priority constraints are given more importance when the layout engine is determining the final layout of the view.
- **Constraint multiplier**: multiplier is used to specify the proportional relationship between two views. For example, if one view has a multiplier of 2 and the other has a multiplier of 1, the first view will be twice the size of the second view.
- **Constraint item relations**: Relations are used to specify the relationship between two views in terms of layout. For example, one view may be constrained to be aligned with the top of another view or have a fixed distance from its edges.

Conclusion

In this chapter, we delved into the fundamental building blocks of your app's user interface - views and controls. We explored the use of storyboards and Interface Builder for creating visually appealing interfaces in Apple apps. We also took an in-depth look at the app launch and view controller life cycles, which are essential to understanding the flow of controllers from initialization to **`deinit`** in every subclass of the **`UIViewController`** class.

Furthermore, we examined the **`UIControl`**, the base class for every control and UI element that is used to design the app's interface. We covered all the major UI components, including **`UITableView`** and **`UICollectionView`**, which are extensively used to handle large sets of data on the Front-end UI. Additionally, we learned about **`UINavigationController`**, which acts as a container stack for other view controllers. We also discussed size classes and autolayout, which are crucial for developers to handle UI components for multiple sizes of devices and make them responsive.

In the next chapter, we will explore SwiftUI, an exciting option for building UIs from interactive Swift code without the use of storyboards or Interface Builder. We will delve deeper into user interface designs with UI coding techniques such as SwiftUI provided by Apple.

Multiple choice questions

1. **UI Control which used to select a single value from the range of values between max and minimum values:**
   a. UIPicker
   b. UIStepper
   c. UISlider
   d. UISegmentControl

2. Which keyword is used for UI variable which connect to storyboard file:

a. UIControl

b. Interface Builder

c. IBOutlet

d. UIStepper

3. Super Keyword used for:

a. To access current class methods

b. To access base class methods

c. To access super class methods

d. None of the above

4. Delegate and Data Source used for:

a. UITableView

b. UIStepper

c. UISlider

d. UIProgressView

5. View which can have multiple row and column:

a. UICollectionView

b. UIStepper

c. UISlider

d. UIControl

6. UINavigation Maintains View as:

a. Queue

b. Stack

c. Tree

d. Graph

7. Which is used for proportional relationship between views:

a. Multiplier

b. Relation

c. Priority

d. Aspect ratio

8. **Which class is used to handle constraint programmatically:**
    a. NSLayout
    b. NSContraint
    c. NSLayoutConstraint
    d. None of the above

Answers

1. c
2. c
3. c
4. a
5. a
6. b
7. a
8. c

Join our book's Discord space

Join the book's Discord Workspace for Latest updates, Offers, Tech happenings around the world, New Release and Sessions with the Authors:

https://discord.bpbonline.com

CHAPTER 8
User Interface Design with SwiftUI

Introduction

In this chapter, you will be shown how UI frameworks were shifted to SwiftUI for designing engaging application user interfaces across Apple platforms. SwiftUI is a brand-new framework that is offered by Apple for the developers. It is a new way to create user interfaces. Basically, by using SwiftUI you can build an application's user interface programmatically. SwiftUI is a new and exceptionally easy way of building user interface designs across all Apple platforms. SwiftUI consists of a set of tools and APIs which are based on Swift. SwiftUI is not just a new framework, it fundamentally changed the way you think about how UI was designed and developed on iOS and other Apple platforms. Apple now encourages the functional programming style for creating UI designs. It is even more easy for you as a developer because you just need to focus on specifying what components are needed in designing the UI and what actions should they perform by programming in a declarative style.

Structure

In this chapter, we will cover the following topics:

- Advantages of SwiftUI over traditional UI frameworks
- Implementation of iOS software development user interface with SwiftUI

Objectives

By the end of this chapter you should be able to create your first UI page without Interface builder and with SwiftUI interactive declarative coding style. Also, you will learn to design complex UI with the help of SwiftUI.

SwiftUI basics

SwiftUl is an incredible user interface designing framework with lots of features. It comes with views property, several controls, and design layouts which helps a developer in making amazing application UI designs.

Key features of SwiftUI

The following are some of the key features of SwiftUI:

- **Declarative syntax**: We declare the elements, properties of the elements by stating them. You get your UI by declaratively stating it, you get what you type. SwiftUI is a powerful framework that simply organizes code in an easy-to-read format.
- **Design tools**: SwiftUI provides amazing tools for designing in the native component's library, through which you can easily drag and drop different controls directly in canvas. You can also replace or update them dynamically resulting in an automatic modification in the code editor according to the changes in canvas. From the preview, you can see what is going on with the project and how changes are made.
- **Native**: This is an incredible feature that you can view the demo model/prototype of your application on any platform of Apple with just a few lines of code. Isn't it amazing to design an application prototype for the Apple platform and at the same time viewing it on iPad, Mac, and even Apple Watch? Apple has paid close attention to bringing controls and environment-specific experiences to SwiftUI. This feature has allowed us to make application prototypes with all gesture and haptics-based interactions in the Apple platforms.
- **Dynamic type, localization, dark mode, and accessibility**: SwiftUI offers features like dark mode, localization, and accessibility tools including voice-over, display customization captions and audio descriptions, and guided access. Incredibly anything you prototype with SwiftUI automatically supports these features as well.

This framework provides a friendly environment for the developer to build UI designs with the help of event handlers for handling different events, exceptions, and for delivering taps, signs, and different types of input of application. It offers different tools to manage the dataflow from the application's model to the views and controls that will be viewed and interacted with by end-users. SwiftUI is the future of development as it provides one single platform to write and publish UI code for all Apple devices.

Let us learn a few basic concepts about SwiftUI. Knowing these concepts are equally important as writing better code.

What is a declarative framework?

What does it mean with the declarative framework? We state SwiftUI the elements for our design we want, no matter how it gets and implements these elements. We declare the elements, properties of the elements. So, it is easier to design the user interfaces with declarative Swift syntax. As compared to the previous UI frameworks like UIKit, you can build the same UI design with way less code. It means that the UI code is easier and more natural to write.

View protocol

A View is a simple protocol with a property 'body' which is a mandatory property. It is type also implements the View protocol. It represents the part of your app's user interface, and it provides properties that you can use to organize views. You can create your custom views by declaring types that fit into the View protocol and combine them with SwiftUI views for presenting different control values like texts, images, custom shapes using stacks, lists, and more. You must implement the *body property* to provide the content for your custom view. To customize the rendering and interactivity of views, you can apply powerful modifiers to built-in views or your own.

Getting started with SwiftUI

Figure 8.1 depicts how to create a project **SwiftUI**:

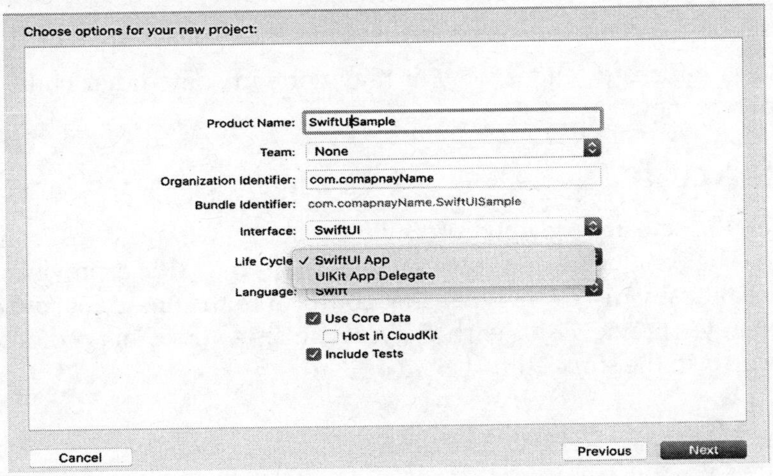

Figure 8.1: *Create Project SwiftUI*

While you create a new project you need to first select SwiftUI in interface and SwiftUI App in lifecycle instead of default selections, which will create a default set for you to start designing UI components with SwiftUI.

```
var body: some View {
    return Text("Hello World")
}
```

The previous code in Swift will create a view with text **Hello World**, with a variable body which would be passed in **ContentView.swift** struct. Let's further add more property to this simple text.

```
import SwiftUI

struct ContentView: View {
    var body: some View {
        Text("Hello, World!")
    }
}

struct ContentView_Previews: PreviewProvider {
    static var previews: some View {
        ContentView()
    }
}
```

What is SwiftUI view?

Let us compare UIView of UIKit vs View of SwiftUI:

- As we discussed earlier, View is protocol rather than a class in SwiftUI.
- View always returns a render view, it may contain some other child view but must return a parent view.

Previews in Xcode

Preview Provider: To create preview of SwiftUI code, we need to conform protocol **PreviewProvider**. The Xcode preview system uses the same API to preview which is used by SwiftUI. Xcode statically discovers types that conform to the **PreviewProvider** protocol in your app and generates previews for each provider it discovers. This protocol does not run when code is executed in the simulator.

Combining Views using stacks

Next step in SwiftUI is to understand if there is no single element to return from the body and relatively multiple views and elements need to be shown. When creating a SwiftUI view, you describe its content, layout, and behavior in the view's body property; however, the body property only returns a single view. You can combine and embed multiple views in *stacks*, which group views together horizontally, vertically, or back-to-front.

- **VStacks**: VStacks represents vertical alignment of views in stack manner. In the vertical stack of views – the three text views would be placed one above the other.

```
struct ContentView: View {
    var body: some View {
```

```
        VStack(alignment: .leading) {
            Text("Header")
                .font(.title)
            Text("First")
                .font(.subheadline)
            Text("Second")
            .font(.subheadline)
        }
    }
}
```

- **HStacks**: HStacks represents horizontal alignment of views and other elements in stack manner. In the horizontal stack of views - the three text views would be placed side by side to each other.

```
struct ContentView: View {
    var body: some View {
        HStack(alignment: .top) {
            Text("Title")
                .font(.title)
            Text("Content 1")
                .font(.subheadline)
            Text("Item 1")
            .font(.subheadline)
        }
    }
}
```

- **ZStacks**: The ZStack is in a category of its own because it groups views together, seen back-to-front, along the z- or depth axis. Views will overlap in a ZStack, which means that it is great for creating UI stacks that overlay other views and assign each successive child view a higher z-axis value than the one before it, meaning later children appear on top of earlier ones.

```
let colors: [Color] = [.orange , .red, .green,  .purple , .yellow, .blue]
struct ContentView: View {
    var body: some View {
        ZStack {
```

```
                    ForEach(0..<colors.count) {
                        Rectangle()
                            .fill(colors[$0])
                            .frame(width: 100, height: 100)
                            .offset(x: CGFloat($0) * 10.0,
                                    y: CGFloat($0) * 10.0)
                    }
                }
            }
        }
```

Figure 8.2: *ZStack Design View*

Grids with ScrollView

In SwiftUI, two new view styles are lazy VGrid and lazy HGrid that SwiftUI provides us with to build a super custom grid-based interface. The axis of the layout is the only contrast between them. In the vertical direction, the lazy VGrid populates the space open. On the other side, in the horizontal direction, lazy HGrid arranges its children. In these two views, axis is the only distinction. It is similar to **`UICollectionView`** of **`UIKit`**.

```
struct ContentView: View {
    private var columns: [GridItem] = [
        GridItem(.fixed(100), spacing: 16),
        GridItem(.fixed(100), spacing: 16),
        GridItem(.fixed(100), spacing: 16)
    ]
    var body: some View {
        ScrollView {
            LazyVGrid(
                columns: columns,
```

```
                alignment: .center,
                spacing: 16,
                pinnedViews: [.sectionHeaders, .sectionFooters]
            ) {
                Section(header: Text("Section 1").font(.title)) {
                    ForEach(0...10, id: \.self) { index in
                        Color.green
                    }
                }

                Section(header: Text("Section 2").font(.title)) {
                    ForEach(11...20, id: \.self) { index in
                        Color.orange
                    }
                }
            }
        }
    }
}
```

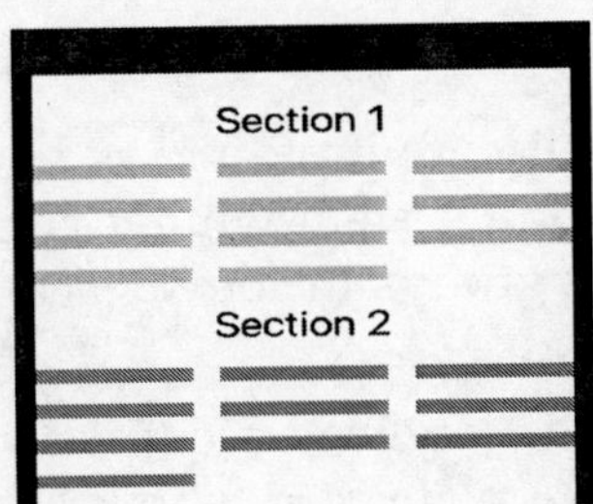

Figure 8.3: Grid with two sections

GridItem: To customize the arrangement of objects in the lazy HGrid and lazy VGrid views, you can use **GridItem** instances. Each grid object defines the layout properties, such as spacing and orientation, that all objects in a given column or row will be sized and arranged by the grid view.

Container views

There are mainly four types of containers provided by Apple in the SwiftUI framework. Although you can create your own custom containers if required or default containers won't work as expected.

- **List**: A grouping control container that is used for data entry, such as in settings or inspectors. In a way suitable for the network, SwiftUI makes shapes. For starters, forms appear as grouped lists on iOS. List in SwiftUI is similar to **UITableView** in **UIKit** Framework:

```
var body: some View {
    List {
        HStack {
          Text("1.").frame(width: 20.0, height: nil, alignment: .leading)
            Text("Name - John Mathew \nAge - 32")
        }
        HStack {
          Text("2.").frame(width: 20.0, height: nil, alignment: .leading)
            Text("Name - Marry Saldom \nAge - 24")
        }
    }
}
```

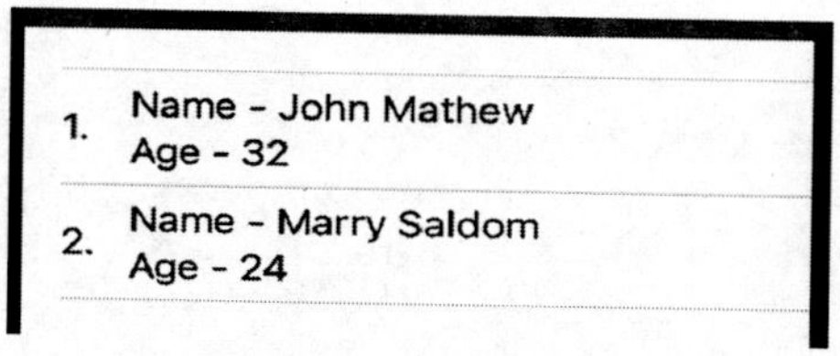

1.	Name - John Mathew Age - 32
2.	Name - Marry Saldom Age - 24

Figure 8.4: *List View*

- **Group**: When you want to list multiple views you can use VStack but that has a limitation that SwiftUI building system will let you design to add up to 10 views in VStack so there you can use groups inside VStack to add more than 10 elements to designs.
- **GroupBox**: The GroupBox is a stylized view with an optional icon connected to a logical content classification. A plain card with title and content is the default style on iOS. Let's have a look at that. SwiftUI provides us with the **GroupBoxStyle** protocol that enables us to fully alter the look and feel of every instance of GroupBox. For all the use-cases we require, we can build numerous types. A framework that conforms to the **GroupBoxStyle** protocol is created to create your own GroupBox style. The sole prerequisite is **GroupBoxStyle**. You must build a **makeBody** feature which accepts the **GroupBoxStyleConfiguration** type instance and returns a new view. **GroupBoxStyleConfiguration** provides us with the GroupBox mark as well as the material. Within the **makeBody** feature, you can use them as you like.

```
Struct HeartGroupBoxStyle: GroupBoxStyle {
    func makeBody(configuration: Configuration) -> some View {
        Vstack(alignment: .leading) {
```

```
                configuration.label
                configuration.content
            }
        }
    }
    struct ContentView: View {
        var body: some View {
            GroupBox(
                label: Label("Heart Rate - ", systemImage: "heart.fill")
                    .foregroundColor(.red)
            ) {
                Text("Your heart rate is 80 BPM.")
            }.groupBoxStyle(HeartGroupBoxStyle())
        }
    }
```

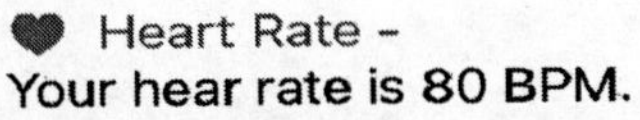

Heart Rate -
Your hear rate is 80 BPM.

Figure 8.5: GroupBox

- **Section**: Much like **`UITableView`** in UIKit, SwiftUI's listview has built-in support for sections and section headers. Start by placing a section around it and optionally adding a header and footer to add a section around those cells.

```
struct TaskRow: View {
    var body: some View {
        Text("Task Link ")
    }
}
struct ContentView: View {
    var body: some View {
        List {
            Section(header: Text("Important Tasks")) {
                TaskRow()
                TaskRow()
            }
            Section(header: Text("Other Tasks")) {
```

```
                        TaskRow()
                        TaskRow()
                    }
                }
            }
        }
```

Figure 8.6: Section in List

Working with Form and Navigation in SwiftUI

The SwiftUI type is a container that allows you to group controls for data entry, such as text fields, toggles, steppers, pickers and others. In this tutorial, we are going to explore and apply each type of data entry control to a form. We can learn now how to build and use forms in SwiftUI by constructing a basic UI type setup.

Wrap the content view in *NavigationView* to create a simple form with a text field, and then embed a form within it. By inserting a toggle with an option to keep our account private and making a section called **`Profile`** containing both the **`TextField`** and a Toggle, you can further change our form.

```
struct ContentView: View {
    @State var username: String = ""
    @State var isPrivate: Bool = true
    @State var notificationsEnabled: Bool = false
    @State private var previewIndex = 0
    var previewOptions = ["Always", "When Unlocked", "Never"]
    var body: some View {
        NavigationView {
            Form {
                Section(header: Text("PROFILE")) {
```

```
        TextField("Username", text: $username)
        Toggle(isOn: $isPrivate) {
            Text("Private Account")
        }
    }

    Section(header: Text("NOTIFICATIONS")) {
        Toggle(isOn: $notificationsEnabled) {
            Text("Enabled")
        }
        Picker(selection: $previewIndex, label: Text("Show Previews"))
{
            ForEach(0 ..< previewOptions.count) {
                Text(self.previewOptions[$0])
            }
        }
    }

    Section(header: Text("ABOUT")) {
        HStack {
            Text("Version")
            Spacer()
            Text("0.1.1")
        }
    }

    Section {
        Button(action: {
            print("Perform an action here...")
        }) {
            Text("Reset All Settings")
        }
    }
```

```
            }
            .navigationBarTitle("Settings")
        }
    }
}
```

Creating a new segment called **`Alerts Now`**. The segment will include a toggle to turn on and off alerts and a picker to select options to preview notifications. Create three new variables to keep track of the toggle range, the picker's chosen index, and a list of choices for the picker. Finally, to the very bottom of the form, let's add a button, allowing you to reset all the options to default values.

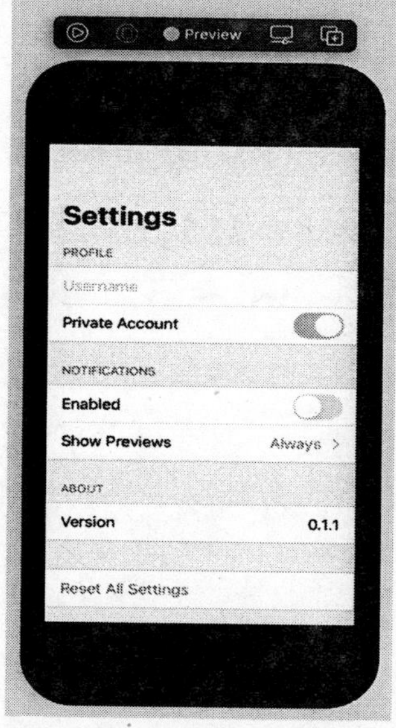

***Figure 8.7**: Form with Navigation*

SwiftUI drawing and animations

In this section, we will discuss how we can draw different shapes with the help of default available shapes as well as draw custom shapes with path components. SwiftUI provides us with some simple shapes that we can use in our app for drawing. They are:

- Rectangle
- Rounded rectangle
- Ellipse
- Circle
- Capsule

The shape doesn't know anything about its supposed size and position. This is why, as long as we provide the shape with a **.frame** it tries to fill out the whole view. Here we will understand how we can make use of default shapes. Let us provide a **RoundedRectangle** with a certain width and height. We also define another fill color than the default black, and the below code will show a rounded rectangle with green color:

```
struct ContentView: View {
    var body: some View {
        RoundedRectangle(cornerRadius: 20)
            .frame(width: 250, height: 100)
            .foregroundColor(.green)
    }
}
```

If you want a shape not to be completely filled with a color, but just want to build some sort of boundary out of it. You can do this by using a certain line width for your boundary by using the **.stroke** modifier (like the first one). Using another stroke form is also possible, such as using a dashed-line as the boundary. Like this:

```
struct ContentView: View {
    var body: some View {
        RoundedRectangle(cornerRadius: 20)
         .stroke(style: StrokeStyle(inewidth: 7, lineCap: .square, dash: [15], 
dashPhase: 2))
        .frame(width: 250, height: 100)
        .foregroundColor(.green)
    }
}
```

Figure 8.8: Shaded Rectangle

Drawing custom shapes with path

Reusability is the secret to recognizing the distinction between Path and Shape: paths are built to do one particular thing, while shapes have the freedom of drawing space and can also embrace parameters to enable us to further modify them.

Take a quick look at what paths in SwiftUI are. You can imagine a path like a set of drawing instructions, including lines, curves and other segments like arcs. This is why a shape is doing nothing different than using a specific path to define its appearance. Insert a Path instance followed by its corresponding closure. Inside the closure we can actually define how our Path should go. SwiftUI will fill out the resulting view with a black color. Now draw our square by adding several lines to our Path. We can do this by using absolute X- and Y-coordinates. Before drawing the first line, we move the *cursor* right upper corner of our imaginary square.

```
struct MySquare: Shape
{
    func path(in rect: CGRect) -> Path {
        var path = Path()
        path.move(to: CGPoint(x: 200, y: 0))
        path.addLine(to: CGPoint(x: 200, y: 200))
        path.addLine(to: CGPoint(x: 0, y: 200))
        path.addLine(to: CGPoint(x: 0, y: 0))
        path.closeSubpath()
        return path
    }
}
struct ContentView: View {
    var body: some View {
        MySquare()
        .frame(width: 250, height: 250)
    }
}
```

The given code will draw a simple black square which is by default completely filled, as shown in the following figure:

Figure 8.9: *Square Rectangle*

Drawing curved shapes in SwiftUI

We will take a look at how curved shapes can be formed. We'll be able to create interesting shapes like raindrop. A structure called **`Raindrop`** is proclaimed here and conforms to the **`Shape`** protocol. We initialize the **`Raindrop`** shape and add a **`.stroke`** and **`.frame`** to it within our SwiftUI window. We begin pushing our *cursor* within our Raindrop's route to the center of the upper edge of the rect.

```
struct Raindrop: Shape {
    func path(in rect: CGRect) -> Path {
        Path { path in
            path.move(to: CGPoint(x: rect.size.width/2, y: 0))
             path.addQuadCurve(to: CGPoint(x: rect.size.width/2, y: rect.size.
height), control: CGPoint(x: rect.size.width, y: rect.size.height))
        }
    }
}
struct ContentView: View {
    var body: some View {
        Raindrop()
            .stroke(lineWidth: 4)
            .frame(width: 200, height: 200)
    }
}
```

First, we want to draw the correct downward curve. We use the **addQuadCurve** approach to do this. This function applies to the direction of a so-called **Bézier curve**. We first need to define an endpoint for the curve for such a Bézier curve, so to really do the curve, we need to have a control point for the Bézier curve. Such a point of control is used to measure the curve's intensity and direction. For this, you don't need to know calculus. Only take a peek at the infographic below and get a feel for this:

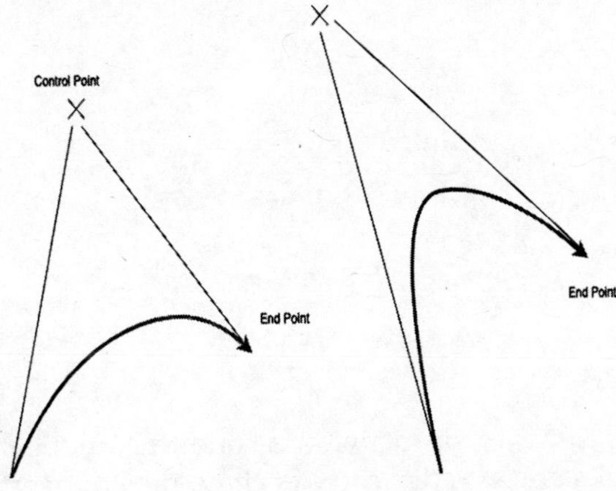

Figure 8.10: *Draw Curve*

```
struct Raindrop: Shape {

    func path(in rect: CGRect) -> Path {
        Path { path in
            path.move(to: CGPoint(x: rect.size.width/2, y: 0))
             path.addQuadCurve(to: CGPoint(x: rect.size.width/2, y: rect.size.
height), control: CGPoint(x: rect.size.width, y: rect.size.height))
            path.addQuadCurve(to: CGPoint(x: rect.size.width/2, y: 0), control:
CGPoint(x: 0, y: rect.size.height))
        }
    }
}
struct ContentView: View {
    var body: some View {
        Raindrop()
            .fill(LinearGradient(gradient: Gradient(colors: [.white, .blue]),
startPoint: .topLeading, endPoint: .bottom))
        .frame(width: 200, height: 200)
    }
}
```

Let us complete our **Raindrop** form by drawing another curve that points to where we began to sketch. When we're done with our **Raindrop** form, by swapping the **.stroke** modifier, we can fill out this shape within our SwiftUI view. You may fill the form with a gradient, for example, as seen in the code above. And your **Raindrop** shape is expected to look like the picture as follows:

Figure 8.11: *Draw Drop*

Animation views

You can animate updates to views, or to a view's condition, independently by using SwiftUI, no matter where the results are. The difficulty of these mixed, overlapping, and interruptible animations is managed by SwiftUI for you.

An interpolating spring animation that uses a damped spring model to create values within the range [0, 1] that are then used to interpolate within the range of the animated property [from, to]. By incorporating the impacts of each animation, it maintains speed through simultaneous animations. Let us take a working example with an image of a ball which will bounce on tap. That image value can be toggled whenever a tap gesture is called.

```
struct ContentView: View {
    @State private var bounceBall: Bool = false
    var body: some View {
        VStack
        {
            Image("ball")
            .resizable()
            .frame(width: 150, height: 150)
            .foregroundColor(.black)
            .clipShape(Circle())
           .animation(Animation.interpolatingSpring(stiffness: 90, damping: 1.5).
repeatForever(autoreverses: false))
            .offset(y: bounceBall ? -200 : 200)
            .onTapGesture {
                self.bounceBall.toggle()
            }
        }
    }
}
```

Architecture views

Architecture views used when we want transitions of views with better management of UI flow is required. In such case we can use mainly three architectural views other than Navigation views are:

- **TabBar view**: A view that moves between various views of children using elements of the immersive user interface is used as **TabBar** view. Place views in **TabView** to create a user interface with tabs and add the **tabItem(:)** modifier to the contents of each tab. A tab view with three tabs is generated as follows:

```
struct ContentView: View {
    var body: some View {
        TabView {
            Text("The Home Tab")
```

```
                .tabItem {
                    Image(systemName: "heart.fill")
                    Text("Home")
                }
            Text("Featured Tab")
                .tabItem {
                    Image(systemName: "star.fill")
                    Text("Featured")
                }
            Text("The Profile Tab")
                .tabItem {
                    Image(systemName: "person.fill")
                    Text("Profile")
                }
        }
        .font(.headline)
    }
}
```

Home
Featured
Profile

Figure 8.12: TabBar View

- **Split view**: A layout container that arranges its children in a horizontal or vertical line and allows the user to resize them using dividers placed between them.

```
struct ContentView: View {
  let  requestUrls  =  ["https://Google.com",  "https://bpbonline.com",
"https://twitter.com"]
    var body: some View {
          GeometryReader { geo in
           NavigationView {
               List(self.requestUrls, id: \.self) { url in
```

```
                    NavigationLink(destination: RequestDetailView(url:
url)) {
                        Text(url)
                    }
                }
                .navigationBarTitle("Links")

                Text("Nothing Selected.")
            }
            .padding(.leading, geo.size.height > geo.size.width ? 1 : 0)
        }
    }
}
// Detail view
struct RequestDetailView: View {
    let url: String
    var body: some View {
        Text("Detail view of request with url: \(url).")
    }
}
```

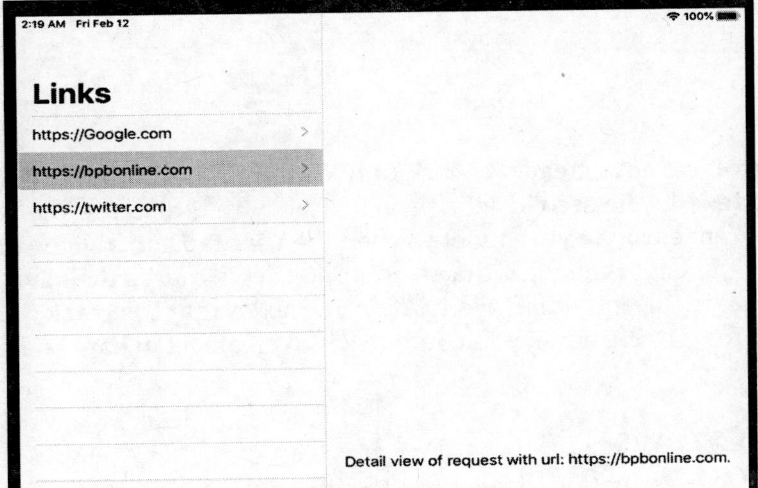

Figure 8.13: Split View

- **Navigation Stack:** **`NavigationStack`** is a new view in SwiftUI that allows you to create a stack of views that can be navigated between. It is a more flexible and powerful alternative to the **NavigationView** view, and it can be used to create a variety of navigation patterns. To use **NavigationStack**, you first need to create a new instance of the view. You can then add views to the stack by using the **push()** method. The **push()** method takes a view as its argument, and it will push that view onto the top of the stack.

You can also remove views from the stack by using the **pop()** method. The **pop()** method will remove the top view from the stack, and it will return the view that was removed. Here is an example of how to use **NavigationStack** to create a simple navigation pattern:

```
@State private var currentView = 0
var body: some View {
    NavigationStack {
        Text("View 1")
            .tag(1)
            .onTapGesture {
                self.currentView = 2
            }
        Text("View 2")
            .tag(2)
            .onTapGesture {
                self.currentView = 1
            }
        }
    }
}
```

In the given example, we have created a stack of two views. The first view is a Text view that displays the text **View 1**. The second view is a Text view that displays the text **View 2**. We have also added a **TapGesture** to each view. When the user taps on a view, the **currentView** state is updated to the tag of the view that was tapped. This causes the **NavigationStack** to update the view that is currently displayed. You can use **NavigationStack** to create a variety of navigation patterns. For example, you could use it to create a tab bar, a navigation drawer, or a modal sheet.

Presentation views

There are mainly two presentation views used to either inform the user or to give options to choose, those are:

- **Action view**: When you want the user to respond in response to the status of the app or the device, use a warning. Using the **alert(isPresented:content:)** view modifier, you display an alert to generate an alert that occurs if the bound value **isPresented** is valid. A personalized instance of the Alert form is generated by the content closure you include for this modifier. In the example below, when tapped, a button shows a basic warning by updating the local **showAlert** property that links to the alert.

```
struct ContentView : View {
    @State private var showAlert = false
    var body: some View {
        Button("Tap to view alert") {
            self.showAlert = true
        }
        .alert(isPresented: $showAlert) {
            Alert(
                title: Text("Unable to Save Data"),
                message: Text("The connection to the server was lost."),
                primaryButton: .default(
                    Text("Try Again"),
                    action: saveData
                ),
                secondaryButton: .destructive(
                    Text("Delete"),
                    action: saveData
                )
            )
        }
    }

    func saveData() {
        // Save data code
    }
}
```

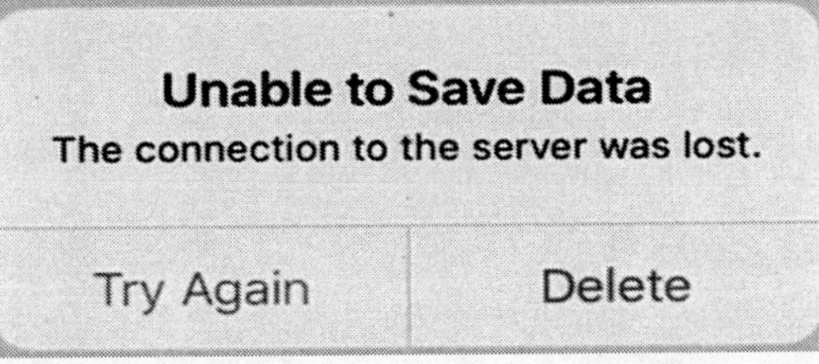

Figure 8.14: Alert View

Action Sheet view: When you want the user to make a decision between two or more choices, in reaction to their own action, use an action sheet. By using the **actionSheet(isPresented:content:)** view modifier, you display an action sheet to construct an action sheet that occurs whenever the **isPresented** binding value is valid. A personalized instance of the **ActionSheet** form is generated by the content closure you include for this modifier. To include the alternatives, build an **ActionSheet.Button** instance to differentiate between the ordinary options, the destructive options, and the user's initial action cancellation.

```
struct ContentView : View {
    @State private var showActionSheet = false
    var body: some View {
        Button("Tap to view action sheet") {
            self.showActionSheet = true
        }
        .actionSheet(isPresented: $showActionSheet) {
            ActionSheet(title: Text("Resume Workout Recording"),
                        message: Text("Choose a destination for workout data"),
                        buttons: [
                            .cancel(),
                            .destructive(
                                Text("Overwrite Workout"),
                                action: overwrite
                            ),
                            .default(
                                Text("Append Workout"),
                                action: overwrite
                            )
                        ]
            )
        }
    }

    func overwrite() {
        // overwrite data code
    }
}
```

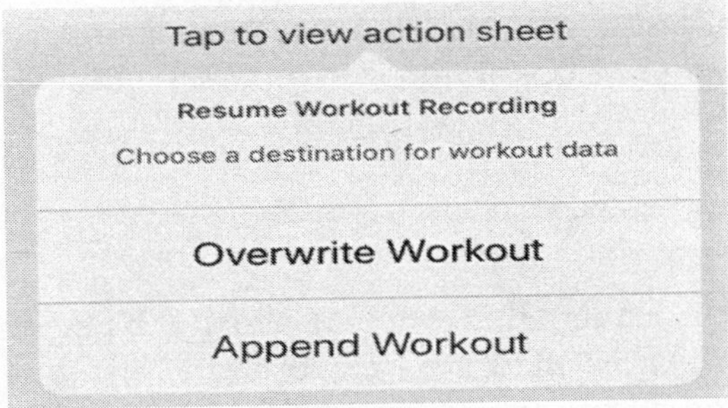

***Figure 8.15:** Action Sheet*

SF symbols

SF symbols is a versatile icon system introduced by Apple, providing a vast collection of icons that are designed to integrate seamlessly with Apple's user interface guidelines. These symbols are available in a variety of weights and scales, making them suitable for different display sizes and contexts. In SwiftUI, you can easily incorporate SF Symbols into your app's interface, enhancing its visual appeal and ensuring a consistent user experience. Here's an example of how you can use SF symbols in SwiftUI:

```
struct ContentView: View {
    var body: some View {
        VStack {
            Image(systemName: "heart.fill")
                .font(.system(size: 100))
                .foregroundColor(.red)

            Text("Liked")
                .font(.title)
                .fontWeight(.bold)
        }
    }
}
```

In the given code, we have a **`ContentView`** that contains an image view. The image uses the SF symbol **`heart.fill`** as the system name, representing a filled heart icon. By setting the font size to **`.system(size: 100)`**, we control the size of the SF symbol. Additionally, we apply the **`color.red`** to the image, making it appear red. Below the image, we have a text view displaying the label **`Liked`**. We can adjust the font size and style using the available modifiers. In this example, we set the font to .title and apply a bold font weight.

By leveraging SF symbols in SwiftUI, you gain access to a comprehensive library of icons that align with Apple's design language. These symbols are scalable and adaptable to different display sizes, ensuring a consistent visual experience across various Apple platforms. SF symbols offer a wide range of possibilities to enhance your app's UI and communicate information effectively.

Conclusion

It is surely an incredible improvement that Apple has made. It has simplified building a robust and flexible design system. Apple platforms are friendly, and their controls and platform-specific experiences are loved by everyone because of their presentation. SwiftUI is genuinely native, so your applications can straightforwardly access the proven technologies of every platform with a limited amount of code and a collaborative design canvas.

It is a powerful platform for UI designers and developers who are compulsive about designing user interfaces and about building real apps across all supported Apple platforms, like (iOS, macOS, tvOS, iPad, and watchOS). While the code does not suit a one-size, the controls and methods involved can apply to all platforms. It provides an easy and friendly environment for beginners as well, but it is also filled with tricks of the trade and cool workflows for developing the best UIs and interactions.

Multiple choice questions

1. **View in SwiftUI is a __________.**
    a. Protocol
    b. Class
    c. struct
    d. UIKit component
2. **Why is the path used?**
    a. Add Line
    b. Draw curve
    c. Default shape
    d. Custom shape
3. **Alertview in SwiftUI is __________.**
    a. Show info to user
    b. show option to choose
    c. Draw curve
    d. A Shape
4. **Is the ActionSheet in SwiftUI __________.**
    a. Show info to user
    b. show option to choose

c. Draw curve

d. A Shape

5. RoundRectangle in SwiftUI is ________________.

a. Custom Shape

b. Default Shape

c. Draw by curve

d. Class

6. Interpolating Spring is used in SwiftUI as ____________________.

a. show option to choose

b. Animation Component

c. Draw curve

d. Custom Shape

Answer

1. a

2. a

3. a

4. b

5. b

7. b

Chapter 9
Concurrency in Swift and SwiftUI

Introduction

Swift includes built-in assistance for building parallel and asynchronous code in a systematic manner. Although only one part of the program is executed at once, asynchronous programming can be paused and continued later. Your software may continue to work on long-running tasks like getting data from the network or processing files while making progress on short-term tasks like refreshing its **user interface** (**UI**). A computer with four cores may run four pieces of code concurrently, with each core handling one of the jobs. Parallel code refers to code that runs in numerous places at once. It is simpler to create this code in a memory-safe manner that performs several actions at once when a program employs parallel and asynchronous code. It also suspends activities that are waiting for an external system.

Structure

In this chapter, we will cover the following topics:

- Concurrency in Swift
- Task and task groups
- Concurrency with SwiftUI

Objectives

By reading this chapter, you will be able to learn about concurrency in iOS with built-in support. Also, you will learn more about tasks, task groups, and actors, which will help you do both synchronous and asynchronous tasks better overall.

Concurrency in Swift

Swift lets you describe your goal so that some of it can be checked at compile time. For example, you can use actors to access data that can be changed in a secure way. Concurrency does not always make slow or flawed code faster or more reliable. In fact, increased concurrency could make it more difficult to debug your code. Swift's language-level concurrency support can help you find problems at compile time if you use it in code that needs to run at the same time. This common mix of parallel and asynchronous programming is called **concurrency** and is talked about in the rest of this chapter.

If you have previously developed concurrent programming, you may be used to using threads. Although Swift's concurrency architecture is based on threads, you don't deal with them directly. In Swift, an asynchronous function has the option to release the thread it is now using, allowing another asynchronous function to use it while the first one is stalled. Swift does not say which thread an asynchronous function will run on when it starts running again. Let us understand with and example as shown below:

```
listContacts(fromContact: "Contact Book") { contactNames in
    let sortedNames = contactNames.sorted()
    let name = sortedNames[0]
    downloadContactInfo(named: name) { contactPhoto in
        show(contactPhoto)
    }
}
```

Even in this simple case, you have to write nested closures because the function must be written as a set of handlers for when it's done. When written this way, it may be hard to write code with deep layers or that is more complicated.

Defining and calling asynchronous functions

A unique type of function or method that may be paused mid-execution is known as an **asynchronous** function or asynchronous method. Unlike conventional, synchronous functions and methods, which either run to completion, throw an error, or never return, this one works. Although an asynchronous function or method can still accomplish one of those three things while waiting for anything, it can also halt in the middle of the process. In the body of an asynchronous function or method, you point out each of these places so that execution can be stopped there.

The **async** keyword is added to the declaration of a function or method to show that it is asynchronous. This is similar to how the **throws** keyword is used to show that a function throws. Async is written before the return arrow (**->**) if the function or method returns a value:

```
func listContacts(fromContact name: String) async -> [String] {
    let contactResult = // ... some code asynchronous with networking ...
    return contactResult
}
```

Execution pauses when an asynchronous method is called until it completes its work. To indicate a potential moment of suspension, you type **await** before the call. This is similar to using **try** when calling a function that throws to show how the flow of the program might change if there is an error. The only time the execution flow is halted inside an asynchronous method is when you call another asynchronous method, the suspension is never implicit or preemptive, and thus every potential suspension point is indicated with await:

```
let contactNames = await listContacts(fromContact: "Contact Book")
let sortedNames = contactNames.sorted()
let name = sortedNames[0]
let contact = await downloadContactCard(named: name)
show(contact)
```

Asynchronous sequence

When all of the array's elements are ready, the **listContacts(fromContact:)** method from the last section returns the whole array at once. To wait for each item in the collection one at a time, you could also use an asynchronous sequence. Here is an example of iterating over an asynchronous sequence:

```
import Foundation
let taketask = FileHandle.standardInput
for try await line in taketask.bytes.lines {
    print(line)
}
```

Swift also allows unstructured concurrency in addition to the structured concurrency options outlined in the preceding sections. In contrast to activities that are part of a task group, unstructured tasks lack a parent task. You have the entire freedom to handle whatever unstructured tasks your program requires, but you are also solely liable for their accuracy. To generate an unstructured task that executes on the current actor, use the **Task.init(priority:operation:)** initializer. Call the **Task.detached(priority:operation:)** class method to create an unstructured task that is not associated with the current actor, also known as a **detached task**. Both of these actions give you back a task that you can do something with, like wait for it to finish or stop it.

Calling asynchronous function in parallel

Calling an asynchronous function with await runs only one piece of code at a time. While the asynchronous code is running, the caller waits for that code to finish before moving on to run the next line of code. For example, to get the first three photos from a gallery, you could wait for three calls to the **downloadContactCard(named:)** function as follows:

```
let firstContact = await downloadContactCard(named: contactNames[0])

let secondContact = await downloadContactCard(named: contactNames[1])

let thirdContact = await downloadContactCard(named: contactNames[2])

let contacts = [firstContact, secondContact, thirdContact]

show(contacts)
```

This method has a significant flaw in that only one **downloadContactCard(named:)** call is ever active at the same time, despite the fact that the download is asynchronous and allows other tasks to be completed while it is being completed. Before the next picture begins downloading, the previous one has already finished downloading. These processes do not need to wait, however; each picture may be downloaded separately or even simultaneously.

When defining a constant, place async in front of let, and then write await each time the constant is used to call an asynchronous function, allowing it to execute concurrently with the code surrounding it as shown below:

```
async let firstContact = downloadContactCard(named: photoNames[0])

async let secondContact = downloadContactCard(named: photoNames[1])

async let thirdContact = downloadContactCard(named: photoNames[2])

let contacts = await [firstContact, secondContact, thirdContact]

show(contacts)
```

In this case, none of the three calls to **downloadContactCard(named:)** wait for the preceding one to finish before starting the subsequent one. They can both operate at once if the system has adequate resources. Since the code does not pause to await the function's output, none of these function calls are tagged with await. The program needs the results from these asynchronous calls at that time, so you write **await** to stop execution until all three photos have downloaded. Otherwise, execution proceeds until the line where images are specified. You may consider the variations between these two strategies as follows:

- When the code on the lines after it relies on the output of an asynchronous function, call it with await. As a result, tasks are completed in order.
- Use **async-let** to invoke asynchronous functions if you would not require the output right away. This results in tasks that can be done concurrently.
- Other code may execute while they are paused using both await and **async-let**.
- In both scenarios, you use the **await** keyword to signal that, if necessary, execution will halt until an asynchronous function returns.

Both of these methods may be combined in the same code.

Task and TaskGroups

A task is a unit of work that can be done at different times by your software. All asynchronous code is executed as a job. The **async-let** syntax, which we talked about in the previous section, makes your child task for you. You can also make a task group and add child tasks to it. This gives you more control over priority and cancellation and lets you create a variable number of tasks.

A hierarchy of tasks is used. Each task in a set of tasks has a single parent task, and each task can have children. This method is called **organized concurrency** because it shows how tasks and task groups work together. Swift can take care of some behaviors for you, like propagating cancellation, and find some mistakes at build time, even though you are still partly responsible for accuracy.

```
await includeTaskGroup(of: Data.self) { taskG in
    let pNames = await getListOfPhotos(inGallery: "Winter Holiday")
    for name in pNames {
        taskG.addTask { await downloadPhoto(named: name) }
    }
}
```

Unstructured concurrency

Swift also allows unstructured concurrency in addition to the structured concurrency options outlined in the preceding sections. In contrast to activities that are part of a task group, unstructured tasks lack a parent task. You have the entire freedom to handle any unstructured tasks that your program requires, but you are also solely liable for their accuracy. Call the **Task.init(priority:operation:)** initializer to generate an unstructured task that executes on the current actor. Call the **Task.detached(priority:operation:)** class method to create an unstructured task that is not associated with the current actor, also known as a **detached task**. Both of these actions return a task with which you may interact, such as by waiting for its outcome or aborting it.

```
let newContact = // ... new contact data ...
let handle = Task {
    return await add(newContact, toContactBookNamed: "Office Group")
}
let result = await handle.value
```

Task cancellation

A cooperative cancellation approach is used in swift concurrency. At the relevant moments throughout its execution, each task checks to see whether it has been cancelled and takes the required action. That often signifies one of the following things, depending on the task you are doing:

- Throwing an error like **`CancellationError`**
- Returning nil or an empty collection
- Returning the partially completed work

If the job has been cancelled, use **`Task.checkCancellation()`**, which throws a **`CancellationError`**, or check the value of **`Task.isCancelled`** and handle the cancellation in your code. For instance, a job that is downloading pictures from a gallery would need to finish the download and shut off the network. Call **`Task.cancel`** in order to manually propagate the cancellation.

Actors

Your application may be divided into separate, concurrent parts using tasks. While it is safe for jobs to operate concurrently since they are segregated from one another, there are occasions when information sharing is necessary. You may securely transfer information across concurrent programs thanks to actors.

Actors are reference types like classes, hence the discussion of value types and reference types in *classes are reference types* also applies to actors. Actors, as opposed to classes, only let one job at a time to access their changeable state, making it safe for code in numerous tasks to interact with a single instance of an actor. Here is an actor who takes temperature readings as an illustration:

```
actor TempeLogger {
    let textLabel: String
    var measure: [Int]
    private(set) var maxValue: Int
    init(textLabel: String, measurement: Int) {
        self.textLabel = textLabel
        self.measure = [measure]
        self.maxValue = measurement
    }
}
```

When introducing an actor, use the word **`actor`** before its description in braces. The **`TemperatureLogger`** actor limits the **`max`** property so that only code inside the actor can change the maximum value. It also has attributes that code outside the actor can use. The initializer syntax for actors is the same as that for structures and classes. When accessing a property or method of an actor, you can use wait to show where the likely suspension point is:

```
let log = TempeLogger(textLabel: "Indoors", measurement: 34)
print(await log.maxValue)
// Prints "34"
```

In this case, reaching **logger.max** might result in a suspension. If code from another job is already interacting with the logger, this code stops while it waits to access the property, since the actor only lets one task at a time access the changeable state.

When accessing the properties of the **actor**, code that is part of the actor does not write wait. Here is an example of a method that adds a new temperature to a **TempeLogger**:

```
extension TempeLogger
{
    func updateTemperature(with measurement: Int) {
        measurements.append(measurement)
        if measurement > maxValue {
            maxValue = measurement
        }
    }
}
```

Since the **updateTemperature(with:)** function is already using the actor, accessing variables like **maxValue** with await is not recommended. This technique also demonstrates one of the reasons why actors let just one job interact with their variable state at once: Some state changes cause an actor to breach invariants momentarily. The maximum temperature is changed every time the **TemperatureLogger** actor takes a new measurement. The actor also keeps a list of temperatures. After an update, the temperature logger is out of sync for a short time after adding the new value but before updating max. By not letting multiple tasks interact with the same instance at the same time, problems like the following will not happen:

- Your code calls the function **updateTemperature(with:)**. The measurements array is first updated.
- Function somewhere reads the array of temps and the maximum value before your code can change max.
- To complete the upgrade, your code must be changed.

In this scenario, since access to the actor was interleaved in the midst of the call to **updateTemperature(with:)**, when the data was momentarily faulty, the code executing elsewhere would read the wrong information. If you use Swift actors, you can avoid this problem because you can only do one thing to their state at a time, and that code can only be stopped at places where waiting indicates a pause. No other code is able to access the data while an update is in progress since the **updateTemperature(with:)** does not include any suspension points.

Sendable types

A **sendable** type is one that may be transferred across concurrent domains. It could, for example, be sent back as the result of a job or given as a parameter when an actor method is run. Due to the usage of simple value types in the prior examples in this chapter, which are always safe to share for the data being sent across concurrent domains, the sending ability was not covered in those cases. Some types, on the other hand, are unsafe to pass across concurrent domains. If, for example, you send instances of a class between tasks, a class with changeable properties that does not serialize access to those properties could lead to unexpected and wrong results.

Declaring conformance to the **Sendable** protocol identifies a type as being **sendable**. This protocol has no coding constraints but does have semantic restrictions enforced by Swift. There are generally three ways a type may be **sendable**:

- The type is a value type, and its changeable state consists of additional **sendable** data, such as a structure with stored **sendable** attributes or an enumeration with associated **sendable** values.
- The type has no mutable state, and its immutable state is composed of other **sendable** data, such as a structure or class whose attributes are read-only.
- The type contains code that safeguards its mutable state, such as a class designated **@ MainActor** or a class that serializes access to its attributes on a specific thread or queue.

Some forms are always **sendable**, like structures with only **sendable** attributes and enumerations with only **sendable** values. For example:

```
struct TempMeasuring: Sendable {
    var measurement: Int
}
extension TempLogger {
    func addReading(from reading: TempMeasuring) {
        measurements.append(reading.measurement)
    }
}
let log = TempLogger(label: "Water Bottle", measurement: 75)
let read = TempLogger(measure: 35)
await log.addReading(from: read)
```

Because **TempMeasuring** is a structure with only **sendable** attributes and is not marked as public or **@usableFromInline**, it is automatically **sendable**. Here is a variant of the structure where **sendable** protocol adherence is assumed:

```
struct TempMeasuring {
    var measurement: Int
}
```

Concurrency with SwiftUI

SwiftUI is a powerful tool for creating user interfaces, but it can also be used to manage concurrent tasks. In this chapter, we will explore the different ways to use concurrency in

SwiftUI and how to handle different types of tasks. Concurrency in SwiftUI means being able to run multiple tasks or threads at the same time. This makes better use of system resources and makes the user interface more responsive. Apple's framework for making user interfaces for iOS, iPadOS, macOS, watchOS, and tvOS is called SwiftUI. It includes the **`@State`** property wrapper and the **`ObservableObject`** protocol, which can be used to handle multiple tasks at the same time.

The **`@State property`** wrapper and the **`ObservableObject`** protocol are both used for managing state in a SwiftUI app. The **`@State`** property wrapper is used for simple, local state that is specific to a single view. The **`ObservableObject`** protocol, on the other hand, is used for shared state that is passed down the view hierarchy. Both of these tools allow for automatic updates to the user interface when states change, eliminating the need for manual updates and reducing the risk of concurrency-related bugs.

It is also worth noting that SwiftUI uses a declarative syntax, which means that the developer describes the desired end state of the user interface, and the framework takes care of the implementation details. This makes it easier to reason about the concurrent state of the app and reduces the risk of concurrency-related bugs.

There are mainly two ways to handle concurrency in SwiftUI:

- Observable object
- Main Actor

Observable object

In SwiftUI, the most common way to handle asynchronous tasks is through the use of the **`@ StateObject`** and **`@ObservableObject`** property wrappers to manage concurrent tasks. You can create objects that are up-to-date in the background and usable by multiple views using these property wrappers. For example, the following code creates a class that is marked as an **`@ObservableObject`** and a view that displays the value of the object:

```
class MyObject: ObservableObject {
    @Published var value = 0
}
struct MyView: View {
    @ObservedObject var myObject: MyObject
    var body: some View {
        Text("Value: \(myObject.value)")
    }
}
```

In this example, the **`MyObject`** class is marked as an **`@ObservableObject`** and the value property is marked as a **`@Published`** property. The **`MyView`** struct is marked as an **`@ObservedObject`**, and the **`myObject`** property is an instance of the **`MyObject`** class. When the value property of the **`MyObject`** class is updated, the **`MyView`** struct will be updated as well.

Main actor

The main queue is used by the global actor **`@MainActor`** to carry out its task. Since the UI will always run on the main queue and call **`MainActor`**, methods or types annotated with **`@ MainActor`** can change it securely. **`Run()`** lets you send a custom task to the primary actor and, by extension, the primary queue. Both of these features seem easy to use on the surface, but as you will discover, there is a great deal of intricacy behind the surface.

Let us first examine the use of **`@MainActor`**, which causes any or all methods of a type to run on the main actor automatically. **`ObservableObject`** classes and other types that can change your user interface will find this very helpful.

```
import SwiftUI
struct MainActor: View {
    @State private var name = "John Doe"
    @State private var age = 25
    var body: some View {
        VStack {
            Text("Name: \(name)")
            Text("Age: \(age)")

            Button(action: {
                self.name = "Jane Smith"
                self.age = 30
            }) {
                Text("Change Actor")
            }
        }
    }
}
struct ContentView: View {
    @mainactor var actor: MainActor

    var body: some View {
        actor
    }
}
```

In this example, we have two structs: **`MainActor`** and **`ContentView`**. **`MainActor`** is a struct that defines the properties and behavior of our main actor. It has two properties, **`name`** and **`age`**, both of which are marked as **`@State`** so that they can be modified by the user. It also has a button that allows the user to change the name and age of the main actor. **`ContentView`** is the structure that is displayed to the user. It has an **`@mainactor`** property called *actor* that is of type **`MainActor`**. This means that the main actor property is a reference to the **`MainActor`** struct and its properties and behaviors in the body of the **`ContentView`** struct, and we simply display the **`MainActor`** struct, which is the main actor.

When the user taps the **Change Actor** button, the name and age of the main actor will be updated, and the changes will be reflected in the **`ContentView`**. This is because the **`ContentView`** is directly referencing the **`MainActor`** struct and its properties.

Conclusion

In this chapter, we talked about concurrency, which is an important part of making software, and how Swift and SwiftUI give developers a lot of tools to deal with it. By letting multiple tasks run at the same time, concurrency with async-await can greatly improve the performance and user experience of iOS apps. By using async/await, developers can write code that is more readable and easier to maintain, while also ensuring that the app remains responsive to user input. Tasks let you make independent pieces of work that can be done at the same time, and task groups let you group and manage several tasks at once. By utilising these features, developers can create highly efficient and responsive applications that can handle large amounts of data and perform complex operations in a timely manner.

Swift's async and await keywords let you make tasks that run at the same time. SwiftUI's **`@ ObservedObject`** and **`@StateObject`** property wrappers let you control how data flows between threads in a user interface. Also, the Combine framework has a way to deal with events and streams of data that happen at different times. This makes it easier to deal with concurrency in a functional and reactive way. Overall, Swift and SwiftUI give developers a strong set of tools for managing concurrency, which makes it easier for them to make apps that are responsive and work well.

In the next chapter, we will start learning about storage and databases with SQLite and CoreData, which are used in iOS app development with the Swift language.

Multiple choice questions

1. **Which is thread safe class from below?**
   a. Singleton Class
   b. Actor Class
   c. TaskGroup
   d. None of the above

2. **How to make a collection of tasks to work together to form a result?**
    a. Actor
    b. TaskGroup
    c. Observer State
    d. None of the above
3. **_____________ is used for concurrency in SwiftUI.**
    a. Main Actor
    b. TaskGroup
    c. State Change
    d. None of the above
4. **Which are the types which are sent back as parameters when a concurrent task is done?**
    a. Safe data types
    b. Sendable Types
    c. TaskGroup
    d. None of the above
5. **How to show a function is asynchronous?**
    a. Add await
    b. Add async
    c. Add Actor
    d. None of the above
6. **The StateObject wrapper used to manage ___________.**
    a. Synchronous task
    b. Concurrent task
    c. Tasks added to TaskGroup
    d. None of the above
7. **Task Cancellation involves _______.**
    a. Cancellation Error
    b. Throwing Error
    c. Incomplete task
    d. All of the above

8. **Main Actor is used for _______?**
    a. Securely running the task on Main Queue
    b. Running task on other Queue
    c. Global tasking run on Secondary thread
    d. None of the above
9. **One job at a time to access their changeable state is done by ____________.**
    a. TaskGroup
    b. Actor
    c. Observable State
    d. None of the above
10. **Which one allows you to write asynchronous tasks with structured concurrency?**
    a. Async - await
    b. GCD
    c. Operations
    d. None of the above

Answers

1. b
2. b
3. a
4. b
5. b
6. b
7. d
8. a
9. b
10. a

Chapter 10
Storing Data with SQLite and Core Data

Introduction

In the initial stages of mobile development, when network capabilities were not explored for handheld devices, there were extensive requirements to save and persist data in mobile memory. When simple operations such as reading from a file in a directory and writing to a file in a directory were explored, those were good enough only for small data sizes, but when data started increasing gradually on the file, a few problems started, in front of developers, such as searching results becoming slow, and the increasing size of data files was another big issue for handheld devices with limited memory allocations. There are distinct strategies to pick from for iOS storage. However, the decision depends on when and how much knowledge you choose to hold. Most of the time, the implementation of local storage in iOS apps requires more than one process, as the device needs various persistence specifications. Online surfing, user habits, and device configuration gathered this information. The most commonly used approaches in iOS for the implementation of local storage are:

- User defaults
- Property list
- SQLite
- Core data
- Swift data

Structure

In this chapter, we will cover the following topics:

- CRUD operations in mobile applications
- Core Data **Object Relational Management** (**ORM**)
- SwiftData for persistent storage

Objectives

By reading this chapter, you should be able save user inputs and experiences to persistent data, which will show on UI after retrieval of persistent data with SQLite and CoreData. Also, you will be able to save and retrieve user credentials in the keychain to perform auto login.

UserDefaults

An access to the default user account, where you persistently store key-value pairs during launches of your app. The **`UserDefaults`** class provides a programmatic interface for communicating with the default framework. The default framework enables a program to modify its actions to fit the needs of a user. You may allow users to determine their desired measuring units or media playback speed, for example. Apps store these preferences in a user's default database by assigning values to a series of parameters. The parameters are referred to as defaults because they are often used to decide the default state of an app at runtime or the default way it behaves.

```
let defaults = UserDefaults.standard

        defaults.set(30, forKey: "Age")

        defaults.set(true, forKey: "TouchID")

        defaults.set(CGFloat.pi, forKey: "PiValue")

        defaults.set("John Huge", forKey: "Name")

        defaults.set(Date(), forKey: "waitTill")
```

Here you can see in the above code that the **`UserDefaults`** class provides convenience methods for accessing common types such as floats, doubles, integers, boolean values, and dates.

It remains straightforward when it comes to reading back data, but it has a significant clause that if the configuration cannot be found, **`UserDefaults`** will return a default value. You need to know what these default values are so that you do not mistake them for the actual values that you set. Here they are:

- **`integer(forKey:)`** returns an integer if the key exists, or 0 if not.
- **`bool(forKey:)`** returns a boolean if the key existed, or false if not.
- **`float(forKey:)`** returns a float if the key exists, or 0.0 if not.
- **`double(forKey:)`** returns a double if the key existed, or 0.0 if not.

- **`object(forKey:)`** returns **`AnyObject?`** so you need to conditionally typecast it to your data type.

```
let defaults = UserDefaults.standard
        let age = defaults.integer(forKey: "Age")
        let touchID = defaults.bool(forKey: "TouchID")
        let pi = defaults.double(forKey: "PiValue")
        print(age)
        print(touchID)
        print(pi)
```

Property list

Property list or **plist** is a simple form of xml data that can be kept in key-value pair form of data with file extension **`.plist`**. Here you can see how you can create plist file in your project as shown in *Figure 10.1*-

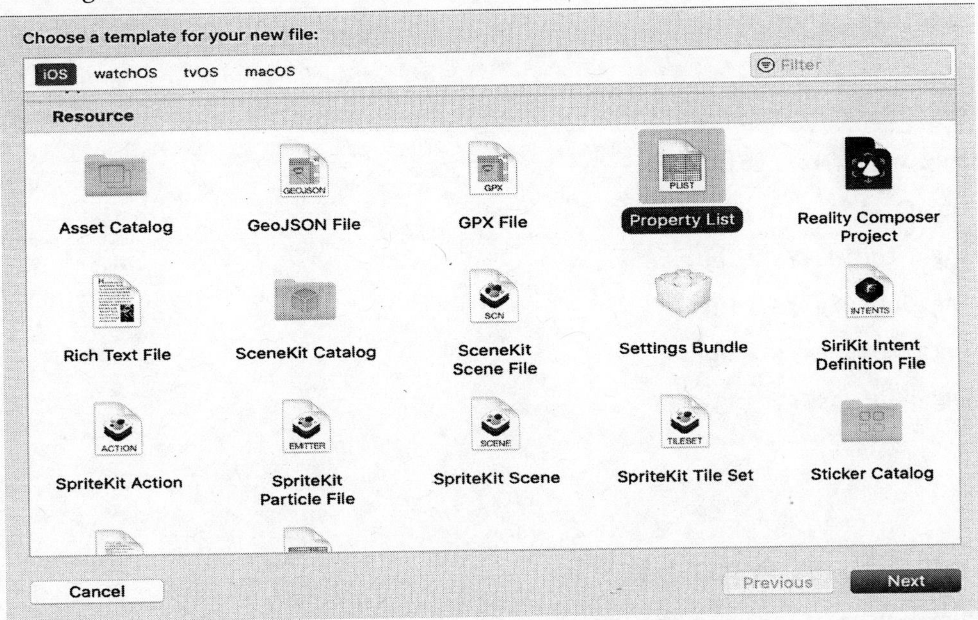

***Figure 10.1:** Creating plist file in your project*

The plist root item could have two types- Dictionary and Array. When you choose one type of root item you could add more child items of types – Dictionary, Array, Boolean, Data, Date, ,String and Number. In Xcode you can see a plist's XML structure by right-clicking on a **`.plist`** file, and choosing **Open As | Source Code**. Let us see how a plist looks with data as well as as source code as shown in *Figure 10.2*.

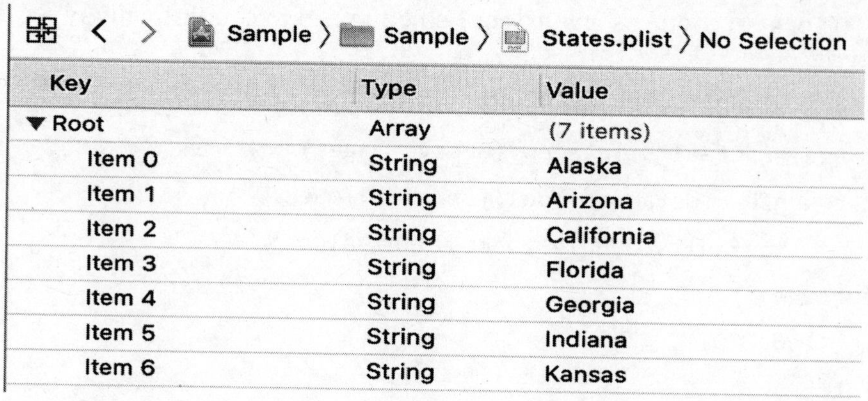

Sample 〉 Sample 〉 States.plist 〉 No Selection

Key	Type	Value
▼ Root	Array	(7 items)
Item 0	String	Alaska
Item 1	String	Arizona
Item 2	String	California
Item 3	String	Florida
Item 4	String	Georgia
Item 5	String	Indiana
Item 6	String	Kansas

Figure 10.2: Screenshot showing how a plist looks with data as well as as source code

```
<?xml version="1.0" encoding="UTF-8"?>
<!DOCTYPE plist PUBLIC "-//Apple//DTD PLIST 1.0//EN" "http://www.apple.com/DTDs/
PropertyList-1.0.dtd">
<plist version="1.0">
<array>
    <string>Alaska</string>
    <string>Arizona</string>
    <string>California</string>
    <string>Florida</string>
    <string>Georgia</string>
    <string>Indiana</string>
    <string>Kansas</string>
</array>
</plist>
```

Reading a Plist with Swift

Property lists are great for your app to save quick, static key-value info. Here is how you can read the Swift plug-in:

```
func getPropertyList(withName name: String) -> [String]?
    {
        if  let path = Bundle.main.path(forResource: name, ofType: "plist"),
            let xml = FileManager.default.contents(atPath: path)
        {
```

```
            return (try? PropertyListSerialization.propertyList(from: xml,
options: .mutableContainersAndLeaves, format: nil)) as? [String]
        }
        return nil
    }
if let states = getPropertyList(withName: "States") {
            print(states)
        }
// Output: ["Alaska", "Arizona", "California", "Florida", "Georgia", "Indiana",
"Kansas"]
```

Let us take a look what happens in the code:

- We are deserializing the xml data as a property list within the conditional clause. The properties list is returned as an array, but we will have to cast it to **`[String]`** because **`Any type`** is returned by **`propertyList(from:options:format:)`**.
- The feature returns zero when the conditional fails, or the type casting fails, or when the **`propertyList(from:options:format:)`** call throws an error. If not, it returns an array of the form **`[String]?`** so, we use optional binding again to get the non-optional array states when we call **`getPropertyList(withName:)`**.

Writing Data To Plist

Adding data to plist and editing any data or key -value pair to plist is similar to writing to file at a specific path location, which we will discuss in detail in the next chapter *File handling in iOS with FileManager*.

SQLite

SQLite is a library of applications that offers a framework for relational database management. In terms of configuration, database management, and resources needed, the lite in SQLite means lightweight. SQLite is capable of building databases in memory that are very easy to work with.

The following notable features are available for SQLite: self-contained, server-less, zero-configuration, transactional. SQLite is self-contained, ensuring that it requires limited operating system or external library support. In any environment, this makes SQLite accessible, especially on embedded devices such as iPhones, Android phones, game consoles, mobile media players, etc. SQLite uses dynamic table forms. It means that in any column, regardless of the data type, you can store any value. SQLite facilitates a single database connection to concurrently view various database files. This brings several fun features, such as joining tables in multiple databases or copying data with a single command within databases.

Working with SQLite in Swift

Here we will make a single class to manage all SQlite file and CRUD operations. This Class includes the creating database, creating table, insert in that table, read from that table and delete from that table functions.

```
import Foundation

import SQLite3

class DBManager

{


    let dbPath: String = "DB.sqlite"

    var db:OpaquePointer?

}
```

In the above code we import the library SQLite3 to perform all sqlite operations. First variable **dbPath** has the name of the database file with its extension **.sqlite** and a variable of **opaquePointer** type will keep the reference of **db** in code at the time of execution.

Create and connect to DataBase

Establish a database link before anything. This feature is named **sqlite3 open()**, which opens or generates a new file for the database. It returns an **OpaquePointer**, which is a Swift sort for C pointers, if it is efficient. You would have to grab the returned pointer when you call this function in order to communicate with the database. Many of the SQLite functions return the result code of Int32, which is normally a constant in the library of SQLite. SQLITE OK, for instance, represents the result code zero.

```
func openDatabase() -> OpaquePointer?
    {
        let fileURL = try! FileManager.default.url(for: .documentDirectory, in: .userDomainMask, appropriateFor: nil, create: false)
            .appendingPathComponent(dbPath)
        var db: OpaquePointer? = nil
        if sqlite3_open(fileURL.path, &db) != SQLITE_OK
        {
            print("error opening database")
            return nil
        }
```

```
        else
        {
            print("Successfully opened connection to database at \(dbPath)")
            return db
        }
    }
```

Creating a table

You can create a table now that you have a link to a database file. In order to store data, you will work with a very basic table. Here, the person table will have three columns : Id with int type and Primary Key, Name of text type, Age of int type. Before preparing sqlite3, create table statement we would need to frame SQL query for create table with given column so query would be:

Query: CREATE TABLE IF NOT EXISTS person(Id INTEGER PRIMARY KEY,name TEXT,age INTEGER)

```
func createTable()
{
        let createTableString = "CREATE TABLE IF NOT EXISTS person(Id INTEGER
PRIMARY KEY,name TEXT,age INTEGER);"
        var createTableStatement: OpaquePointer? = nil
        if sqlite3_prepare_v2(db, createTableString, -1, &createTableStatement,
nil) == SQLITE_OK
        {
            if sqlite3_step(createTableStatement) == SQLITE_DONE
            {
                print("person table created.")
            } else {
                print("person table could not be created.")
            }
        } else {
            print("CREATE TABLE statement could not be prepared.")
        }
        sqlite3_finalize(createTableStatement)
}
```

Let us understand given code for creating table step-by-step:

1. First, take the defined constant table query and create a reference pointer in the next stage.

2. **sqlite3_prepare_v2()** compiles the SQL statement into byte code and returns a status code. To ensure the statement is correctly compiled, you match the returned status code. This mechanism moves on to the next step. Otherwise, you should print a message noting that the declaration was not compiled.
3. **sqlite3_step()** executes the compiled statement. You only move once in this situation, since this argument has a single consequence.
4. Finally, we call sqlite3 **finalize()** on your compiled statement to delete it and prevent leakage of resources.

```
class DBManager
{
    init()
    {
        db = openDatabase()
        createTable()
    }
    let dbPath: String = "DB.sqlite"
    var db:OpaquePointer?
>>>>
```

Inserting data

After the initial steps of opening the database and creating a table, we will insert some records into the person of **db.sqlite** so that later we can perform a retrieve operation and show that data. On the UI side, you will create a simple form with two or three input fields (you can choose Id to be autoincrement and maintain that as unique with programming logic, or you can take it as input too).

Query: INSERT INTO person (Id, name, age) VALUES (?, ?, ?)

```
func insert(id:Int, name:String, age:Int)
    {
         let insertStatementString = "INSERT INTO person (Id, name, age) VALUES
(?, ?, ?);"
        var insertStatement: OpaquePointer? = nil
         if sqlite3_prepare_v2(db, insertStatementString, -1, &insertStatement,
nil) == SQLITE_OK {
            sqlite3_bind_int(insertStatement, 1, Int32(id))
           sqlite3_bind_text(insertStatement, 2, (name as NSString).utf8String,
-1, nil)
```

```
        sqlite3_bind_int(insertStatement, 3, Int32(age))

        if sqlite3_step(insertStatement) == SQLITE_DONE {
            print("Successfully inserted row.")
        } else {
            print("Could not insert row.")
        }
    } else {
        print("INSERT statement could not be prepared.")
    }
    sqlite3_finalize(insertStatement)
}
```

Let us understand the given code for inserting records into database, step-by-step:

- Initially in the first step you will compile the statement and verify that everything is working well..
- The name of the method, **sqlite3_bind_int()**, means that you bind an **Int** to the argument. The first function parameter is the argument to be added to, while the second is a non-zero-based index for the position of the **?** and value itself is the third and final parameter. This binding call returns a status code, but for now, you assume it is successful.
- To execute the sentence and check that it has been completed, use SQlite3 **step()**. While finalizing the assertion, if several connections were to be added, you would keep the argument and reuse it with different values.

Read and retrieve data

There might be multiple records that we need to store in objects class Person. So, let us first create a new class with the same variable as columns and default initialization for table person in the database:

```
class Person
{

    var name: String = ""
    var age: Int = 0
    var id: Int = 0

    init(id:Int, name:String, age:Int)
    {
```

```
        self.id = id
        self.name = name
        self.age = age
    }
}
```

Now, we will read the records from **db.sqlite**, which was stored by insert Person values via a calling function written for insertion of records. The query statement for retrieving and reading of records from database would be, **"SELECT * FROM person"**. Here, * refers to all the records. You can use other SQL query statements with conditions as well to practice this topic more precisely.

```
func read() -> [Person] {
        let queryStatementString = "SELECT * FROM person;"
        var queryStatement: OpaquePointer? = nil
        var psns : [Person] = []
      if sqlite3_prepare_v2(db, queryStatementString, -1, &queryStatement, nil)
== SQLITE_OK {
            while sqlite3_step(queryStatement) == SQLITE_ROW {
                let id = sqlite3_column_int(queryStatement, 0)
                  let name = String(describing: String(cString: sqlite3_column_
text(queryStatement, 1)))
                let year = sqlite3_column_int(queryStatement, 2)
                psns.append(Person(id: Int(id), name: name, age: Int(year)))
                print("Query Result:")
                print("\(id) | \(name) | \(year)")
            }
        } else {
            print("SELECT statement could not be prepared")
        }
        sqlite3_finalize(queryStatement)
        return psns
    }
```

Let us understand the steps of the given code for retrieving records:

1. Prepare the statement with the given query string. Now we will execute the statement. Here we are checking the status of code **SQLITE_ROW** which actually means that you retrieved a row record when you stepped through the result.

2. Now, you are reading the values in the return lines. Provided what you know about the layout of the table and your question, you can access the columns values of the row. The first column is an Int, so you use **sqlite3_column_int()** and pass a zero-based column index and a comment. The returned value is allocated to the locally scoped id constant.

Deleting data

While deleting a record we will perform the delete SQL query statement which will require a where condition to identify identical record to delete for which we will use Id (Id has property of primary key which is useful for selecting a unique person record from person table).

Query: DELETE FROM person WHERE Id = ?

```
func deleteByID(id:Int)
{
        let deleteStatementStirng = "DELETE FROM person WHERE Id = ?;"
        var deleteStatement: OpaquePointer? = nil
         if sqlite3_prepare_v2(db, deleteStatementStirng, -1, &deleteStatement,
nil) == SQLITE_OK {
            sqlite3_bind_int(deleteStatement, 1, Int32(id))
            if sqlite3_step(deleteStatement) == SQLITE_DONE {
                print("Successfully deleted row.")
            } else {
                print("Could not delete row.")
            }
        } else {
            print("DELETE statement could not be prepared")
        }
        sqlite3_finalize(deleteStatement)
 }
```

CoreData

We use Core Data to store permanent data for offline use of your program, to archive temporary data, and to add undo capability on a single device to your app. You describe the types and relationships of your data using Core Data's Data Model editor and create the respective class descriptions. To have the following functionality, Core Data will then handle object instances at runtime. Developers are usually confused between Core data and SQLite. You need to understand that core data is not a database. Core Data is an object graph and persistence architecture supported by Apple. It makes it easy to serialize data structured into XML, binary, or SQLite stores through the relational entity-attribute model. Refer to the following figure:

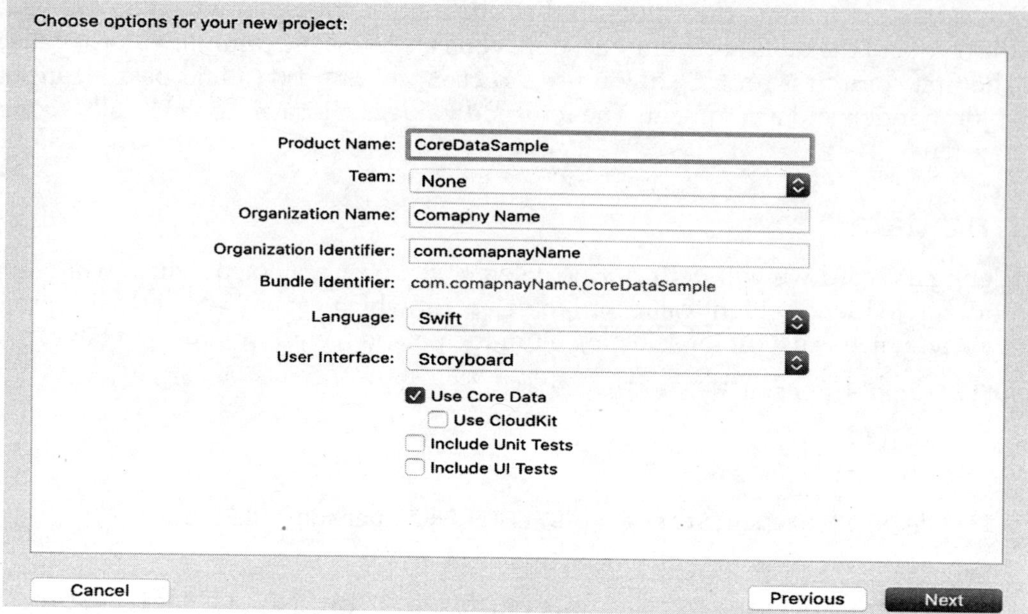

Figure 10.3: *Choosing options for your new project*

Difference between SQLite and Core Data

Let us dive deep into the differences of SQLite and Core Data in the following table:

	SQLite	Core Data
1	Have data constrained features.	Do not have any data constrained features, if required to implement by business logic.
2	Stored on disk and directly operates on data.	Operates on in memory data and regularly syncs to disk.
3	Drop table and edit table operation can be done without loading into memory.	In memory, data load is required before table drop and edit.
4	Slow as compared to Core data.	Fast as compared to SQLite, to perform all operations.

Core Data Create Schema

When you want to use core data for saving your records and data then you need to select core data option while creating a new project from Xcode, that will give you default code setup in **`appdelegate.swift`** file as well as **`<ProjectName>.xcdatamodel`** file (a file view where you can create the database schema with properties). Let us see first the code of **`appdelegate.swift`** in terms of core data, how that can help in creating and managing persistent storage for app:

```
lazy var persistentContainer: NSPersistentContainer = {
        let container = NSPersistentContainer(name: "CoreDataSample")
        container.loadPersistentStores(completionHandler: { (storeDescription, error) in
            if let error = error as NSError? {
                fatalError("Unresolved error \(error), \(error.userInfo)")
            }
        })
        return container
    }()
    func saveContext () {
        let context = persistentContainer.viewContext
        if context.hasChanges {
            do {
                try context.save()
            } catch {
                let nserror = error as NSError
                fatalError("Unresolved error \(nserror), \(nserror.userInfo)")
            }
        }
    }
```

Whenever **persistentContainer** is called to perform CRUD operation on the database, it actually loads all data into memory from sqlite file managed internally and automatically by core data ORM. We should not try to access or interact with sqlite databases directly. In fact, core data sync regularly to storage, whenever we perform insert, update and delete also retrieval of data is fast due to in memory persistent storage.

Now, let us take a look at the **.xcdatamodel** file, how you can play with that:

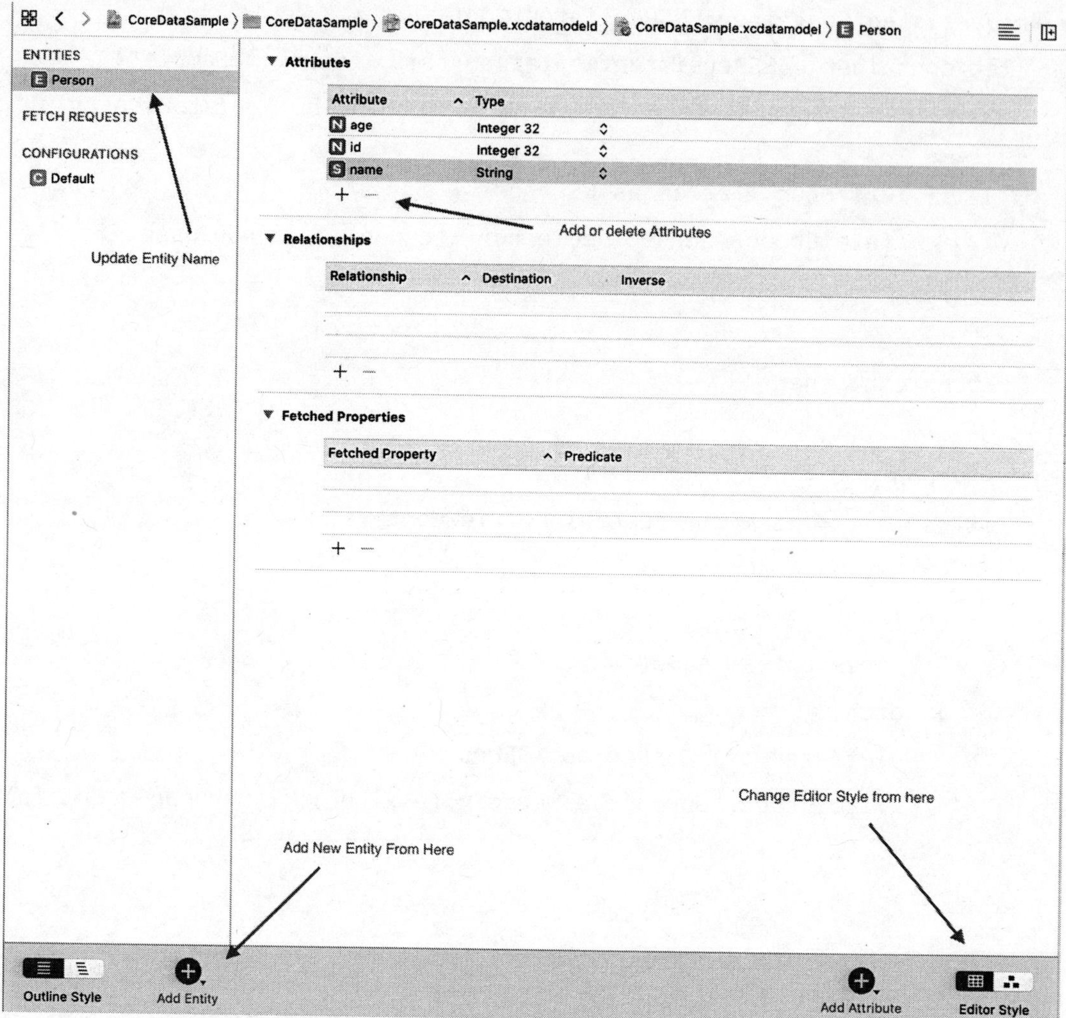

Figure 10.4: .xcdatamodel file

You can view the database model either in the form of entity attribute table style as well as pictorial form, to clearly view the relationship between the entities if there is any. From the **Add Entity** action you can add more tables (here we are talking in terms of SQLite, and in core data or ORM it is not termed as a table but as one entity). In the **Attributes** section, you can add attributes with their types. Further, you need to add an **`NSManagedObject`** subclass with respect to the entity **Person**. However, that is not required to be added manually but could be done automatically like shown below:

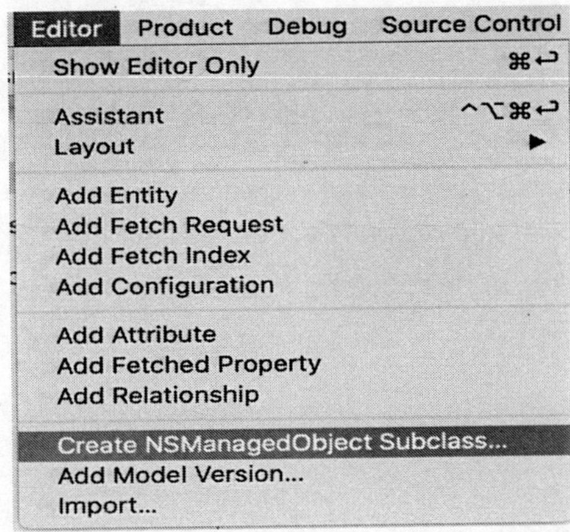

***Figure 10.5:** Creating NSManagedObject Subclass*

When you select **Editor | Create NSManagedObject Subclass** from the menu, in a few next steps the Xcode system will create an extension subclass for Person Entity (as per the case we took in earlier part of this chapter).

> **Note: Remember, in case if you update the attributes of an entity, you need to create these extension subclasses again with similar steps.**

```
import CoreData
extension Person {
    @nonobjc public class func fetchRequest() -> NSFetchRequest<Person> {
        return NSFetchRequest<Person>(entityName: "Person")
    }
    @NSManaged public var id: Int32
    @NSManaged public var name: String?
    @NSManaged public var age: Int32
}
```

Insert data

We need to create records into the database similar to SQLite but this time with the help of Core data ORM. From `appdelegate` object we will get the persistent storage context which actually loads the entire data copy into memory and regularly gets sync to on desk memory. `NSEntityDescription` helps in code to get Person entity so that we can perform insert objects on this entity which we did with a loop so multiple records can be inserted and then we save that context so that records are permanently stored into the database.

```
func insertData(){

        guard let appDelegate = UIApplication.shared.delegate as? AppDelegate
else { return }
        let managedContext = appDelegate.persistentContainer.viewContext
        let personEntity = NSEntityDescription.entity(forEntityName: "Person",
in: managedContext)!

        for i in 1...5 {

                let person = NSManagedObject(entity: personEntity, insertInto:
managedContext)
            person.setValue(i, forKeyPath: "id")
            person.setValue("Mike \(i)", forKey: "name")
            person.setValue(20 + i, forKey: "age")
        }
        do {
            try managedContext.save()

        } catch let error as NSError {
            print("Could not save. \(error), \(error.userInfo)")
        }
    }
```

Retrieve data

When we pass the entity name into **NSFetchRequest**, it prepares the fetch request to perform a retrieve operation. In case you want to apply some condition while fetching records, you can apply with **NSPredicate** which we will see while we perform delete operation further. Now you can fetch from context with a **fetchrequest** statement that will give all results and records of Person entity. To check whether it is correct or not you can check via printing name attributes or any other attribute as well.

```
func retrieveData()
    {
         guard let appDelegate = UIApplication.shared.delegate as? AppDelegate
else { return }
            let managedContext = appDelegate.persistentContainer.viewContext
```

```
            let fetchRequest = NSFetchRequest<NSFetchRequestResult>(entityName:
"Person")
            do {
                let result = try managedContext.fetch(fetchRequest)
                for data in result as! [NSManagedObject] {
                    print(data.value(forKey: "name") as! String)
                }

            } catch {

                print("Failed")
            }
      }
```

Delete data

Similar to other operations, initially we will take persistent store context and prepare a fetch request with **NSFetchRequest** adding a predicate condition to it that deletes the record whose name attribute is similar to name given in code. If there are non-zero fetch results then we will delete the first record from the context, even if you want to delete all records which you fetched from fetch request you can use for/while loop to perform delete operation on each result.

```
func deleteData()
    {
          guard let appDelegate = UIApplication.shared.delegate as? AppDelegate
else { return }
         let managedContext = appDelegate.persistentContainer.viewContext
            let fetchRequest = NSFetchRequest<NSFetchRequestResult>(entityName:
"Person")
         fetchRequest.predicate = NSPredicate(format: "name = %@", "Mike 3")
         do
         {
             let test = try managedContext.fetch(fetchRequest)
             let objectToDelete = test[0] as! NSManagedObject
             managedContext.delete(objectToDelete)
             do{
                 try managedContext.save()
             }
```

```
            catch
            {
                print(error)
            }
        }
        catch
        {
            print(error)
        }
    }
```

SwiftData

SwiftData is a new framework released in iOS 17 that offers a declarative, Swift-first API for working with data persistence in iOS applications. SwiftData can simply convert a Swift class into a persistent model and is ideal for usage with SwiftUI. SwiftData allows you to rapidly add persistence to your project with minimal code and no external dependencies. SwiftData allows you to create code that is quick, efficient, and secure by using current language features such as macros, allowing you to define the whole model layer for your project. The framework is in charge of storing the underlying model data and, if desired, synchronising it across various devices. SwiftData might be used to construct a lightweight caching mechanism and give limited offline capabilities to an app that retrieves data from a distant web service.

To implement SwiftData, you must have Xcode 15 and above, which will use the latest Swift version 5.9. SwiftData makes use of the expressivity that Swift's new language macros offer to create a seamless API interface. It works easily with SwiftUI and is compatible with other platform features like CloudKit and Widgets. The **`@Model`** macro is an important part of SwiftData's functionality. It allows you to design the schema of your data model straight from your Swift code. SwiftData schemas are conventional Swift code with a twist: when appropriate, you may annotate your properties with extra information.

```
import SwiftData
@Model
class HolidayPlan
{
    var name: String
    var tripDestination: String
    var endDate: Date
    var startDate: Date
}
```

It can adapt fundamental value types like String, Int, and Float as well as complicated kinds like structs, enums, and codable types. All of these are immediately accessible as characteristics. SwiftData also enables you to create ties between your model types using relationships and collections of model types.

Using metadata on your properties, you may change how SwiftData constructs your schema. **`@Attribute`** can be used to apply uniqueness requirements, while **`@Relationship`** can be used to govern the selection of inverses and set delete propagation rules.

Model container

The ModelContainer is the backing store for your model categories. It can operate with the default configurations, or it can be modified with configuration and migration options. To construct a model container, it is sufficient to specify the model types that will be stored. Using a configuration, you can make modifications to your URL, CloudKit, group container identifiers, and migration options. Once your container is configured, you can use model contexts to retrieve and save data as shown in below code:

```
let container = try ModelContainer(
    for: [HolidayPlan.self],
    configurations: ModelConfiguration(url: URL("path"))
)
```

Model Context

ModelContext keeps track of modifications to your models and provides multiple operations on them. It is your primary interface for monitoring updates, retrieving data, recording modifications, and even undoing those modifications. After constructing your model container in **`SwiftUI`**, you will generally retrieve the **`ModelContext`** from your view's environment, as shown in the below code:

```
import SwiftUI
struct ContextView : View {
    @Environment(\.modelContext) private var context
}
```

Predicate with SwiftData

SwiftData also has access to new Swift native types like predicate and fetch descriptor, which provide a fully type-checked contemporary replacement for **`NSPredicate`** as well as major improvements to Swift's native sort descriptor. With Xcode's autocomplete support, implementing your predicates is simple.

```
let day = Date()
let holidayPredicate = Predicate<HolidayPlan> {
```

```
    $0.destination == "My City" &&
        $0.name.contains("Mariage") &&
        $0.startDate > day
}
```

In the same manner, other capabilities, such as fetch, update, and delete, of SwiftData can be explored in detail, as introduced in iOS 17 with Xcode 15.

Conclusion

In this chapter, we initially started with how we can save small key value pairs in plist as well as in NSUserDefaults. Both permanent storage and temporary storage have their own significance and applications. Further, we discussed in detail CRUD operations on SQLite databases and their comparison with Core data. From the outset, writing powerful Core Data code allows you to plan the app for potential big datasets. Even if your app is running at the beginning, as your database and model expand, it will quickly slow down. You are now making the Core Data code more effective by using background sense, smart fetch requests, and batch delete requests. There are further complex operations that we can perform with improvements to core data monitoring, including adding predicates and dynamic database relationships. The situation further complicates as you use more core data. In iOS 17, SwiftData is introduced to make core data-like features compatible with SwiftUI.

In the next chapter, we will discuss file management and handling in detail for iOS App development.

Multiple choice questions

1. **NSUserDefault key-value pair in real save in form of ____________.**
   a. JSON
   b. xml
   c. plist
   d. sqlite
2. **From the given options, ORM used in ______________.**
   a. Plist
   b. NSUserDefault
   c. Core Data
   d. sqlite
3. **A fetch request is used to __________________.**
   a. Delete
   b. Update

c. Retrieve

d. Insert

4. Xcdatamodel is used in ________________.

a. NSUserDefault

b. SQLite

c. Core Data

d. Plist

5. Sqlite3_prepare_v2 is used for ____________.

a. Preparing statement

b. Deleting statement

c. Updating Data

d. In Core data

6. What is Core Data?

a. A database management system

b. A web development framework

c. A persistence framework provided by Apple for iOS and macOS app development.

d. A programming language

7. Which data model format does Core Data use?

a. XML

b. JSON

c. SQLite

d. Object Graph Model

8. What is the primary purpose of Core Data?

a. Storing user interface elements

b. Managing app resources such as images and sounds

c. Managing and persisting data in an app's model layer

d. Handling network requests and API communication

9. Which API does Core Data provide to interact with the underlying data store?

a. CoreGraphics

b. CoreDataAPI

c. SQLiteAPI

d. NSPersistentContainer

10. What is a managed object context in Core Data?

   a. A container for fetching and manipulating data objects

   b. A graphical representation of the data model

   c. A class used to define the data schema

   d. A mechanism for mapping objects to the underlying database tables

Answer

1. b
2. c
3. c
4. c
5. a
6. c
7. d
8. c
9. d
10. a

Join our book's Discord space

Join the book's Discord Workspace for Latest updates, Offers, Tech happenings around the world, New Release and Sessions with the Authors:

https://discord.bpbonline.com

CHAPTER 11
File Handling in iOS

Introduction

In iOS, Apple defines rules and regulations with specific locations to save files. For years, in iOS there was no managed access to files. It was only through the photos app for images, or it was possible via iCloud which could be accessed from a desktop browser, and you can download image files on a machine via photos. But that gives no information about how these files are managed in a folder or directory. From iOS 11, file management via iOS users changed altogether with the introduction of Files app. In this chapter, we will discuss in detail how you can make files and save them in applications' directory and expose those files to other apps (such as File app by Apple or other developers file management app). You must be aware every device has its limited local memory which can hold limited amounts of data in terms of file size. Such case explores the idea of further syncing those files to iCloud (the Apple service to save data and files securely on an Apple server integrated with the user's Apple ID).

Structure

In this chapter, we will cover the following topics:

- File management approaches in iOS
- iCloud file syncing from app to cloud
- Enable your app for sharing files to other apps

Objectives

The chapter will help you save your app data and information to file and place that file to document directory in any file format. Further, you will be able to sync your app files to iCloud. So in case a user changes their device they will be able to get their files again with respect to the same app.

File system basics

While you execute and run an iOS app in device or simulator, your app creates a Sandbox file system as shown in *Figure 7.1*:

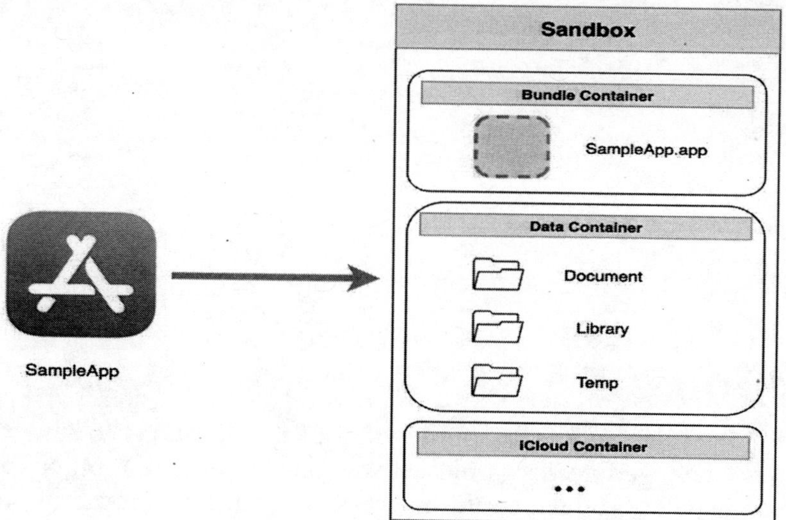

Figure 11.1: *App Sandbox File System Architecture*

iOS App Sandbox system have mainly three containers:

- App bundle container
- Data container
- iCloud container

App bundle container

This app bundle contains the application which is signed at the time of installation. A signed bundle cannot be tampered so it provides security from any time of manual or automated attacks. This directory has all the resources such as **`image`**, **`assets`**, **`info.plist`**, and so on, of the iOS application. The contents of the bundle directory are not backed up by iTunes or iCloud. But in case of In-App purchase, iTunes performs a sync to identify the old purchases for that app. We cannot write anything in the app bundle directory and only can access files with the bundle path. Let us see how you can get the paths of bundle and access the files of bundle:

```
let bundlePath = Bundle.main.bundlePath
print(bundlePath)
let infoFilePath = Bundle.main.path(forResource: "Info", ofType: "plist")
print(infoFilePath)
```

Data container

Data containers have three directories where users can save app data and files into it. This container contains respective folders for these directories:

- Document directory
- Library
- Temp

Document directory

In document directory, either you can create files at top level, or you can create a subfolder or directory to store those files for better management and quick access. Apple reserves some subdirectory names for its own apps such as `Inbox`. So, you need to take care of names while creating a subdirectory in the `document` directory. As a developer, you should save only those files here which you want users to access.

Enable file sharing

When file sharing of an application is enabled then the directory is exposed, and all its files become visible in Files applications and the user can put their files in the spotlight. All content of the directory is persisted as well as included in iCloud and iTunes backups. Storage settings UI under your app's **Document and Data** reported the disk space used in the directory. To enable File sharing for your app, you need to add **Application supports iTunes file sharing** or **UIFileSharingEnabled** with YES in `info.plist` file and to enable **Open in Place** add **LSSupportsOpeningDocumentInPlace** or **Support Opening Document in place key** with **YES** in `info.plist`. Refer to the following figure:

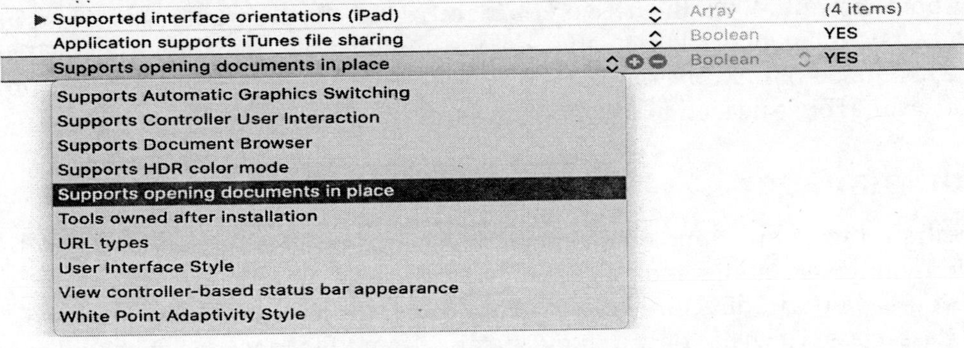

Figure 11.2: File Open Permissions

```
<key>UIFileSharingEnabled</key>
    <true/>
    <key>LSSupportsOpeningDocumentsInPlace</key>
    <true/>
```

Library - application support directory

You can save those files here which can be used by the app but not be visible by users like your database file. Either you can directly save files on top level or sub-directory can be used as well. All contents of the directory are persisted as well as included in iCloud and iTunes backups. Storage settings UI under your app's **Document and Data** reported the disk space used in the directory.

Library - cache

Files stored in cache can be discarded by the OS system whenever memory is low. This is a good place to save those files which can be re-downloaded whenever needed. Contents of this cache directory are not included into the backups. When the device is on low disk space then iOS starts clearing cache. The file storage is not reported into the storage settings Ui under your app's **Document and Data**.

Temp directory

This directory is used to store temporary files which are not needed for a longer time. Although the system removes such files periodically, it is good to have a habit to remove it by programming (further in this chapter we will study those techniques).

iCloud container

iCloud container or drive is the best place to put a document or file. Whenever connection to the Apple server will be established, those files will be available on all the devices synced with the Apple account. When the network is inaccessible, the program reads and writes data locally, and when the network is available, data is immediately uploaded to the iCloud disk. Due to the likelihood of multiple machines accessing the files in the iCloud drive at the same time, file coordination is needed to prevent any conflicts.

App file manager

Now we will start work on an app file manager which could be used across your multiple apps and would require very minimal or less changes while used in other apps. This file manager will help you to perform directory, folder, subfolder and files operations. There will be one singleton class (class which has only a single instance), **AppFileManager** which will implement three protocols, where every protocol has its own purpose.

- **`AppFileStatusChecking`** protocol
- **`AppFileSystemMetaData`** protocol
- **`AppFileManipulation`** protocol

AppFileStatusChecking protocol

We will write a protocol which will check the file status. A status could be writable, readable and, exists or not.

```
protocol AppFileStatusChecking
{
    func isWritable(file at: URL) -> Bool
    func isReadable(file at: URL) -> Bool
    func exists(file at: URL) -> Bool
}
```

The status function gets the URL of files which needs to be checked and returns the status in Boolean values. Let us implement the **`AppFileStatusChecking`** protocol:

```
extension AppFileStatusChecking
{
    func isWritable(file at: URL) -> Bool
    {
        if FileManager.default.isWritableFile(atPath: at.path)
        {
            print(at.path)
            return true
        }
        else
        {
            print(at.path)
            return false
        }
    }

    func isReadable(file at: URL) -> Bool
    {
        if FileManager.default.isReadableFile(atPath: at.path)
        {
            print(at.path)
            return true
```

```
        }
        else
        {
            print(at.path)
            return false
        }
    }

    func exists(file at: URL) -> Bool
    {
        if FileManager.default.fileExists(atPath: at.path)
        {
            return true
        }
        else
        {
            return false
        }
    }
}
```

Apple's Foundation framework contains the **FileManager** inbuilt class whose single instance can be accessed by **FileManager.default** which can be used to access functions to identify status of files.

AppFileSystemMetaData protocol

File meta info is not always required while you develop a general app, but it is good to have this feature. **AppFileSystemMetaData** protocol will develop two main features:

- List all the files from the directory given as input
- Get attributes of the file at a given path.

```
protocol AppFileSystemMetaData
{
    func list(directory at: URL) -> Bool

    func attributes(ofFile atFullPath: URL) -> [FileAttributeKey : Any]
}
extension AppFileSystemMetaData
{
    func list(directory at: URL) -> Bool
```

```
    {
        let listing = try! FileManager.default.contentsOfDirectory(atPath:
at.path)

        if listing.count > 0
        {
            print("\n----------------------------")
            print("LISTING: \(at.path)")
            print("")
            for file in listing
            {
                print("File: \(file.debugDescription)")
            }
            print("")
            print("----------------------------\n")

            return true
        }
        else
        {
            return false
        }
    }

    func attributes(ofFile atFullPath: URL) -> [FileAttributeKey : Any]
    {
      return try! FileManager.default.attributesOfItem(atPath: atFullPath.
path)
    }
}
```

List function of protocol will get all the contents of the directory with the **contentsOfDirectory** function of **FileManger** and attributes of file with **attributesOfItem** function.

AppFileManipulation protocol

Before manipulations of files and folders, we need to have the paths of different directories. Let us get path of all directories:

```
enum AppDirectories : String
{
    case Documents = "Documents"
    case Inbox = "Inbox"
    case Library = "Library"
    case Temp = "tmp"
}
protocol AppDirectoryNames
{
    func documentsDirectoryURL() -> URL
    func inboxDirectoryURL() -> URL
    func libraryDirectoryURL() -> URL
    func tempDirectoryURL() -> URL
    func getURL(for directory: AppDirectories) -> URL
        func buildFullPath(forFileName name: String, inDirectory directory: AppDirectories) -> URL
}
```

In **AppDirectoryNames** protocol, we defined the functions to get the path of all possible default directory as well as to get the path of a custom directory:

```
extension AppDirectoryNames
{
    func documentsDirectoryURL() -> URL
    {
                return FileManager.default.urls(for: .documentDirectory, in: .userDomainMask).first!
    }

    func inboxDirectoryURL() -> URL
    {
    return FileManager.default.urls(for: .documentDirectory, in: .userDomainMask)[0].appendingPathComponent(AppDirectories.Inbox.rawValue)
    }

    func libraryDirectoryURL() -> URL
    {
```

```
        return FileManager.default.urls(for: FileManager.SearchPathDirectory.
libraryDirectory, in: .userDomainMask).first!
    }

    func tempDirectoryURL() -> URL
    {
        return FileManager.default.temporaryDirectory
    }

    func getURL(for directory: AppDirectories) -> URL
    {
        switch directory
        {
        case .Documents:
            return documentsDirectoryURL()
        case .Inbox:
            return inboxDirectoryURL()
        case .Library:
            return libraryDirectoryURL()
        case .Temp:
            return tempDirectoryURL()
        }
    }

    func buildFullPath(forFileName name: String, inDirectory directory:
AppDirectories) -> URL
    {
        return getURL(for: directory).appendingPathComponent(name)
    }
}
```

Now we will define the main protocol for file and directory operations such as write, read, rename, delete, move, copy, and so on. **AppFileManipulations** will extend the **AppDirectoryNames** protocol as well.

```
protocol AppFileManipulation : AppDirectoryNames
{
```

```
    func writeFile(containing: String, to path: AppDirectories, withName name: String) -> Bool
    func readFile(at path: AppDirectories, withName name: String) -> String
    func deleteFile(at path: AppDirectories, withName name: String) -> Bool

    func renameFile(at path: AppDirectories, with oldName: String, to newName: String) -> Bool
    func moveFile(withName name: String, inDirectory: AppDirectories, toDirectory directory: AppDirectories) -> Bool
    func copyFile(withName name: String, inDirectory: AppDirectories, toDirectory directory: AppDirectories) -> Bool
    func changeFileExtension(withName name: String, inDirectory: AppDirectories, toNewExtension newExtension: String) -> Bool
}
```

You would require a path of directory and name of file when you want to write, read and delete the file and when you want to either move the file or copy the file from one path/place to another path/place that will take two directories as input in functions.

Write file

While performing write file operations there are two options, one is to write string data passed as input. It would require you to convert that string into UTF data and write as file. Second way is to directly pass file data as input to write on path as file.

Copy file

Copy file requires a path of file which needs to be copied and another or may be the same path where file needs to be copied. Copy file name logic could be implemented by you here (in the following code) number one (1) is added by default on every new copy of file:

```
extension AppFileManipulation
{
    func writeFile(containing: String, to path: AppDirectories, withName name: String) -> Bool
    {
        let filePath = getURL(for: path).path + "/" + name
        let rawData: Data? = containing.data(using: .utf8)
        return FileManager.default.createFile(atPath: filePath, contents: rawData, attributes: nil)
    }
```

```
    func writeFile(containing: Data, to path: AppDirectories, withName name: String) -> Bool
    {
        let filePath = getURL(for: path).path + "/" + name
            return FileManager.default.createFile(atPath: filePath, contents: containing, attributes: nil)
    }
    func writeFileIn(folder: String, containing: Data, to path: AppDirectories, withName name: String) -> Bool
    {
        let filePath = getURL(for: path).path + "/" + folder + "/" + name
        let fileManager = FileManager.default
        if let tDocumentDirectory = fileManager.urls(for: .documentDirectory, in: .userDomainMask).first {
            let filePath =  tDocumentDirectory.appendingPathComponent("\(folder)")
            if !fileManager.fileExists(atPath: filePath.path) {
                do {
                    try fileManager.createDirectory(atPath: filePath.path, withIntermediateDirectories: true, attributes: nil)
                } catch {
                    NSLog("Couldn't create document directory")
                }
            }
            NSLog("Document directory is \(filePath)")
        }
            return FileManager.default.createFile(atPath: filePath, contents: containing, attributes: nil)
    }
    func readFile(at path: AppDirectories, withName name: String) -> String
    {
        let filePath = getURL(for: path).path + "/" + name
        let fileContents = FileManager.default.contents(atPath: filePath)
        let fileContentsAsString = String(bytes: fileContents!, encoding: .utf8)
        print(fileContentsAsString!)
```

```
        return fileContentsAsString!
    }

    func deleteFile(at path: AppDirectories, withName name: String) -> Bool
    {
        let filePath = buildFullPath(forFileName: name, inDirectory: path)
        do
        {
            try FileManager.default.removeItem(at: filePath)
            return true
        }
        catch
        {
            print(error)
        }
        return false
    }

    func renameFile(at path: AppDirectories, with oldName: String, to newName: 
String) -> Bool
    {
        let oldPath = getURL(for: path).appendingPathComponent(oldName)
        let newPath = getURL(for: path).appendingPathComponent(newName)
        do {
            try FileManager.default.moveItem(at: oldPath, to: newPath)
            return true
        } catch {
            return false
        }
    }

    func moveFile(withName name: String, inDirectory: AppDirectories, toDirectory 
directory: AppDirectories) -> Bool
    {
```

```
        let originURL = buildFullPath(forFileName: name, inDirectory: inDirectory)
            let destinationURL = buildFullPath(forFileName: name, inDirectory: 
directory)
        try! FileManager.default.moveItem(at: originURL, to: destinationURL)
        return true
    }

    func copyFile(withName name: String, inDirectory: AppDirectories, toDirectory 
directory: AppDirectories) -> Bool
    {
        let originURL = buildFullPath(forFileName: name, inDirectory: inDirectory)
            let destinationURL = buildFullPath(forFileName: name+"1", inDirectory: 
directory)
        try! FileManager.default.copyItem(at: originURL, to: destinationURL)
        return true
    }

    func changeFileExtension(withName name: String, inDirectory: AppDirectories, 
toNewExtension newExtension: String) -> Bool
    {
        var newFileName = NSString(string:name)
        newFileName = newFileName.deletingPathExtension as NSString
            newFileName = (newFileName.appendingPathExtension(newExtension) as 
NSString?)!
        let finalFileName:String =  String(newFileName)

        let originURL = buildFullPath(forFileName: name, inDirectory: inDirectory)
        let destinationURL = buildFullPath(forFileName: finalFileName, inDirectory: 
inDirectory)

        try! FileManager.default.moveItem(at: originURL, to: destinationURL)

        return true
    }
}
```

Change file extension

When you want to change an extension of a file with a file name and new extension, it would first be required to frame a new name with that new extension and rewrite that file with that new name and further old extension file can be deleted.

Now we need to implement our actual singleton class and use all these defined protocols in **AppFileManager**:

```
class AppFileManager: NSObject, AppFileStatusChecking, AppFileManipulation,
AppFileSystemMetaData
{
    static let sharedInstance: AppFileManager = {
        let instance = AppFileManager()
        return instance
    }()

    override init() {
        super.init()
    }
}
```

Class **AppFileManager** extends and uses all protocols which we used earlier and initialized the singleton instance. Now you can make functions as per your application requirements.

Save file

When you need to save an image file or PDF file, you would be required to pass the file data with path. The path could be at the directory top level or could be passed with the folder name to accommodate file in subdirectory. In the following code, if we not required to save file in folder we would send that as empty string so that we can take decision to write file directly on path or with folder path.

```
func savefile(folder: String, fileName: String, image: Data) -> Bool
    {
        if folder == ""
        {
          return writeFile(containing: image, to: .Documents, withName: fileName)
        }

        return writeFileIn(folder: folder, containing: image, to: .Documents,
withName: fileName)
    }
```

Delete file

When you want to delete a file from any directory or path, then first you need to check whether that file exists on that path or not. If that exists on the path, you can proceed with the delete file operations.

```
func fileExist(folder: String, file: String) -> Bool
    {
            return folder == "" ? exists(file: buildFullPath(forFileName: file, inDirectory: .Documents)) : exists(file: buildFullPathWith(folder: folder, forFileName: file, inDirectory: .Documents))
    }
func deleteFile(folder: String, fileName: String) -> Bool
    {
            let filePath = folder == "" ? buildFullPath(forFileName: fileName, inDirectory: .Documents) : buildFullPathWith(folder: folder, forFileName: fileName, inDirectory: .Documents)
        if fileExist(folder: folder, file: fileName)
        {
            do
            {
                try FileManager.default.removeItem(at: filePath)
                return true
            }
            catch
            {
                print(error)
            }
        }
        return false
    }
```

Get file list

If you want to get all files saved on the top level of the **document** directory, you will need to get directory contents which will give you an array of files. Further, if you want you can filter that directory content for more precise results.

```
func getFileList() -> [String]
    {
```

```
        var documentsUrl =  FileManager.default.urls(for: .documentDirectory,
in: .userDomainMask).first!
        do {
            // Get the directory contents urls (including subfolders urls)
        let directoryContents = try FileManager.default.contentsOfDirectory(at:
documentsUrl, includingPropertiesForKeys: nil, options: [])
            print(directoryContents)

            // if you want to filter the directory contents you can do like this:
          var pdfList = directoryContents.filter{ $0.pathExtension == "pdf"} as [URL]
          let txtList = directoryContents.filter{ $0.pathExtension == "txt"} as [URL]
          let csvList = directoryContents.filter{ $0.pathExtension == "csv"} as [URL]
          let gpxList = directoryContents.filter{ $0.pathExtension == "gpx"} as [URL]
            pdfList.append(contentsOf: txtList)
            pdfList.append(contentsOf: csvList)
            pdfList.append(contentsOf: gpxList)
            var fileList: [String] = []
            for item in pdfList {
                let str = item.absoluteString.components(separatedBy: "/")
                fileList.append(str.last!)
            }
            print("PDF list:", fileList)
            return fileList

        } catch {
            print(error.localizedDescription)
        }
        return []
    }
```

In the above programming example, four types of file extensions would be considered to be in the file list. If your app requires more such different extension files as well, you can use it in a similar way.

How to use AppFileManager?

You can use **AppFileManager** as a singleton class. Let us see some of the example code as follows:

```
if WSFileManager.sharedInstance.deleteFile(folder: folderName, fileName: filename)
```

```
{
    print("File Deleted")
}
self.list = WSFileManager.sharedInstance.getFileList()
```

Conclusion

In this chapter, we discussed in detail the sandbox structure of an iOS app and how folders and files could be kept in those default directories. We read and write files on disk in the document directory folder or subfolder to manage them better. Accessing data on disk is one of the slowest operations a machine can perform, in contrast to other operations. Reading files from a disk-based hard drive can take anything from a few milliseconds to several minutes, depending on the size and number of files. Make sure the code runs as well as possible under a range of workloads, from mild to moderate. Using the Instruments app to capture any baseline measurements if the app slows down or becomes less sensitive while dealing with files. Instruments inform you how much time the app spends dealing with files and help you keep track of different file-related events.

Multiple choice questions

1. `FileManager.default` is ______________.
    a. Factory Instance
    b. Singleton Instance
    c. Protocol
    d. Extension
2. **What does** `appendingPathComponent` **do?**
    a. Add New Files
    b. Check if File Exist
    c. Add new path or folder
    d. Make file visible
3. **What does** `contentsOfDirectory` **return?**
    a. Size of files
    b. Name of files on path
    c. Size of directory
    d. Singleton Instance

4. **If you can download content again and would not require saving that permanently then you will save that file in _________.**
    a. Document Directory
    b. Temp Directory
    c. Sub Directory of Document directory
    d. In App Bundle
5. **If you want to delete a file, what would you check first before deleting?**
    a. Document Directory is empty or not
    b. Size of file
    c. File Exist at given path or not
    d. Cache is empty or not

Answer

1. b
2. c
3. b
4. b
5. c

Join our book's Discord space

Join the book's Discord Workspace for Latest updates, Offers, Tech happenings around the world, New Release and Sessions with the Authors:

https://discord.bpbonline.com

CHAPTER 12
Core Location with MapKit

Introduction

In today's time, with the advancements in technology, geo-positional systems are an essential part of mobile hardware, and this GPS can help to write such apps which show users' current location, positions on maps, the distance between two or multi-geo positional points, etc. Apple embedded the Core Location framework, which natively integrates with the GPS hardware of iOS-supported iPhones and iPads in such a manner that developers can use this to build apps with features of native maps and the user's location. Core Location provides services that determine a device's geographic location, altitude, and orientation or its position relative to a nearby iBeacon device. The framework gathers data using all available components on the device, including Wi-Fi, GPS, Bluetooth, a magnetometer, a barometer, and cellular hardware. Including location-based information in your app is an excellent way to keep your users connected to their surroundings. Location-based information should improve the overall user experience, whether you use it for practical purposes (such as navigation) or entertainment.

Structure

In this chapter, we will cover the following topics:

- Standard and significant location updates
- Show user location on Apple and Google Maps
- Geo position region monitoring

Objectives

In this chapter, you will gain valuable knowledge and skills to enhance your positional location capabilities. With an emphasis on both accuracy and efficiency, you will learn how to obtain significant positional location using advanced techniques. Additionally, you will delve into map kit operations involving core location points, allowing you to harness the power of geospatial data effectively. Moreover, you will be equipped with the expertise to perform geo-position region monitoring, which will enable you to track and monitor specific geographical areas with precision. Overall, mastering these concepts will empower you to excel in location-based applications and services, enriching your understanding of geolocation technologies.

CLLocationManager

The Core Location services are configured, started, and stopped using instances of the **`CLLocationManager`** class. A location manager object is capable of supporting the following location-related tasks:

- **Standard and significant location updates**: Track big or small changes in the user's current location with a configurable degree of precision.
- **Region monitoring**: When the user enters or leaves specific areas of interest, location events are generated.
- **Beacon ranging**: Detect and locate nearby beacons.
- **Compass headings**: Report heading changes from the onboard compass.

Add location permissions to app

Your app would require location permission from the user. There are mainly two types of location authorization for different purposes and requirements of the app:

- **When in Use**: In this type of location authorization, your app will receive location events when the user is using it, and if your app goes into the background, it will stop receiving the location updates and events. You can add this property to the **`info.plist`** of your app as *Privacy: Location When In Use Usage Description* with a proper explanation of why your app requires this permission. Here we will use xml code for adding privacy policy reason for When in Use location as shown below:

```
<key>NSLocationWhenInUseUsageDescription
</key>
<string>
    To include location data with the Report.
</string>
```

Alternatively, you can add the above code with the change of reason as per your app **`info.plist`** source code.

- **Always use:** In this type of location authorization, your app receives location events and updates, even if the app is in the foreground or background. You can add the **`info.plist`** of your app as *Privacy - Location Always Usage Description* property with a proper explanation of why your app required this permission. Here we will use xml code for adding privacy policy reason for Always Use location as shown below:

```
<key>NSLocationAlwaysUsageDescription
</key>
<string>
    To include location data with Project Report.
</string>
```

Alternatively, you can add the above code with the change of reason as per your app **`info.plist`** source code.

App location manager

Now we will start building a singleton class that will be single-handedly responsible for managing user location and start/stop tracking user location.

Setup location manager

The location manager must set a delegate as a self-object, invoked when the app gets the user's real-time location in latitude and longitude. Here we will setup location manager properties as shown below code:

```
var locationManager : CLLocationManager!
var kMinUpdateDistance = 5.0
 /*
    Setting up Location Manager Properties
    - type, filter, accuracy, enabled check
    */
   func setupLocationManager()
   {
       locationManager = CLLocationManager()
       locationManager.delegate = self
       locationManager.activityType = CLActivityType.automotiveNavigation
       locationManager.distanceFilter = kMinUpdateDistance
```

```
        locationManager.desiredAccuracy = kCLLocationAccuracyBestForNavigation
        locationManager.pausesLocationUpdatesAutomatically = false
        locationManager.allowsBackgroundLocationUpdates = false
    }
```

- **Activity type**: The location manager uses the information in the activity type field to decide when location updates should be automatically halted. When the user's position is unlikely to change, pausing updates allows the system to conserve energy.
  - o **Automotive Navigation: It** is used specifically during vehicular navigation to track location changes to the automobile.
  - o **Fitness**: It tracks fitness activities such as walking, running, cycling, and so on.
  - o **Airborne**: The location manager is being used specifically during airborne activities.
  - o **Other Navigation:** It is used to track movements for other types of vehicular navigation that are not automobile related.
- **Distance filter**: Before an update event is created, a device must travel horizontally a minimum distance (measured in meters). This distance is measured relative to the previously delivered location.
- **Desired accuracy:** Assign a value to this parameter that is appropriate for your use to decrease the impact of your app on battery life. While the location service makes every effort to attain the desired precision, applications must be prepared to work with less precise data. Changes to this property's value have no effect if your app is not permitted to receive precise location data; the accuracy is always **`kCLLocationAccuracyReduced`**. When making an app for navigation purposes, it is advisable to use **`kCLLocationAccuracyBestForNavigation`**.
- **Pause location updates**: The bool value indicates the location manager object's ability to halt location updates. Allowing the location manager to stop updates on the target device helps extend battery life while preserving location data. This must be set to false so location updates will not stop while using the app.
- **Allow background location:** If an app wants to receive location updates while suspended, it must include the **`UIBackgroundModes`** key (with the location value) in its **`Info.plist`** file and set the value to true. Background updates need the availability of the **`UIBackgroundModes`** key with the location value; this property is used to programmatically activate and disable background updates. We need to check if location services of device is enabled or not which will performed by below code:

```
if CLLocationManager.locationServicesEnabled()
{
      requestLocationAuthorization()
}
```

Before requesting user location permissions, we must check for location services, which must be enabled. If location services are not enabled for a device, we need to show an appropriate message so that the user can enable location services on that device. If the location service enabled check returns true, we will proceed with user location permissions as shown in below code:

```
/*
        Check GPS Setting Status
        - Always, WhenIn Use , Not Determined etc

*/
      func requestLocationAuthorization()
      {
          let status = CLLocationManager.authorizationStatus()
          if status == CLAuthorizationStatus.notDetermined {
              locationManager.requestWhenInUseAuthorization()
          }
          else if status == CLAuthorizationStatus.authorizedWhenInUse
          {
              // perform any operation if required
          }
      }
```

In the preceding function, first, we check if authorization for location permission is already given as per requirements, then we can continue; otherwise, we need to request location authorization. It could be of two types:

- **When in use**: This authorization is requested when your app requires user location only when the app is in use and not in the background.
- **Always use**: This type of authorization is given when your app has background modes permissions to be active in the background to get location always.

Check location enabled

In some instances of app features, returning users might not have location enabled, which we need before an important current location event. Then you need a function that will tell you the current location-enabled status, and based on that status, you can show alerts to the user as shown in below code here:

```
/*
        Check for location is enabled or not and return red / green image
*/
    func checklocationEnabled() -> UIImage
    {
```

```
        if CLLocationManager.locationServicesEnabled()
        {
            switch CLLocationManager.authorizationStatus()
            {
            case .notDetermined, .restricted, .denied:
                print("No access")
                return UIImage(named: "RedGPS")!
            case .authorizedAlways, .authorizedWhenInUse:
                print("Access")
                return UIImage(named: "GreenGPS")!
            default:
                print("Access")
                return UIImage(named: "GreenGPS")!
            }
        } else {
            print("Location services are not enabled")
            return UIImage(named: "RedGPS")!
        }
    }
```

Although we already used all these statuses initially, but **checkLocationEnabled** function will give you the status of device location enable conditions. Here we are returning an image green as on location and red as off location. You may use it as you want.

Start and stop location tracking

When tracking a user or object with location, ideally to save battery, sometimes you need to stop or start the location tracking as per the feature implementation requirements. As we studied earlier, getting user location depends on significant location change or distance. Sometimes we need to force an update such that we can get the current location of the device, we can implement this as shown in below code:

```
/*
    Trigger to start GPS Location Tracking
*/
func startTracking()
    {
        locationManager.startUpdatingLocation()
```

```
        updateTimer = Timer.scheduledTimer(timeInterval: 16.0, target: self,
selector: #selector(WSLocationManager.forceUpdateLocation), userInfo: nil,
repeats: true)
    }
```

The location manager can start the location tracking via **startUpdatingLocation**, which will trigger the delegate methods with updated locations that can be retrieved as latitude and longitude points. And to optimize the location we need to stop tracking location at some point of time as shown in below code:

```
/*
    Trigger to stop GPS Location Tracking
 */
func stopTracking()
    {
        locationManager.stopUpdatingLocation()
        if (updateTimer != nil) {
            updateTimer!.invalidate()
            updateTimer = nil
        }
    }
```

When app features do not require location tracking, we can save battery power by stopping unnecessary location tracking. The location manager can stop tracking via **stopUpdatingLocation**. In the above case, a timer forces the location manager to get the current location. This could help if device movement is insignificant, and we require regular location changes. Time calls **forceUpdateLocation**, which simply does **requestLocation** and notifies the app of the current location in the delegate method as shown in below code:

```
// Request Location Update
func forceUpdateLocation()
{
    locationManager.requestLocation()
}
```

Get current user location

When we need a location point of the current location, then with the location object of **LocationManager** we can get the latitude and longitude of geo positional points to mark the destination of the user device as shown in below code:

```
/*
    Get current location latitude and longitude from Location Manager
*/
    func currentUserLocation() -> (Float, Float)?
    {
        var lat: Float
        var long: Float
        if let location = locationManager.location {
            lat = Float(location.coordinate.latitude)
            long = Float(location.coordinate.longitude)
            return (lat, long)
        }
        return nil
    }
```

Location manager delegates

After starting location tracking, the location manager sends location updates as success or failure, which will be listened to by the location manager delegate methods. We will add an extension to our singleton class with **`CLLocationManagerDelegate`** to implement this. Further, we will discuss these methods in detail.

- **`didchangeAuthorization`**: This delegate method informs the delegate of its authorization status when the app creates the location manager and when the authorization status changes.
- **`didUpdateLocations`**: This delegate method creates an array of CLLocation objects to store the location information. At least one item reflecting the current location is always present in this array. The array may contain extra entries if updates were delayed, or numerous locations arrived before they could be provided.
- **`didFailWithError`**: When the location manager finds an error while attempting to retrieve the location or heading data, it calls this function. A CLError is reported if the location service cannot get a location immediately. Continues to attempt despite the code locationUnknown error.

All mentioned cases are implemented here:

```
extension WSLocationManager: CLLocationManagerDelegate
{
    func locationManager(_ manager: CLLocationManager, didChangeAuthorization
status: CLAuthorizationStatus)
    {
        if status == CLAuthorizationStatus.authorizedWhenInUse
```

```
        {
            locationManager.startUpdatingLocation()
            locationManager.startMonitoringSignificantLocationChanges()
        }
    }

    func locationManager(_ manager: CLLocationManager, didUpdateLocations locations: [CLLocation]) {
        userLocation = locationManager.location
        dLog("userLocation \(String(describing: userLocation))")
    }

    public func locationManager(_ manager: CLLocationManager, didFailWithError error: Error)
    {
        dLog("LocationTracker: didFailWithError \(error)")
        if locationManager.location?.coordinate == nil
        {
            userLocation = CLLocation.init(latitude: CLLocationDegrees(0.0), longitude: CLLocationDegrees(0.0))
        }
    }
}
```

Significant location change

When the location manager calls **startMonitoringSignificantLocationUpdate**, this starts the generation of updates based on significant location changes. This method initiates the delivery of location events asynchronously. The first event to be delivered is usually the most recently cached location event (if any), but it may be a newer event in some circumstances.

When the smartphone goes 500 meters or more from its previous notification, apps can anticipate a notice. It should not be expected to get alerts more than once every five minutes. The location manager is far more likely to provide notifications promptly if the device can receive data from the network.

Show current location on map

To show a user's location on a map, you may opt for two ways, one is with Google Maps, and the other is with Native Apple Maps.

Location with Google Maps

First, you must install the iOS SDK for the Google Maps and Places API. Then you need to get API keys for further implementation. You can refer to the developer's Google Maps documentation.

In **AppDelegate.swift**, you need to add the following code:

```
import GooglePlaces

import GoogleMaps
```

Add the following to your application (**:didFinishLaunchingWithOptions:**) method, replacing **YOUR_API_KEY** with your API key:

```
GMSPlacesClient.provideAPIKey("YOUR_API_KEY")

GMSServices.provideAPIKey("YOUR_API_KEY")
```

Add the view controller where you want to implement the mapview:

```
var mapView: GMSMapView!

var placesClient: GMSPlacesClient!
```

In the **didUpdateLocation** delegate method, we can set the camera position object to the map view camera property in such a way that it contains location coordinates with the map's zoom level too.

Here, the zoom level helps to point out the location on the map that we want to show accurately as shown in below code:

```
let location: CLLocation = locations.last!
print("Location: \(location)")


let zoomLevel = locationManager.accuracyAuthorization == .fullAccuracy ? preciseLocationZoomLevel : approximateLocationZoomLevel
let camera = GMSCameraPosition.camera(withLatitude: location.coordinate.latitude, longitude: location.coordinate.longitude, zoom: zoomLevel)
if mapView.isHidden {
   mapView.isHidden = false
   mapView.camera = camera
} else
{
   mapView.animate(to: camera)
}
```

Location with Apple Maps

Apple iOS devices use the native MapKit framework to implement map functions in the app. First, we have to initialize a map view from **MapKit**, which needs to be connected with **MapView** on the app, as shown here:

```
@IBOutlet var mapView: MKMapView!

mapView.delegate = self

mapView.mapType = .standard

mapView.isZoomEnabled = true

mapView.isScrollEnabled = true
```

While setting the properties of the map, we can select map type, zoom enabled, and scroll enabled for smooth transitions on the map. We can set a location if that is available in the location manager as shown here:

```
if let coor = mapView.userLocation.location?.coordinate {

    mapView.setCenter(coor, animated: true)

}

func locationManager(_ manager: CLLocationManager, didUpdateLocations
        locations: [CLLocation]) {

        let locValue:CLLocationCoordinate2D = manager.location!.coordinate

        mapView.mapType = MKMapType.standard

        let span = MKCoordinateSpan(latitudeDelta: 0.05, longitudeDelta: 0.05)

        let region = MKCoordinateRegion(center: locValue, span: span)

        mapView.setRegion(region, animated: true)

        let annotation = MKPointAnnotation()

        annotation.coordinate = locValue

        annotation.title = "You are Here"

        mapView.addAnnotation(annotation)

    }
```

To drop a location pin on the native map, first, we will set up a region on which the map needs to be focused. This map region takes the location as the center and spans objects to show the location properly. Further, we can add a point annotation with the location coordinates and title to show a pin drop on the mapview.

Convert location into placemark address

If you have a **CLLocation** object, use your geocoder object's **reverseGeocodeLocation(:completionHandler:)** function to get a **CLPlacemark** object for that place. You usually transform coordinates into placemarks when you wish to show the user information about a location as shown here:

```
func lookUpCurrentLocation(completionHandler: @escaping (CLPlacemark?)
                    -> Void ) {
      // Use the last reported location.
      if let lastLocation = self.locationManager.location {
          let geocoder = CLGeocoder()

          // Look up the location and pass it to the completion handler
          geocoder.reverseGeocodeLocation(lastLocation,
                      completionHandler: { (placemarks, error) in
              if error == nil {
                  let firstLocation = placemarks?[0]
                  completionHandler(firstLocation)
              }
              else {
               // An error occurred during geocoding.
                  completionHandler(nil)
              }
          })
      }
      else {
          // No location was available.
          completionHandler(nil)
      }
  }
```

Convert a place address to location coordinates

If you have a user-supplied address, use the **CLGeocoder** method to get the associated location data. The **CLGeocoder** class allows you to transform either a user-typed string or a dictionary containing address-related information. This data is sent to Apple servers, which evaluate it and deliver the findings as shown here:

```
func getCoordinate( addressString : String,
        completionHandler: @escaping(CLLocationCoordinate2D, NSError?) ->
Void ) {
        let geocoder = CLGeocoder()
        geocoder.geocodeAddressString(addressString) { (placemarks, error) in
            if error == nil {
                if let placemark = placemarks?[0] {
                    let location = placemark.location!

                    completionHandler(location.coordinate, nil)
                    return
                }
            }

            completionHandler(kCLLocationCoordinate2DInvalid, error as NSError?)
        }
    }
```

Types of core location errors

`CLError` delivered the instances of `NSError` when there was any error specific to location events. We will discuss some of them below:

- **Location unknown**: This indicates the location manager could not obtain a location value.
- **Denied**: This indicates the user was denied access to the location service.
- **Prompt declined**: This indicates the user did not grant the requested temporary authorization.
- **Network**: This indicates the network was unavailable or a network error occurred.
- **Heading failure**: This indicates the heading could not be determined.
- **Geocode canceled** This indicates the geocode request was canceled.
- **Deferred not updating location**: This indicates the location manager did not enter deferred mode because location updates were already disabled or paused.

Monitoring the user's proximity to geographic regions

Monitoring region service of Core location can be used for region monitoring to determine when the user enters or leaves a geographic region. When a user enters or departs a geographical region, region monitoring (geofencing) allows your app to be notified. To execute location-related tasks, you might employ region monitoring. The Reminders app, for example, utilizes them to send out reminders when the user enters or exits a specific place.

When a user passes a set area border, the system monitors it and wakes up your app as needed. Region monitoring is only possible on macOS when the program is open (in the foreground or background), and the user's machine is awake. Before starting the monitoring we will check if monitoring available or not then we will start monitoring for cordinates as shown here:

```
func monitorRegionAtLocation(center: CLLocationCoordinate2D, identifier: String
) {
        // Make sure the devices supports region monitoring.
       if CLLocationManager.isMonitoringAvailable(for: CLCircularRegion.self) {
            // Register the region.
            let maxDistance = locationManager.maximumRegionMonitoringDistance
            let region = CLCircularRegion(center: center,
                 radius: maxDistance, identifier: identifier)
            region.notifyOnEntry = true
            region.notifyOnExit = false

            locationManager.startMonitoring(for: region)

       }
   }
```

Handle region notifications

The delegate object of your location manager receives boundary crossing notifications. The location manager specifically invokes its delegate's **locationManager(:didEnterRegion:)** or **locationManager(:didExitRegion:)** methods. If your app has already been launched, you must immediately create a **CLLocationManager** object and a delegate object to receive these alerts. If a monitoring for location running and a new coordinates entered that region it will notify to delegate methods as shown here:

```
func  locationManager(_  manager:  CLLocationManager,  didEnterRegion  region:
CLRegion) {
       if let region = region as? CLCircularRegion {
            let identifier = region.identifier
            triggerTaskAssociatedWithRegionIdentifier(regionID: identifier)
       }
   }
```

The system waits until it is certain that a boundary crossing has occurred before delivering the notification. The user must cross the barrier at a minimum distance and remain on the same side of the boundary for at least 20 seconds. These criteria assist in avoiding bogus calls to the methods of your delegate object.

Conclusion

The Core Location and Map Kit frameworks offer powerful tools for developers to leverage GPS and map-based features on iOS devices. In this chapter, we explored various functionalities these frameworks provide, including continuous location tracking, obtaining the user's current location, and displaying location coordinates on a map. Both Google Maps and Apple Maps, which the MapKit framework supports, are options for developers when displaying map features. Each map service has its own set of advantages and disadvantages, and the choice should be based on the specific requirements of your app.

Additionally, we delved into location region monitoring, which allows developers to define specific geographic areas and receive notifications when a device enters or exits those regions. This feature is particularly useful for applications that need to locate businesses and events or engage in real-time service and product marketing. It provides timely notifications to users based on their proximity to certain locations.

In the next chapter, we will discuss the multimedia features of iOS, such as the camera, photo gallery, etc.

Multiple choice questions

1. **Which framework is used to get locations in iOS devices?**
   a. iBeacon
   b. Map Kit
   c. Core Location
   d. UIKit
2. **Which delegate method gets an array of updated location coordinates?**
   a. changeAuthrizationStatus
   b. didUpdateLocation
   c. didfailwithError
   d. StartMonitoringRegion
3. **Reverse geocoding is used for?**
   a. To get updated location
   b. Location coordinates to address
   c. Address to Location coordinates
   d. None of the above

4. **`startMonitoringSignificantLocationChanges` method is used for the?**
   a. Start location update
   b. Get location when there is a significant change in location
   c. Monitor region at a location
   d. None of the above
5. **`CLCircularRegion` is used in?**
   a. Start location update
   b. When a significant change in location
   c. Monitor region at location
   d. None of the above
6. **Which class of Core location contains location coordinates?**
   a. CLLocationCoordinate2D
   b. CLCircularRegion
   c. CLGeocoder
   d. MKCoordinateSpan

Answers

1. c
2. b
3. b
4. b
5. b
6. a

Join our book's Discord space

Join the book's Discord Workspace for Latest updates, Offers, Tech happenings around the world, New Release and Sessions with the Authors:

https://discord.bpbonline.com

CHAPTER 13
Camera and Photo Library

Introduction

In recent times, there have been consistent advancements in mobile processing power, leading to regular increases in camera megapixels. The inclusion of multimedia features in mobile applications significantly enhances their overall visual appeal while providing users with the ability to capture photos using the native camera or select images from their photo gallery. Moreover, users can also record videos using these features and seamlessly integrate them into the app. This chapter will provide a comprehensive understanding of utilizing the native camera functionality to capture photos within your app as well as leveraging the image picker to retrieve images from the device's gallery.

It is worth noting that implementing extensive customizations in the camera stream or adding intricate modifications to the camera functionality lies beyond the scope of this book. However, the chapter will equip you with the necessary knowledge to effectively utilize the available camera and gallery features to enhance your app's multimedia capabilities.

Structure

In this chapter, we will cover the following topics:

- Loading photo library into app with image picker
- Take an image using camera

Objectives

After reading this chapter, you will be able to make use of the image picker for loading the photo library and native camera app when you want to add an image from mobile resources such as the photo library and camera for the purpose of user image, image upload, album image, and so on, or any other such feature of your app, as well as be able to make use of Image picker for loading the photo library and native camera app.

Add photo library and camera permissions

Before starting any coding for either loading the photo library or camera, you need to add permissions to **`Info.plist`** with a detailed, specific reason explaining why and for which feature you want access to the camera and photo library for your app. If there is no proper explanation, then there is a high chance that while going through **App Store Review** at Apple's side, your app may get rejected. To add these permissions first go to **`Info.plist`** and add row as shown below:

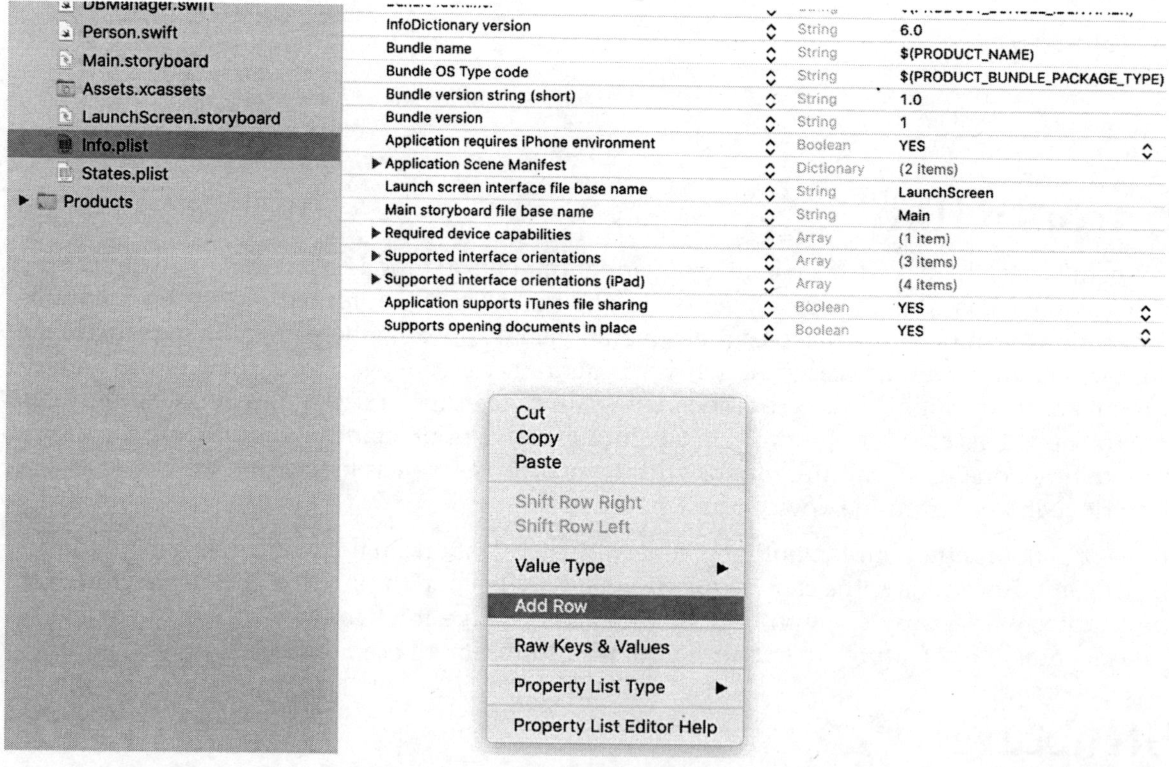

Figure 13.1: *Add Media Permissions*

The following *Figure 13.2* shows options for which we need to mention the reason in detail for asking permissions:

Key	Type	Value
▼ Information Property List	Dictionary	(18 items)
Localization native development region	String	$(DEVELOPMENT_LANGUAGE)
Privacy - Camera Usage Description	String	To Upload User Image
Executable file	String	$(EXECUTABLE_NAME)
Bundle identifier	String	$(PRODUCT_BUNDLE_IDENTIFIER)
InfoDictionary version	String	6.0
Bundle name	String	$(PRODUCT_NAME)
Bundle OS Type code	String	$(PRODUCT_BUNDLE_PACKAGE_TYPE)
Bundle version string (short)	String	1.0
Bundle version	String	1
Application requires iPhone environment	Boolean	YES
▶ Application Scene Manifest	Dictionary	(2 items)
Launch screen interface file base name	String	LaunchScreen
Main storyboard file base name	String	Main
▶ Required device capabilities	Array	(1 item)
▶ Supported interface orientations	Array	(3 items)
▶ Supported interface orientations (iPad)	Array	(4 items)
Application supports iTunes file sharing	Boolean	YES
Supports opening documents in place	Boolean	YES

***Figure 13.2:** Add Reason for Media Permissions*

When next in that new row you will start writing the word **Privacy**, select the option **Privacy - Camera Usage Description**. Further, this will give you the option to write a string or statement where you need to explain the reason behind using this camera feature in your app. If you are writing code for practice, you can write any sample string it will not affect your overall functionality and is limited to App Store review cautions. In a similar way, select the option for **Privacy - Photo Library Usage Description** for accessing images from the photo library of devices.

Other than directly adding them to the **.plist**, you can add them by opening the **.plist** file as code and adding the below codes to it. Which will work in the same way as we manually added permissions:

```
<key>NSCameraUsageDescription</key>

<string>This app wants to take pictures.</string>

<key>NSPhotoLibraryUsageDescription</key>

<string>This app wants to use your photos.</string>
```

Add option to choose camera and gallery

Now, we will give options to choose one of the operations either to take pictures from camera or image gallery:

```
@IBAction func imagePickerAction(selectedButton: UIButton)

        {
```

```
        let alert = UIAlertController(title: "Choose Image", message: nil,
preferredStyle: .actionSheet)
            alert.addAction(UIAlertAction(title: "Camera", style: .default,
handler: { _ in
                self.openCamera()
        }))
            alert.addAction(UIAlertAction(title: "Gallery", style: .default,
handler: { _ in
                self.openGallery()
        }))
        alert.addAction(UIAlertAction.init(title: "Cancel", style: .cancel,
handler: nil))
        self.present(alert, animated: true, completion: nil)
    }
```

With the help of action button operation users will be able to choose one of the choices out of camera and gallery. Now we will perform **openCamera** and **openGallery** code operation using **UIImagePickerViewController**.

```
func openCamera()
    {
        if UIImagePickerController.isSourceTypeAvailable(UIImagePickerController.
SourceType.camera) {
            let imagePicker = UIImagePickerController()
            imagePicker.delegate = self
            imagePicker.sourceType = UIImagePickerController.SourceType.camera
            imagePicker.allowsEditing = false
            self.present(imagePicker, animated: true, completion: nil)
        }
        else
        {
            let alert  = UIAlertController(title: "Warning", message: "You don't
have camera", preferredStyle: .alert)
            alert.addAction(UIAlertAction(title: "OK", style: .default, handler:
nil))
            self.present(alert, animated: true, completion: nil)
        }
    }
```

In the previous code, first we will check if the source type as camera is available, if it is not available code will throw a message warning of not having a camera by this device. You will be able to test this code only on devices which have a camera and not in a simulator.

```
func openGallery()
    {
      if UIImagePickerController.isSourceTypeAvailable(UIImagePickerController.
SourceType.photoLibrary){
            let imagePicker = UIImagePickerController()
            imagePicker.delegate = self
            imagePicker.allowsEditing = true
                  imagePicker.sourceType = UIImagePickerController.SourceType.
photoLibrary
            self.present(imagePicker, animated: true, completion: nil)
        }
        else
        {
            let alert  = UIAlertController(title: "Warning", message: "You don't
have permission to access gallery.", preferredStyle: .alert)
           alert.addAction(UIAlertAction(title: "OK", style: .default, handler: nil))
            self.present(alert, animated: true, completion: nil)
        }
    }
```

In the preceding code first we will check if the source type as photo library is available, if it is not available code will throw a message warning of not having permissions to access photo library. You will be able to test this code on devices as well as on simulators.

Allow editing

Adding this property to the **`UIImagePickerController`** instance, if given as **`TRUE`** then allows the user to resize, zoom in and zoom out the selected image before taking that into the app as the final selected image.

Source types

The type of picker interface that the controller will display. Set this value to the appropriate source type before executing the picker interface. If the source type you provide is not accessible, an exception is raised. If you modify this property while the picker is displayed, the picker interface will update to reflect the new value. There are mainly two source types that are as follows:

- Camera
- Photo library

UIImagePickerController delegate

When either a camera opens or photo gallery after selecting and finalizing a picture it returns that image in **didFinishPickingMediaWithInfo** delegate method. In the form of **InfoKey.OriginalImage** and in case the user does not select or capture any image then this will be returned in the **imagePickerControllerDidCancel** delegate method as follows:

```
extension WSImageViewController: UINavigationControllerDelegate,
UIImagePickerControllerDelegate
{
    //Mark:- UIImagePicker delegate
        func imagePickerController(_ picker: UIImagePickerController,
didFinishPickingMediaWithInfo info: [UIImagePickerController.InfoKey : Any])
    {
        imagePicker.dismiss(animated: true, completion: nil)
       projectImage.image = info[UIImagePickerController.InfoKey.originalImage]
as? UIImage
      let imageName: String = WSCacheManager.sharedInstance.project.value(forKey:
"pName") as! String
        let fileName = String(format: "%@.png",imageName.replacingOccurrences(of:
" ", with: ""))
        let resizedImage = WSUtility.shared.resize(info[UIImagePickerController.
InfoKey.originalImage] as! UIImage)
     }

    func imagePickerControllerDidCancel(_ picker: UIImagePickerController)
    {
        imagePicker.dismiss(animated: true, completion: nil)
    }
}
```

Working with movies

The default camera interface allows you to modify videos that have already been saved. Trimming a movie starts or ends at the beginning or end, and then saves the reduced movie. The **videoMaximumDuration** parameter may be used to change the default duration limit of 10 minutes for movie capture.

UIVideoEditorController

A view controller that manages the system interface for trimming video frames and encoding a previously recorded movie. A video editor manages user interactions and provides the filesystem path of the edited movie to your delegate object. The features of the **`UIVideoEditorController`** class are available only on devices that support video recording. Use a video editor when your intent is to provide an interface for movie editing. The **`UIVideoEditorController`** class only supports portrait mode. This class is not meant to be subclassed and should be used as it is. Do not change the view hierarchy for this class because it is private. The use of overlay views to change the look of this class is not supported. We will check whether the edit view controller can edit the provided video before initializing the edit controller. Then, we will allocate the video to the video path property and assign delegate properties:

```
if UIVideoEditorController.canEditVideo(atPath: video.path) {
            let editController = UIVideoEditorController()
            editController.videoPath = video.path
            editController.delegate = self
            present(editController, animated:true)
      }
```

Here, we will create an extension of the controller in which we executed the above code and implement the **`UIVideoEditorControllerDelegate`** methods. There are mainly three delegates, as explained as follows:

- **`didSaveEditedVideoToPath`**: When the system has completed saving an edited video, this delegate method is called. The parameter **`editedVideoPath`** contains the path to the edited video files.
- **`videoEditorControllerDidCancel`**: When the user cancels a video editing process, this delegate method is invoked.
- **`didFailWithError`**: When the video editor is unable to load or save a movie, this delegate method is invoked. An incorrect filesystem path or an invalid media format might cause a movie to fail to load into the video editor. It's possible that saving will fail due to a lack of disk space or other factors.

```
extension WSViewController: UIVideoEditorControllerDelegate {
        func videoEditorController(_ editor: UIVideoEditorController,
           didSaveEditedVideoToPath editedVideoPath: String) {
           dismiss(animated:true)
        }
       func videoEditorControllerDidCancel(_ editor: UIVideoEditorController) {
           dismiss(animated:true)
        }
```

```
        func videoEditorController(_ editor: UIVideoEditorController,
                    didFailWithError error: Error) {
            print("an error occurred: \(error.localizedDescription)")
            dismiss(animated:true)
        }
    }
```

In every case above, we will dismiss the editor controller so we can get control and handle the code appropriately with correct reasoning.

Working with Live Photos

For live photos, the **PHLivePhoto** class functions in the same way as the **UIImage** or **NSImage** classes do for static pictures. A **UIImage** or **NSImage** object does not represent the data file from which an image is loaded, but rather a ready-to-use picture that can be presented in a view. Similarly, a **PHLivePhoto** object represents a live photo that is ready to be displayed with motion and sound. This class may be used to import displayable Live Photo objects from data obtained elsewhere (such as images posted through a social network) and to assign Live Photos to **PHLivePhotoView** objects for display.

Implement camera features in your app

You can use the iOS Camera app to take photographs and videos with both the front and back cameras. The Camera app also allows still capture of depth data, portrait effects matte, and live photos, depending on your device. We'll teach you how to include these capabilities into your own camera app. It takes advantage of the built-in front and back cameras on the iPhone and iPad.

```
private let session = AVCaptureSession()
```

Configure a capture session

The camera and microphone are examples of capture devices that **AVCaptureSession** accepts data from. Following receipt of the data, **AVCaptureSession** marshals it to the relevant outputs for processing, finally producing a video file or still picture. In **viewDidLoad**, our app creates a session and assigns it to the preview view:

```
previewView.session = session
```

Setting up a capture session

At least one capture input and output are required for every capture session. Media sources, such as the cameras and microphone installed into an iOS device or a Mac, are used as capture inputs. Capture outputs create media, such as picture and video files, using data given by capture inputs. Select an appropriate **AVCaptureDevice**, create a matching **AVCaptureDeviceInput**, and add it to the session to utilize a camera for video input (to take images or movies):

```
captureSession.beginConfiguration()
let videoDevice = AVCaptureDevice.default(.builtInWideAngleCamera,for: .video,
position: .unspecified)
guard let videoDeviceInput = try? AVCaptureDeviceInput(device: videoDevice!),
          captureSession.canAddInput(videoDeviceInput)
          else { return }
captureSession.addInput(videoDeviceInput)
```

Display a camera preview

In the same way that a typical camera viewer allows the user to see the camera before snapping a photo or starting video recording, the user wants to see the camera before snapping a photo or starting video recording. Connecting an **AVCaptureVideoPreviewLayer** to your capture session, which shows a live video stream from the camera while the session is active, can offer such a preview as follows:

```
class PreviewView: UIView {
        override class var layerClass: AnyClass {
            return AVCaptureVideoPreviewLayer.self
        }
        var videoPreviewLayer: AVCaptureVideoPreviewLayer {
            return layer as! AVCaptureVideoPreviewLayer
        }
    }
```

Rear and front facing cameras switching

When a user touches a button in the UI, the **changeCamera** function handles switching between cameras. It employs a discovery session that lists available device types in order of preference and accepts the first device in the array. The **videoDeviceDiscoverySession** in this code, for example, searches for possible input devices on the device on which the program is running:

```
func changeCamera()
    {
        switch currentPosition {
        case .unspecified, .front:
            newVideoDevice = backVideoDeviceDiscoverySession.devices.first

        case .back:
            newVideoDevice = frontVideoDeviceDiscoverySession.devices.first
```

```
        @unknown default:
            print("Error capture position. Again to back, dual-camera.")
              newVideoDevice = AVCaptureDevice.default(.builtInDualCamera, for:
.video, position: .back)
        }
    }
```

Capture a photo

Taking a picture is done while waiting for a session. The method starts with matching the video orientation of the video preview layer to the **AVCapturePhotoOutput** connection. This allows the camera to record exactly what the user sees on the screen:

```
if let photoOutputConnection = self.photoOutput.connection(with: .video) {
        photoOutputConnection.videoOrientation = videoPreviewLayerOrientation!
    }
```

The picture captures the delegate here by using a distinct object, the **PhotoCaptureProcessor**. For Live Photos, when a single capture cycle may include the recording of many frames, this obvious separation of capture cycles is required. This Project snaps a shot with the previously specified settings every time the user hits the center shutter button:

```
func photoCapture()
    {
        var photoSettings = AVCapturePhotoSettings()
        if  self.photoOutput.availablePhotoCodecTypes.contains(.hevc) {
            photoSettings = AVCapturePhotoSettings(format: [AVVideoCodecKey:
AVVideoCodecType.hevc])
        }
        if self.videoDeviceInput.device.isFlashAvailable {
            photoSettings.flashMode = .auto
        }
        photoSettings.isHighResolutionPhotoEnabled = true
        if let previewPhotoPixelFormatType = photoSettings.
availablePreviewPhotoPixelFormatTypes.first {
            photoSettings.previewPhotoFormat = [kCVPixelBufferPixelFormatTypeKey
as String: previewPhotoPixelFormatType]
        }
      if self.livePhotoMode == .on && self.photoOutput.isLivePhotoCaptureSupported {
            let livePhotoMovieFileName = NSUUID().uuidString
```

```
            let livePhotoMovieFilePath = (NSTemporaryDirectory() as
NSString).appendingPathComponent((livePhotoMovieFileName as NSString).
appendingPathExtension("mov")!)
            photoSettings.livePhotoMovieFileURL = URL(fileURLWithPath:
livePhotoMovieFilePath)
        }
        photoSettings.isDepthDataDeliveryEnabled = (self.depthDataDeliveryMode
== .on
            && self.photoOutput.isDepthDataDeliveryEnabled)
        photoSettings.isPortraitEffectsMatteDeliveryEnabled = (self.
portraitEffectsMatteDeliveryMode == .on
            && self.photoOutput.isPortraitEffectsMatteDeliveryEnabled)
        if photoSettings.isDepthDataDeliveryEnabled {
            if !self.photoOutput.availableSemanticSegmentationMatteTypes.
isEmpty {
                photoSettings.enabledSemanticSegmentationMatteTypes = self.
selectedSemanticSegmentationMatteTypes
            }
        }
   photoSettings.photoQualityPrioritization=self.photoQualityPrioritizationMode
                self.photoOutput.capturePhoto(with: photoSettings, delegate:
photoCaptureProcessor)
    }
```

Two arguments are accepted by the **capturePhoto** method:

- The settings your user configures through the app, such as exposure, flash, focus, and torch, are encapsulated in an **AVCapturePhotoSettings** object.
- A delegate that follows the **AVCapturePhotoCaptureDelegate** protocol and responds to the system's following callbacks during photo capture.

Further **AVCapturePhotoCaptureDelegate** methods handle all the listening of events done with either photo or movie captures. Other visual effects, such as animating a preview thumbnail of the taken photo, can be applied in this delegate function. On a per-photo request basis, the camera adds depth and portrait effects matter as auxiliary information. The app displays an option to alter the settings for activating or removing depth data, portrait effects matte, or Live Photos if the device supports them.

You may also require authorization permissions for saving files or taking pictures, which will work the same as explained in the initial part of this chapter. Also, you may consider uploading media files directly to the cloud or different storage apps.

Conclusion

Proper management of memory cache and file handling is crucial for optimizing the user experience and achieving better visual performance in media-enabled apps. In this chapter, we extensively covered the loading and usage of the default camera app for capturing photos and videos. Additionally, we explored implementing similar functionalities in custom camera apps, enabling you to embed a customized camera preview and tailor its functions according to your specific requirements. This level of control allows you to manage the entire camera experience within your app.

In the upcoming chapter, you will delve into the domain of machine learning and gain insights into Apple's implementation of the CoreML framework, which greatly simplifies iOS app development processes.

Multiple choice questions

1. **UIVideoEditorController is used for?**
   a. Enable Camera session
   b. Edit Videos
   c. Capture photos
   d. None of the above

2. **Which class is the same for Live Photos as UIImage for static photos?**
   a. PHLivePhoto
   b. PHPhotoLive
   c. PLPhotoLive
   d. PHPhoto

3. **How do you get an Image from UIImagePickerController?**
   a. InfoKey.OriginalImage
   b. Key.OriginalImage
   c. Info.Key.OriginalImage
   d. OriginalImage

4. **Which class shows the camera preview?**
   a. PHLivePhoto
   b. AVcaptureDevice
   c. AVCaptureVideoPreviewLayer
   d. AVSession

Answers

1. b
2. a
3. a
4. c

CHAPTER 14
Multithreading in iOS

Introduction

Multithreading in iOS is the ability to run multiple threads as smaller pieces of a program at the same time. This makes applications run faster and respond more quickly. The Threading API, **Grand Central Dispatch** (**GCD**), or Operation Queues can be used to do this. With these tools, tasks like networking and calculations that use a lot of resources can be done in the background while the main thread updates the user interface. This can make the whole user experience much better by reducing lag and making it easier for the app to handle multiple tasks at once.

Structure

In this chapter, we will cover the following topics:

- Grand Central Dispatch
- Processes and threads
- Multithreading with operation

Objectives

By reading this chapter, you will be able to learn about multithreading in iOS. Also, you will be able to learn more about GCD, dispatch queues, and the advantages and disadvantages of operations queues.

Grand Central Dispatch

Grand Central Dispatch (**GCD**) makes it easy for iOS developers to manage and complete complicated tasks. GCD is a low-level **application programming interface** (**API**) that makes it easy and quick to run multiple tasks at the same time. This is one of the most important parts of GCD because it lets developers use the great hardware in iOS devices to do complicated tasks quickly and easily.

The basic concept behind GCD is that it allows developers to create and manage task queues. A task queue is a collection of tasks that are executed in a specific order. Tasks can be added to a queue, and GCD will automatically schedule them to be executed as soon as possible. One of the most important concepts in GCD is the concept of a dispatch queue. A dispatch queue is a list of jobs that need to be done in a certain order. Tasks can be added to a dispatch queue, and GCD will automatically schedule them to be done as soon as possible. There are two types of dispatch queues: serial and concurrent.

A serial dispatch queue can only run one task at a time, but a concurrent dispatch queue can run more than one task at once. The main difference between the two is that a serial dispatch queue will execute tasks in the order that they were added, while a concurrent dispatch queue will execute tasks as soon as they are ready.

DispatchQueue

`DispatchQueue` is managing concurrent tasks in iOS. It makes it easy for developers to create and manage queues of tasks that can be run at the same time. This lets them do more than one thing at once without stopping the main thread.

The **Grand Central Dispatch** (**GCD**) framework includes **`DispatchQueue`**, which is a low-level API for managing tasks that are running at the same time. **`DispatchQueue`** provides a simple and easy-to-use API that allows developers to create and manage queues of tasks and schedule them to be executed either concurrently or serially.

There are mainly three types of dispatch queues.

- Main queue
- Global queue
- Custom queue

Main queue

The main queue, also known as the main dispatch queue, is a unique queue that the system creates and is in charge of overseeing the main thread of execution in an iOS. The main queue is a serial queue, meaning that it executes tasks one at a time in the order they were added. This is important to ensure that tasks are executed in a predictable and consistent manner, and that the user interface remains responsive and stable.

For example, let's say we have a task that updates a label on the main thread with some text. In order to execute this task, we would use the main queue like so:

```
DispatchQueue.main.async {
    label.text = "Access to main Queue"
}
```

In this case, the task of changing the text on the label is put on the main queue and done as soon as the main thread is free. This makes sure that the task runs on the main thread, which is in charge of keeping the user interface up to date.

It's important to note that blocking the main queue can cause the application to become unresponsive or even crash. So, it's usually best to put long-running tasks or heavy computations on background queues and update the main queue, which is where the user interface is. The main queue is a key part of how a Swift application manages the main thread of execution and keeps the user interface responsive and stable.

Global queue

With global queue, multiple tasks can be executed at the same time, without blocking the main thread of the application. This can make an app run and respond much better, especially when it has to deal with a lot of data or do complicated calculations.

One example of using global queues in Swift is for image processing. Suppose we have a large number of images that need to be resized and processed for a photo gallery app. Instead of processing each image sequentially on the main thread, we can use the Queue to perform the tasks concurrently. This means that more than one image can be processed at the same time, which is a big step forward in terms of speed.

To use global queue in Swift, we first need to import the Dispatch framework. We then create a global queue using the **DispatchQueue.global()** method. This queue can be used to perform tasks in a concurrent and asynchronous manner.

For example, to resize an image, we can use the following code:

```
import Dispatch
let globalQueue = DispatchQueue.global()
globalQueue.async {
    // Resize image
    let newImage = resizeImage(image: originalImage, newSize: CGSize(width: 300, 
height: 300))
    // Perform other processing tasks
}
```

In this example, the **globalQueue.async** method is used to resize an image in a way that is both simultaneous and independent of other tasks. This means that the main thread of the application will not be blocked while the image is being resized.

Another example of using global queue in Swift is for network requests. Suppose we have an app that needs to retrieve data from multiple API endpoints. Instead of making the requests sequentially on the main thread, we can use global queue to perform the tasks concurrently. This means that multiple network requests can be made at the same time, which leads to a big improvement in performance. To make a network request using global queue in Swift, we can use the following code:

```
import Dispatch
let globalQueue = DispatchQueue.global()
globalQueue.async {
    // Make network request
    let data = fetchData(url: "https://example.com/api")

    // Perform other processing tasks
}
```

In this example, the network request is made at the same time and out of order by using the **globalQueue.async** method. This means that the main thread of the application will not be blocked while the data is being retrieved from the API endpoint.

Custom queue

Custom queue in GCD let us developers create their own queues to manage the execution of tasks. When the default queues that GCD offers are unable to meet an application's needs, this can be helpful.

In GCD, developers can use the **DispatchQueue.init(label:)** initializer to create a custom queue. This initializer takes a label parameter that tells the system how to find the queue. For example, the following code creates a custom queue named **myQueue**:

```
let myQueue = DispatchQueue(label: "myQueue")
```

Once the developer makes the custom queue, they can use it to run tasks using the async or sync methods. The async method adds the task to the queue and returns immediately, while the sync method waits for the task to complete before returning. For example, the following code adds a task to the **myQueue** custom queue using the async method:

```
myQueue.async {
    // Perform task here
}
```

And the following code adds a task to the **myQueue** custom queue using the **sync** method:

```
myQueue.sync {
    // Perform task here
}
```

In addition to creating custom queues, developers can also use GCD to create concurrent queues, which allow multiple tasks to be executed simultaneously. To create a concurrent queue, developers can use the **`DispatchQueue.init(label:attributes:)`** initializer, passing in the .concurrent attribute. For example, the following code creates a concurrent queue named **`myConcurrentQueue`**:

```
let myConcurrentQueue = DispatchQueue(label: "myConcurrentQueue", attributes:
.concurrent)
```

The custom queue feature in GCD with Swift is a very powerful feature that allows developers to create their own queues to manage task execution. This allows for more fine-grained control over how tasks are executed in an application and can be useful in situations where the default queues provided by GCD do not meet the specific needs of an application.

Quality of Service

Quality of Service (**QoS**) in Swift refers to the ability to prioritize certain network requests over others. This lets developers make sure that important requests, like those for important data or real-time updates, get done before less important requests, like those for non-essential data or tasks that run in the background.

To implement QoS in Swift, developers can use the **`DispatchQueue`** class, which lets them create and manage queues of tasks. There are five different QoS classes available:

- **User-interactive**: It is the class with the highest priority, and it's used for tasks that are essential to making sure the user experience is smooth and responsive. Examples include scrolling, animations, and user input.
- **User-initiated**: A high priority class, used for tasks that are initiated by the user and are important to the user's experience. Examples include loading a new view or saving a document.
- **Utility**: A medium priority class, used for tasks that are not essential to the user's experience but are still important. Examples include data backup or image processing.
- **Background**: The lowest priority class, used for tasks that are not essential to the user's experience and can be performed in the background. Examples include sending analytics data or cleaning up old files.
- **Default**: When you are unsure whether or not to assign a priority to a task, you can set it to default. which will behave as if it is somewhere between high and low priority.

Here is an example of how to use QoS with **`DispatchQueue`** in Swift:

```
let queue = DispatchQueue(label: "com.example.app.background", qos: .background)

queue.async {

    // Perform background task

}
```

In this example, we create a new **`DispatchQueue`** with the label **`com.example.app.background`** and the QoS class of background. Any tasks added to this queue will be given the lowest priority and run in the background.

It's important to note that QoS is not a guarantee of the order in which tasks will be executed, but rather a suggestion to the system on how to prioritize them. In practice, the system may still run lower-priority tasks before higher-priority tasks if it determines that it is more efficient to do so. QoS in Swift is a way to prioritize network requests, allowing developers to ensure that important requests are given priority over less important requests. The **DispatchQueue** class is the way to implement QoS in Swift, it allows developers to create and manage queues of tasks with different priority classes.

DispatchGroup

Developers can use **DispatchGroup** to group multiple tasks together and wait for them to finish before proceeding to the next step. This is helpful when working with tasks that don't happen at the same time, like network requests or file operations.

One common use case for **DispatchGroup** is when you need to make multiple network requests and wait for them all to complete before updating the user interface. For example, imagine you have a view controller that needs to display information from three different API endpoints. Without **DispatchGroup**, you would need to create separate completion handlers for each request and manually keep track of when all requests have been completed.

With **DispatchGroup**, however, you can group all of the requests together and wait for them to complete before updating the user interface. Here is an example of how you might use **DispatchGroup** to accomplish this:

```
let group = DispatchGroup()
// Start first request
group.enter()
API.getFirstEndpoint { result in
    // Handle first request result
    group.leave()
}
// Start second request
group.enter()
API.getSecondEndpoint { result in
    // Handle second request result
    group.leave()
}
// Start third request
group.enter()
API.getThirdEndpoint { result in
    // Handle third request result
```

```
    group.leave()
}
// Wait for all requests to complete
group.notify(queue: .main) {
    // Update user interface with results from all requests
}
```

In this example, we create a **DispatchGroup** and start each of the three network requests. Before each request is started, we call a **group.enter()** to indicate that we are starting a new task within the group. Once each request is complete, we call **group.leave()** to indicate that the task has been completed.

Finally, we call **group.notify(queue: .main)** to wait for all tasks within the group to complete. Once all tasks are done, the code in the notify block will be run, letting us update the user interface with the results from all three requests. It's important to note that **DispatchGroup** can also be used for other types of tasks, such as file operations or image processing. In these cases, you would use **group.enter()** and **group.leave()** in a similar fashion to indicate when a task has started and completed.

By using **DispatchGroup**, you can easily wait for multiple tasks to finish before moving on to the next step. This makes it easier to manage complex code that runs in different steps at different times.

DispatchWorkItem

DispatchWorkItem is a type of closure in Swift that is used to represent work that can be executed asynchronously. It provides a convenient way to queue a block of code for execution at a later time, allowing you to take advantage of concurrency and parallelism in your applications.

One of the best things about **DispatchWorkItem** is that it can be easily scheduled to run on a **DispatchQueue**, which is a data structure that manages how tasks are run in a way that is efficient and runs them all at the same time. **DispatchQueues** can be used to manage the execution of tasks in different contexts, such as the main queue for tasks that should be executed on the main thread, or a background queue for tasks that should be executed in the background.

DispatchWorkItem can be created using the **DispatchWorkItem** constructor, which takes a block of code as its argument. Once the **DispatchWorkItem** has been made, it can be run by calling its perform method or scheduled to run on a **DispatchQueue** using the async or sync methods. **DispatchWorkItem** also has a number of other useful features, such as the ability to stop a task from running, wait for a task to finish, or watch a task finish. With these features, you can handle the way your tasks are done in a more flexible and effective way.

Here is an example of how to use **DispatchWorkItem** in Swift:

```
let workItem = DispatchWorkItem {
    // Perform some background task here
}
```

```
let queue = DispatchQueue.global(qos: .background)
queue.async(execute: workItem)
```

In the given example, we make a **DispatchWorkItem** that holds a block of code that should be run in the background. The **DispatchWorkItem** is then scheduled for execution on a **DispatchQueue**, which is a global queue with a background quality of service.

By using **DispatchWorkItem**, you can easily control how your tasks are run and take advantage of Swift's concurrent and parallel programming features. If you are making an app for iOS, macOS, watchOS, or tvOS, **DispatchWorkItem** is a flexible and easy way to keep track of your tasks.

Processes and threads

Processes and threads are two important ideas in iOS programming that are used to control how code runs in an environment with multiple tasks. Now, we will explore the differences between processes and threads, and provide a code example of how they can be used in an iOS app. A *process* is a program that is being executed by the operating system. Each process has its own memory space, and it runs independently of other processes. In iOS, each app is a separate process and runs in its own memory space. This means that an app cannot access the memory of another app, and vice versa.

A thread, on the other hand, is a lightweight unit of execution that runs within a process. A process can have multiple threads, and each thread runs independently of the others. In iOS, each thread has its own stack and program counter, and it can be scheduled to run by the operating system at any time.

The main reason to use threads in iOS is that they let code run at the same time. This means that multiple threads can run at the same time, allowing for better performance and responsiveness in your app.

Run loop scheduling

Run-loop scheduling is a fundamental concept in iOS development. It is responsible for managing the execution of tasks and events in the application. The run loop is a loop that runs on a separate thread and constantly monitors for events such as user input, notifications, and timer events. When an event happens, the run loop sets up the right task to deal with it.

In iOS, the main run loop is responsible for handling events in the main thread. This is where the user interface and most of the application's logic are executed. The **CFRunLoop** class is in charge of the main run loop, and the **CFRunLoopGetMain()** function lets you get to it.

A simple example of using the main run loop is scheduling a timer. The following code creates a timer that fires every second and updates a label with the current time:

```
class ViewController: UIViewController {
    @IBOutlet weak var timeLabel: UILabel!
```

```
    override func viewDidLoad() {
        super.viewDidLoad()
        let timer = Timer.scheduledTimer(timeInterval: 1, target: self, selector: 
#selector(updateTimeLabel), userInfo: nil, repeats: true)
        RunLoop.main.add(timer, forMode: .common)
    }

    @objc func updateTimeLabel() {
        timeLabel.text = DateFormatter.localizedString(from: Date(), dateStyle: 
.medium, timeStyle: .medium)
    }
}
```

In this example, we create a timer using the **Timer** class and schedule it to fire every second. The timer is then added to the main run loop via the **RunLoop** class's **add(_:forMode:)** method. The **forMode:** parameter specifies the run loop mode to add the timer to. In this case, we use the **.common** mode, which is the default mode for the main run loop.

It's also possible to create custom threads and run loops; for that, you could use the **Thread** class and **RunLoop** class respectively.

```
class MyThread: Thread {
    override func main() {
        let runLoop = RunLoop.current
        runLoop.add(Port(), forMode: .default)
        runLoop.run()
    }
}
let thread = MyThread()
thread.start()
```

In this example, we create a custom thread by subclassing the **Thread** class. In the main method of the thread, we create a new run loop, add a **Port** object to it, and start the run loop.

It's important to note that run loop scheduling is a complex topic and this is just a basic example. There are many other features and options available, such as adding input sources, observers, and custom modes, that can be used to fine-tune the behaviour of the run loop. Run loop scheduling is a fundamental concept in iOS development. It allows for the management of the execution of tasks and events in the application. The main run loop is responsible for handling events in the main thread and is managed by the **CFRunLoop** class. The run loop is a loop that runs on a separate thread and constantly monitors for events such as user input, notifications, and timer events. When an event happens, the run loop sets up the right task to deal with it.

Thread class

The **Thread** class in iOS managing concurrent tasks in your application. This class lets you make and control threads that can run independently of the main thread. This lets you do things like background processing, networking, and data manipulation without stopping the user interface.

Here is an example of how you can use the **Thread** class to create a new thread and perform a task on it:

```
let newThread = Thread {
    // Perform task on new thread
    print("Task running on new thread")
}
// Start the thread
newThread.start()
```

In this example, we create a new thread using the **Thread** class and pass a closure as an argument. This closure contains the task that we want to perform on the new thread. We then start the thread using the **start()** method.

It's important to note that the Thread class does not automatically manage the thread's lifecycle. This means that you must manually start and stop the thread as needed. You can use the **isExecuting** and **isFinished** properties to check the current state of the thread.

You can also use the **join()** method to wait for a thread to complete before moving on to the next task. This can be helpful when you need to make sure a background task is done before updating the user interface or doing other things.

```
let newThread = Thread {
    // Perform task on new thread
    print("Task running on new thread")
}
// Start the thread
newThread.start()
// Wait for thread to complete before moving on
newThread.join()
print("Thread has completed")
```

In this example, the **join()** method is called after the thread has been started. The program will wait for the thread to complete before moving on and printing **Thread has completed**.

It's also important to note that when a thread exits, it cannot be restarted. If you need to perform the same task multiple times, you should create a new thread each time. By using threads, you can work on tasks in the background without stopping the user interface. This can make your app more responsive and easier to use.

Multithreading with operations

A high-level Swift API that provides an abstraction over GCD and makes it easier to manage the execution of complex tasks. **NSOperation** and **NSOperationQueue** are two classes in iOS that are used for multithreading. Multithreading lets an application do more than one thing at once, which makes it more efficient and quicker.

NSOperationQueue is a class that manages a collection of **NSOperations**. The **NSOperationQueue** class has a method **addOperation()** that you can use to add an **NSOperation** to the queue. The **NSOperationQueue** class also has a method **setMaxConcurrentOperationCount()** that you can use to set the maximum number of operations that can run simultaneously.

NSOperation

NSOperation is a class that represents a single unit of work. It can be used to encapsulate any task that needs to be performed asynchronously. The **NSOperation** class has a **main()** method that runs on a separate thread. To use **NSOperation**, you need to create a subclass of **NSOperation** and override the **main()** method. In the **main()** method, you can put any code that you want to run on a separate thread. By using **NSOperation** and **NSOperationQueue** together, you can create complex, multithreaded applications. For example, you can create an **NSOperation** that downloads a file from the internet and add it to an **NSOperationQueue**. The **NSOperationQueue** will then run the **NSOperation** on a separate thread. This lets the main thread keep running and respond to user actions. Let us see how we can use the **NSOperation** class to create a custom operation class:

```
class CustomOperation: NSOperation {
    var name: String
    init(name: String) {
        self.name = name
    }
    override func main() {
        print("Starting operation: \(name)")
        for i in 0...10 {
            print("\(name) - iteration: \(i)")
            sleep(1)
        }
        print("Finished operation: \(name)")
    }
```

```
}
```

Further, we will add the operation instances to **NSOperationQueue** instances as shown below:

```
let operationQueue = NSOperationQueue()
let operation1 = CustomOperation(name: "Operation 1")
let operation2 = CustomOperation(name: "Operation 2")
operationQueue.addOperation(operation1)
operationQueue.addOperation(operation2)
operationQueue.start()
```

With the given code, two operations will be done at the same time on separate threads, and their progress will be shown on the console. The **sleep(1)** function is used to simulate some time spent processing, and the **main()** function is where the operation starts. The **NSOperationQueue** handles all the details of creating and managing separate threads for each operation.

BlockOperation

BlockOperation is a subclass of **NSOperation**. It is used to represent a block of code that can be run as an operation in an **NSOperationQueue**. Here's an example of using **BlockOperation** in an **NSOperationQueue**:

```
let operation1 = BlockOperation {
    print("Operation 1 started")
    sleep(3)
    print("Operation 1 finished")
}
let operation2 = BlockOperation {
    print("Operation 2 started")
    sleep(2)
    print("Operation 2 finished")
}
queue.addOperations([operation1, operation2], waitUntilFinished: false)
```

In the given example, we create an **NSOperationQueue** and two **BlockOperations**. Each **BlockOperation** contains a block of code that will be executed when the operation is started. The operations are then added to the queue using the **addOperations** method. Since the **waitUntilFinished** parameter is set to false, the operations will be done at the same time. When you run this code, you'll see that the operations are executed in parallel:

```
Operation 1 started
Operation 2 started
```

```
Operation 2 finished
Operation 1 finished
```

Using **BlockOperation** and **NSOperationQueue**, you can easily add and manage multiple operations in your iOS app. This lets you take advantage of multithreading and improve the performance of your app.

Conclusion

Multithreading is a crucial aspect of iOS development, as it enables developers to create applications that can perform multiple tasks simultaneously. The use of multithreading enables iOS devices to take full advantage of their processing power, providing a smooth and efficient user experience. The Grand Central Dispatch (GCD) and Operation Queue frameworks make it easier for developers to create and manage threads. This lets them make more complex and efficient apps. When you can run multiple tasks at once, long-running tasks have less of an effect on the user interface. This keeps the device responsive at all times. Multithreading is particularly important in today's world, where users expect applications to be fast and responsive. As a result, it has become an important part of iOS development that developers need to know about and use to make high-quality, responsive apps.

In the end, multithreading lets iOS developers make apps that can do more than one thing at once, giving users a quick and responsive experience. With the right tools and methods, developers can use the processing power of iOS devices to their fullest and make applications that are very efficient and complex.

In the next chapter, we will start learning about networking in iOS, which deals with interaction with REST APIs, which are used in iOS app development with the Swift language.

Multiple choice questions

1. **Which queue is responsible for running UI tasks?**
   a. Main Queue
   b. Global Queue
   c. Custom Queue
   d. None of the above

2. **Which of the following is a subclass of NSOperation ?**
   a. NSOperationQueue
   b. DispatchGroup
   c. BlockOperation
   d. None of the above

3. **What would you use if you want to group multiple tasks and get a completion call in the end ?**
    a. Global Queue
    b. Main Queue
    c. DispatchGroup
    d. None of the above
4. **Which one is a low-level API for multithreading?**
    a. DispatchGroup
    b. Grand Central Dispatch
    c. NSOperationQueue
    d. None of the above
5. **Which one is a high-level API for multithreading?**
    a. DispatchGroup
    b. Grand Central Dispatch
    c. NSOperationQueue
    d. None of the above
6. **From the following, which one decides the priority of requests in the global queue?**
    a. High level APIs
    b. Low level APIs
    c. Quality of service (QoS)
    d. None of the above
7. **From the following, which one is the high priority task in the queue?**
    a. default
    b. Utility
    c. Background
    d. User Initiated
8. **From the following, which one is the low priority task in the queue?**
    a. User Initiated
    b. Default
    c. User Interactive
    d. Background

9. **When multiple tasks are executed simultaneously, is called_______**
   a. Synchronous
   b. Asynchronous
   c. Quality of service (QoS)
   d. None of the above
10. How does the Thread class know the task is finished already?
    a. isFinished()
    b. isExecuting()
    c. start()
    d. None of the above

Answers

1. a
2. c
3. c
4. b
5. c
6. c
7. d
8. d
9. b
10. a

Join our book's Discord space

Join the book's Discord Workspace for Latest updates, Offers, Tech happenings around the world, New Release and Sessions with the Authors:

https://discord.bpbonline.com

CHAPTER 15

Networking in iOS Apps

Introduction

When the support for dynamic content and data synchronization from one device, along with remote access from anywhere on the internet via websites or other cloud accounts, is desired, systems need to be built by developers that integrate with server-side implementations. In this chapter, the basics of client-server networking architecture will be discussed, including the access to REST APIs with tools like Postman or Advance Rest Client. The process of data request, sending, and updating from an iOS app to the cloud will also be explored, with the assistance of the Alamofire Library and Apple Networking Frameworks.

Structure

In this chapter, we will cover the following topics:

- REST architecture
- Connection reachability
- AlamoFire
- URLSession

Objectives

By learning this chapter, you should be able to understand the communication and data transfer between client-side apps and servers, that will help you to identify user accounts across multiple clients with credentials which can share data to server and vice versa as well.

REST architecture

The acronym for REST is **Representational State Transfer**, which is an architecture for distributed hypermedia systems used for the portability of user interface data across multiple platforms. **Application Programming Interface** (**API**) is a set of protocols and definitions used for the purpose of service request contract between information providers and consumers and works as middleman for web server content and content consumer client.

A mobile iOS app can implement the client request for RESTful APIs which will enable app to handshake successfully with server securely and further sync data and get content for end user consumption.

Information content type

When we require to use RESTful APIs then communication content needs to be defined such that client and server can parse and understand the data easily. Content Types of APIs is as follows:

- **JSON**: JSON is the most popular content type in client request due to its lightweight structure and easily readable by both humans as well as machine algorithms.
- **XML/XSLT:** XML stands for eXtensible Markup Language. It was created as a language with a basic formal syntax, making it straightforward for both programmes and people to produce and manipulate documents, with a focus on Internet use.
- **Binary file:** Binary file is used when there is a need to send file attachment with text information in API request.
- **Plain text:** Plain text can be sent when there is no need of structured data and used very rarely in the context of best API communication.

HTTP structure

Data is transferred between a server and a client via HTTP messages. There are different kinds of messages: requests, which are delivered by the client to cause the server to do an action, and responses, which are the server's response. HTTP messages are made up of textual data encoded in ASCII that spans many lines. HTTP Structure consists of mainly two components one is Request other response. HTTP requests are messages that the client sends to start an action on the server. The request target, usually a URL, or the absolute path of the protocol, port, and domain are usually characterized by the request context.

Request methods

HTTP specifies a variety of request methods for expressing the desired action for a given resource. These request methods are frequently referred to as HTTP verbs, despite the fact that they can also be nouns. Each of them implements a different semantic, although a number of them have certain similarities. The list of HTTP methods are as follows:

- `GET`: The `GET` method is used to get a representation of a resource. Requests made using the `GET` method should only return data.
- `HEAD`: The `HEAD` method requests a response that is equivalent to a `GET` request, but without the body.
- `POST`: The `POST` method is being used to submit an entity to the given resource, which frequently causes the server's state to change or has side effects.
- `PUT`: All existing representations of the target resource are replaced with the request payload when using the `PUT` method.
- `DELETE`: The `DELETE` method removes the provided resource from the system.
- `CONNECT`: The `CONNECT` method creates a tunnel between the client and the server specified by the destination resource.
- `OPTIONS`: The `OPTIONS` method is used to describe the communication options for the target resource.
- `TRACE`: A message loop-back test is performed via the `TRACE` technique along the way to the target resource.

HTTP headers

HTTP headers allow the client and server to send extra data with an HTTP request or response. A colon (`:`), the value, and then the name of an HTTP header is case-insensitive. Headers can be grouped into mainly four types:

- Request
- Response
- Representation
- Payload

More information about the resource to be obtained, or about the client seeking the resource, can be found in request headers. Additional information about the response, such as its location or the server that sent it, is stored in response headers. The representation headers provide information about the resource's body, such as the MIME type or the encoding/compression used. Payload headers provide representation-agnostic information on payload data, such as content length and transport encoding.

Credentials providing the user agent's authentication information for the realm of the resource being requested make up the authorization field value. The Accept-Encoding request-header element is identical to accept, except it limits the permitted content-codings in the response.

HTTP body

The body of the request is the last component. Requests that fetch resources, such as **GET**, **HEAD**, **DELETE**, or **OPTIONS**, often do not require one. Some requests, such as **POST** requests, transmit data to the server in order to update it. The two headers **Content-Type** and **Content-Length** describe single-resource bodies, which are made up of a single file. Multiple-resource bodies are made up of several parts, each of which contains a distinct piece of information. HTML forms are commonly connected with this.

Connection reachability

When we are required to establish a connection with a server with RESTful APIs for handling and managing user information, mobile devices must work properly with internet connection. Connections lost in between or before API calls may cause several issues to your app. For this we need to check for internet connection reachability as well as our server reachability. There might be cases where the internet connection would work perfectly but the server might be down. To check the internet and server connection, we will write a class named **Reachability**, as shown here:

```
import Foundation
import SystemConfiguration
open class Reachability {

    class func isConnectedToNetwork() -> Bool {

        var zeroAddress = sockaddr_in()
        zeroAddress.sin_len = UInt8(MemoryLayout<sockaddr_in>.size)
        zeroAddress.sin_family = sa_family_t(AF_INET)

        guard let defaultRouteReachability = withUnsafePointer(to: &zeroAddress,
{
            $0.withMemoryRebound(to: sockaddr.self, capacity: 1) {
                SCNetworkReachabilityCreateWithAddress(nil, $0)
            }
        }) else {
            return false
        }

        var flags: SCNetworkReachabilityFlags = []
        if !SCNetworkReachabilityGetFlags(defaultRouteReachability, &flags) {
            return false
```

```
        }

        let isReachable = flags.contains(.reachable)
        let needsConnection = flags.contains(.connectionRequired)

        return (isReachable && !needsConnection)

    }
}
```

Let's understand step by step the given code:

- With the use of the **SystemConfiguration** framework, first we create a socket address which contains IP information while connecting to the network.
- Further **SCNetworkReachabilityCreateWithAddress** returns an object which creates a network establishment. If these operations failed to create a network reachability object then we can return as that there is no network available.
- In some cases we even get that object, but we need to ensure with appropriate flags that the correct internet connection is established or not.
- In such cases we check on **SCNetworkReachabilityGetFlags** to get network status flags. If we get the reachable flag as true and connection required flag as false then we can confirm that an internet connection is available.

```
class func isServerConnectivityAvailable(webSiteToPing: String?,
completionHandler: @escaping (Bool) -> Void) {

        // 1. Check the Internet Connection
        guard isConnectedToNetwork() else {
            completionHandler(false)
            return
        }

        // 2. Check the Server Connection
        var webAddress = "https://www.xyz.com" // Your Server base URL
        if let _ = webSiteToPing {
            webAddress = webSiteToPing!
        }
```

```
        guard let url = URL(string: webAddress) else {
            completionHandler(false)
            print("could not create url from: \(webAddress)")
            return
        }

        let urlRequest = URLRequest(url: url)
        let session = URLSession.shared
       let task = session.dataTask(with: urlRequest, completionHandler: { (data,
response, error) in
            if error != nil || response == nil {
                completionHandler(false)
            } else {
                completionHandler(true)
            }
        })

        task.resume()
    }
```

Let's understand step-by-step the given code:

1. After checking for network connections, we can check whether the server is up or down and available for making server-side requests.
2. Further URL request object is passed to **`URLsession`** singleton, which makes a data task request. (We will discuss **`URLsession`** in detail in the later part of this chapter.)
3. When a data task request returns an error as nil with a properly handled response the server connection is reachable.

Alamofire

Alamofire provides an attractive and reusable HTTP network request interface. It doesn't have its own HTTP networking implementation. Instead, it uses the Foundation framework's URL Loading System, which is provided by Apple. The **`URLSession`** and **`URLSessionTask`** subclasses are at the heart of the system. Alamofire covers these APIs, as well as many others, in a more user-friendly interface and provides a wide range of capabilities for contemporary HTTP networking application development. It's vital to understand where many of Alamofire's basic behaviors come from; therefore you should be familiar with the URL Loading System. The

Alamofire Software Foundation has produced additional component libraries to offer extra functionality to the Alamofire ecosystem in order to keep Alamofire focused exclusively on fundamental networking solutions. There are two as follows:

- **`AlamofireImage`**: Image response serializers, **`UIImage`** and **`UIImageView`** extensions, custom image filters, an auto-purging in-memory cache, and a priority-based picture downloading mechanism are all included in this image library.
- **`AlamofireNetworkActivityIndicator`**: Alamofire is used to control the appearance of the network activity indicator on iOS. It has delay timers that may be configured to assist reduce flicker, and it can handle **`URLSession`** instances that aren't controlled by Alamofire.

API encoding

API encoding refers to the accepted encoding format for data in request. Encoding API allows developers to encode and decode strings using a wide range of character encodings. If your app supports multi language then you have to use utf8 encoding and decoding for proper handling of texts in their provided languages. In general you may use JSON encoding for APIs.

URL encoding

URL encoding is the process of converting characters into a format that can be sent over the Internet. Only the ASCII character set may be used to send URLs over the Internet. Because URLs frequently contain characters that are not part of the ASCII set, they must be transformed to a valid ASCII format. In URL encoding, a *percent* (**`%`**) and two hexadecimal numbers replace safe ASCII characters. Spaces are not allowed in URLs.

Alamofire headers

Alamofire has its own **`HTTPHeaders`** type, which is a case-insensitive and order-preserving representation of HTTP header name value pairs. The **`HTTPHeader`** classes encapsulate a single name value combination and give a range of static header values as shown here:

```
let headers: HTTPHeaders = [
        "Authorization": "Basic VXNlcm5hbWU6UGFzc3dvcmQ=",
        "Accept": "application/json"
    ]
```

For every request, the default Alamofire session gives a default set of headers which includes accept encoding, accept language, user agent, and so on.

Alamofire request

Alamofire allows you to send any **`Encodable`** type as a request parameter. These parameters are then appended to the **`URLRequest`**, which is subsequently transmitted across the network, using a type that follows the **`ParameterEncoder`** protocol. **`JSONParameterEncoder`** and

URLEncodedFormParameterEncoder are two types of **parameterEncoder** that Alamofire supports. The most popular encodings used by contemporary services are covered by these kinds as shown here:

```
struct Login: Encodable {
      let email: String
      let password: String
  }
  let login = Login(email: "test@test.test", password: "Password")
  AF.request("https://samplesiteurl.org/post",
             method: .post,
             parameters: login,
             encoder: JSONParameterEncoder.default
             headers: headers).response { response in
      debugPrint(response)
  }
```

In the given code you can see request parameters as method type, login parameters, encoder and headers, and so on. All these parameters are optional and one or more of them can be removed from request if required.

Alamofire response handling

Regardless of the content of the answer, Alamofire considers any completed request to be successful. If the response has an unsatisfactory status code or MIME type, using **validate()** before a response handler causes an error to be produced. Also you may manually validate as shown here:

```
AF.request("https://samplesiteurl.org/get")
     .validate(statusCode: 200..<300)
     .validate(contentType: ["application/json"])
     .responseData { response in
         switch response.result {
         case .success:
             print("Validation Successful")
         case let .failure(error):
             print(error)
         }
     }
```

AlamofireImage

Before the first download request is completed, application logic may attempt to download an image many times. The image is frequently downloaded many times as a result of this. **AFImage** gracefully handles this situation by combining the duplicate downloads. **AFImage** may combine duplicate image filters in addition to duplicate downloads. When two image filters with the same identifier are connected to the same download, the image filter is only run once, and both completion handlers receive the same image. For a variety of reasons, it may be essential to cancel an image download. Using the **RequestReceipt** type and the **cancelRequestForRequestReceipt** function, **AFImage** can intelligently manage cancellation logic in the **ImageDownloader**. Each request for a download generates a **RequestReceipt**, which can be used to cancel the request later. The **UIImage** extensions, image filters, image cache, and image downloader were all created to be versatile and stand-alone while still serving as the backbone of the **UIImageView** extension. The **UIImageView** APIs are succinct, easy to use, and offer a lot of capability thanks to the robust support of various classes, protocols, and extensions. We can use **UIImage** extension for image download as shown here:

```
let imageView = UIImageView(frame: frame)
let url = URL(string: "https://sampleImagesite.org/image/png")!
imageView.af.setImage(withURL: url)
```

In case you want to show a default placeholder image then you can use image view extension as shown here:

```
let placeholderImage = UIImage(named: "placeholder.png")
imageView.af.setImage(withURL: url, placeholderImage: placeholderImage)
```

Image downloader

We may leverage Image Downloader features which are also part of **AlamofireImage** to adjust cache capacities, download priority, request cache rules, timeout durations, and so on. The **ImageDownloader** class is in charge of downloading images in a prioritized queue in parallel. All of the downloading and response image serialization is handled by an internal Alamofire **SessionManager** object. An **ImageDownloader** object's startup utilizes a default **URLSessionConfiguration** with the most common parameter values by default. We can set parameters of Image Downloader as shown here:

```
let imageDownloader = ImageDownloader(
        configuration: ImageDownloader.defaultURLSessionConfiguration(),
        downloadPrioritization: .fifo,
        maximumActiveDownloads: 4,
        imageCache: AutoPurgingImageCache()
    )
```

After initialization of image downloader further URL with **URLRequest** needs to be set in the same object to perform the custom image downloading as shown here:

```
let downloader = ImageDownloader()
    let urlRequest = URLRequest(url: URL(string: "https://sampleImagesite.org/
image/jpeg")!)
    downloader.download(urlRequest) { response in
        print(response.request)
        print(response.response)
        debugPrint(response.result)
        if case .success(let image) = response.result {
            print(image)
        }
    }
```

AlamofireNetworkActivityIndicator

On iOS, you may control the activity indicator using non-safe app extension APIs. This logic could not be included in the Alamofire framework in order for Alamofire to continue to be used in app extensions. It will show a spinner in the status bar when an API call is made. You can just set it enable, as shown here:

```
NetworkActivityIndicatorManager.shared.isEnabled = true
```

To minimize flickering, start and stop delays must be introduced to make the activity indicator experience as pleasant as possible for the user. In the shared manager, there are two such delay timers. The start delay is a time interval that specifies the minimum amount of networking activity that should take place before the activity indicator appears. The completion delay is a time interval that specifies how long no networking activity should be monitored before the activity indication is dismissed. This permits the activity indicator to remain visible while several network requests are being processed, as shown here:

```
NetworkActivityIndicatorManager.shared.completionDelay = 0.2
NetworkActivityIndicatorManager.shared.startDelay = 1.0
```

URLSession

The **URLSession** class and its subclasses offer an API for receiving and uploading data to URL-based destinations. Your program might also use this API to carry out background downloads when it isn't running or, in the case of iOS, when it is in suspended mode. To handle authentication and receive events like redirection and task completion, use the associated **URLSessionDelegate** and **URLSessionTaskDelegate**. Your program creates one or more **URLSession** instances, each of which manages a group of linked data-transfer activities. If you're making a web browser, for example, your program may establish one session for every session or window, or one for interactive usage and another for background downloads. Your program adds a series of tasks to each session, each of which represents a request for a certain URL.

Operation queue

Based on their priority and readiness, an operation queue calls its queued operation objects. When you add an operation to a queue, it will stay in the queue until it completes its duty. You can't delete an operation from a queue once it's been added. The **OperationQueue** class is capable of supporting both **key-value coding** (KVC) and **key-value observation** (KVO). These attributes can be used to control other sections of your program. Operation queues start the execution of their operations by using the dispatch framework. As a result, regardless of whether the operation is synchronous or asynchronous, queues always invoke it on a different thread. Let's create an operation queue and its configurations:

```
fileprivate var operations = [Int: DownloadOperation]()
private let queue: OperationQueue = {
            let _queue = OperationQueue()
            _queue.name = "download"
            _queue.maxConcurrentOperationCount = 1
            return _queue
        }()
```

Add operation in operation queue

At any one moment, an operation object may only be in one operation queue, and it cannot be added if it is actively executing or completed. If any of the error conditions are true for any of the operations in the ops parameter, this function raises an **NSInvalidArgumentException** exception. The requested operation is added to the queue and remains there until it is completed with completed method returns true as shown here:

```
func addDownload(_ url: URL) -> DownloadOperation
{
     let operation = DownloadOperation(session: session, url: url)
     operations[operation.task.taskIdentifier] = operation
     queue.addOperation(operation)
     return operation
}
func cancelAll()
{
     queue.cancelAllOperations()
}
```

Types of URL sessions

For simple requests, **URLSession** has a singleton shared session (which does not contain a configuration object). It's not as flexible as sessions you design, but it's a nice place to start if you only have a few needs. The shared class function is used to access this session. Create a **URLSession** with one of three settings for different types of sessions:

- A default session is similar to a shared session, but it allows you to customize it. You may also delegate the default session to a delegate to get data progressively.
- Ephemeral sessions are identical to shared sessions except that they don't save caches, cookies, or credentials to memory.
- While your programme isn't operating, background sessions allow you to execute content uploads and downloads in the background.

URLSessionConfiguration

When establishing a **URLSession** object to upload and download data, a **URLSessionConfiguration** object sets the behavior and policies to employ. When uploading or downloading data, the initial step is always to create a configuration object. This object is used to set the timeout settings, caching rules, connection requirements, and other information that will be used with the **URLSession** object. The type of configuration used to generate a URL session has a significant impact on the behavior and capabilities of the session. Default sessions function similarly to shared sessions (until further customized); except they allow you to access data progressively via a delegate. The default method on the **URLSessionConfiguration** class may be used to establish a default session setup, as shown here:

```
lazy var session: URLSession = {

            let configuration = URLSessionConfiguration.default

               return URLSession(configuration: configuration, delegate: self,
delegateQueue: nil)

}()
```

Ephemeral sessions are identical to regular sessions except that they don't save caches, cookies, or credentials to disk. The ephemeral method on the **URLSessionConfiguration** class may be used to generate an ephemeral session configuration.

Types of URL session tasks

You may build tasks within a session that upload data to a server and then receive data from the server as a file on storage memory or one or more **NSData** objects in memory. There are four sorts of tasks available in the **URLSession** API, as follows:

- **NSData** objects are a tool that data activities use to send and receive data. Data tasks are designed for brief, interactive server queries.
- Upload tasks are similar to data tasks in that they deliver data and allow for background uploads even when the app isn't open.

- While the programme isn't operating, download tasks retrieve data in the form of a file and allow background downloads and uploads.
- WebSocket tasks use the RFC 6455 defined WebSocket protocol to send and receive messages via TCP and TLS.

URLSession delegate

All tasks in a session share a common delegate object. This delegate is used to offer and collect information when certain events occur, such as:

- When authentication fails.
- When data arrives from the server.
- When data becomes available for caching.

Using the methods described in **URLSessionTaskDelegate**, each task you create using the session calls back to the session's delegate. By filling a separate task-specific delegate, you may intercept these callbacks before they reach the session delegate as shown here:

```
extension DownloadManager: URLSessionDownloadDelegate
{
   func urlSession(_ session: URLSession, downloadTask: URLSessionDownloadTask, didFinishDownloadingTo location: URL)
   {
      operations[downloadTask.taskIdentifier]?.urlSession(session, downloadTask: downloadTask, didFinishDownloadingTo: location)
   }
   func urlSession(_ session: URLSession, downloadTask: URLSessionDownloadTask, didWriteData bytesWritten: Int64, totalBytesWritten: Int64, totalBytesExpectedToWrite: Int64)
   {
      operations[downloadTask.taskIdentifier]?.urlSession(session, downloadTask: downloadTask, didWriteData: bytesWritten, totalBytesWritten: totalBytesWritten, totalBytesExpectedToWrite: totalBytesExpectedToWrite)
   }
}
// MARK: URLSessionTaskDelegate methods
extension DownloadManager: URLSessionTaskDelegate {
  func urlSession(_ session: URLSession, task: URLSessionTask, didCompleteWithError error: Error?)
   {
      let key = task.taskIdentifier
```

```
        operations[key]?.urlSession(session, task: task, didCompleteWithError:
error)
            operations.removeValue(forKey: key)
    }
```

App transport security

App Transport Security (**ATS**) is a networking feature on Apple platforms that enhances privacy and data integrity for all applications and app extensions. All HTTP connections established with the URL Loading System—typically using the `URLSession` class—must use HTTPS, according to ATS. It also applies additional security tests on top of the **Transport Layer Security** (**TLS**) protocol's default server trust evaluation. ATS blocks connections that do not meet the minimal security requirements.

Conclusion

Communication of app clients from the server with the help of REST APIs gives enhanced capabilities to app developers to sync with other clients data and stream data from devices to the server backend. Sometimes you may need to implement a third-party library and its data to showcase on your after authentication would also require similar capabilities which we discussed in this chapter in detail. Alamofire is an advanced level library which hides all the difficult steps for you and can give advanced performance with cache handling, proper data handling, Image downloading, error handling, file data management etc.

Although Almofire takes care of no internet and server not responding, it's good to handle it separately as we discussed initially in this chapter. In case you want more configuration and deep level integration for making REST API requests then you may use `URLsession` provided by apple in its Network framework.

In the next chapter we will discuss in detail about the best App Architectures practices and design patterns to enhance your coding level and make scalable mobile apps.

Multiple choice questions

1. **Which of the following is NOT the request method type in HTTP ____________.**
    a. GET
    b. POST
    c. DELETE
    d. IDENTITY

2. **Reachability is used for ____________.**
    a. Internet Connectivity
    b. Make Request

c. Download Image
d. Call API

3. AlamofireImage used for ____________.

a. Make API Request
b. Image Download
c. Cancel Request
d. Cache Handling

4. URL Encoding is required to ________________.

a. Remove unsupported characters
b. Apply API encoding
c. Apply Cache
d. File download handling

5. Operation Queue is used for ____________.

a. To add task / operations in queue
b. Downloading Images
c. Cache Handling
d. None of the Above

6. Image Downloader is part of ________________.

a. Alamofire
b. AlamofireImage
c. AlamofireActivityIndicator
d. None of above

Answers

1. d
2. a
3. b
4. a
5. a
6. b

CHAPTER 16

Mobile App Architectures, Patterns, and Anti-Patterns

Introduction

When an application scales up in size and features then there might be architectural design issues or loopholes. This needs to be addressed carefully with respect to code reusability, clean code and correct use of object-oriented programming and protocol-oriented programming. Many of the Cocoa environment's structures and processes make good use of design patterns, such as abstract designs that tackle recurrent issues in a specific context. This chapter covers the key design patterns implemented in Cocoa, with an emphasis on Model View Controller and MVVM. The major goal of this chapter is to raise your knowledge of Cocoa and mobile application design patterns that may be utilized in iOS application development and to urge you to apply these patterns in your own iOS applications. Further, we will discuss the redux architecture in iOS which gained popularity after React native app development was introduced as well as three main core architectures with the mobile app development perspective.

Structure

In this chapter, we will cover the following topics:

- Design patterns in iOS
- Anti-design patterns in iOS
- Mobile app architecture case studies
- Mobile app architectures
- Redux architecture in iOS

Objectives

By learning this chapter, you should be able to develop a complete commercial iOS application with clean, reusable, structured architecture designs such that if that application scales to a large size that should not impact the overall quality of the application.

Design patterns in iOS

Design patterns have always aided in the development of software that is controllable, tested, reusable, and optimized. It aids in the modularization of apps, ensuring that each component is distinct and responsible for a particular task. They significantly enhance the readability of the code, which is critical for conveying software code. Furthermore, using well-proven design principles, the software development process got speed up. Mobile apps are becoming larger and virtually identical in terms of functionality to their desktop and web counterparts, necessitating the consideration of design patterns prior to going into development mode. There are four types of design patterns category which consists of many popular design patterns used in Swift iOS as follows:

- Creational patterns
- Structural patterns
- Behavioral patterns

  Let us discuss these patterns in detail for further understanding of better code reusability and architecture.

Creational patterns

Object generation processes are addressed in design patterns, with the goal of creating things that are appropriate for the context. The most basic type of object generation may cause design issues or contribute to the design's complexity. This challenge is solved by creational design patterns, which regulate the creation of objects in some way. There are mainly five design patterns that come in creational patterns as follows:

- Prototype pattern
- Factory pattern
- Abstract factory pattern
- Builder pattern
- Singleton design pattern

Prototype pattern

This design pattern is used to create a new item by cloning an existing object known as a prototype. When you clone an item, all of its attributes are transferred to another object. This design pattern should be utilized when you need to construct an object but do not know the class hierarchy as follows:

```
protocol Fruit {
    func set(price: String?)
    func clone() -> Fruit
}
class Orange: Fruit {
    var count: Int
    var price: String?

    init(count: Int) {
        self.count = count
    }

    func set(price: String?) {
        self.price = price
    }

    // function definition for cloning the object
    func clone() -> Fruit {
        return Orange(count: self.count)
    }
}
let prototype = Orange(count: 6)
let redOrange: Orange = prototype.clone() as! Orange
print(redOrange.count) // 6
redOrange.set(price: "$4")
print(redOrange.price!) // $4
```

Factory pattern

It is the most popular design pattern. It essentially abstracts the construction of an item. Any instance returned by the factory would be of the type **`Interface`** (in Swift protocol), which every factory candidate class must implement. At runtime, the type of object created is determined. This design approach makes it easier to add or delete new kinds from the codebase.

```
protocol Fruit {
    func getPrice() -> String
    func getCount() -> Int
```

```
}
class Orange: Fruit {
    func getPrice() -> String {return "$5"}
    func getCount() -> Int {return 2}
}
class Banana: Fruit {
    func getPrice() -> String {return "$2"}
    func getCount() -> Int {return 5}
}
class Grapes: Fruit {
    func getPrice() -> String {return "$3.5"}
    func getCount() -> Int {return 1}
}
```

Here we made three different types of fruit classes which actually class **Fruit**. In this case, superclass methods are overridden in other fruit child classes that can be differentiated via a simple **enum** as shown in the following code:

```
// Enum of Fruit Type
enum FruitType {
    case orange, banana, grapes
}
// A factory class with static method
class FruitFactory {
    // Return object of class that implements Fruit protocol
    static func getFruit(forType type: FruitType) -> Fruit? {
        switch type {
        case .orange:
            return Orange()
        case .banana:
            return Banana()
        case .grapes:
            return Grapes()
        }
    }
}
```

```
let orange = FruitFactory.getFruit(forType: .orange)
orange?.getPrice() // "$5
orange?.getCount() // 2
```

Abstract factory pattern

This design pattern provides an interface for building families of related items without naming their concrete classes. They are frequently built using the Factory Method pattern. It shows the interface rather than the implementation. Abstract Factory is similar to a procedure that we will use to build objects on a concrete class:

```
protocol ApplianceFactory {
    static func createTable() -> Table
    static func createChair() -> Chair
}
protocol Table {
    func count() -> Int
}
protocol Chair {
    func count() -> Int
}
class Factory: ApplianceFactory {
    static func createChair() -> Chair {return MyChair()}
    static func createTable() -> Table {return MyTable()}
}
private class MyChair: Chair {
    func count() -> Int {return 4}
}
private class MyTable: Table {
    func count() -> Int {return 1}
}
let chair = Factory.createChair()
chair.count() // 4
```

Builder pattern

This design pattern separates the process of creating items from the actual use of the products. Because it does not expose implementation details, you may use the Builder approach for creating public APIs. It has the ability to conceal complexity. It hides a complicated operation behind a simple API.

```
protocol ShoeShop {
    func produceShoe()
}
// class that conforms to Shoe Shop protocol
class Nike: ShoeShop {
    func produceShoe() {
        print("Shoe Produce")
    }
}
class Director {
    let shoeShop: ShoeShop

    init(shoeShop: ShoeShop) {
        self.shoeShop = shoeShop
    }
    func produce() {
        shoeShop.produceShoe()
    }
}
let nike = Nike()
let director = Director(shoeShop: nike)
print(director.produce())
```

Singleton design pattern

The **static** keyword is used in Swift to define Singleton classes. It implies that the object will only be instantiated once. Static properties are lazily initialized, which means they will not be created until they are invoked. This object has a single copy and is shared by all other objects. Singletons assure that there is only one object of its kind and offers a single point of access to it for any other code. Singletons have nearly the same advantages and disadvantages as global variables. They are extremely useful, yet they destroy the modularity of your code:

```
class Automobile {
    static let sharedInstance = Automobile()
    // private initialization
```

```
    private init() {}

    func getName() -> String {
        return "Car"
    }
    func getModel() -> String {
        return "Honda Amaze"
    }
}
```

Every time when we want to access the class automobile, we will not create any factory object of this class rather access via a static initialization shared instance that will restrict developers to use multiple instances of the class.

```
print(Automobile.sharedInstance.getName()) // Car
print(Automobile.sharedInstance.getModel()) // Honda Amaze
```

Structural patterns

The goal of streamlining the app design process while identifying the simplest technique for linking objects and classes is known as **structural design pattern**. By identifying the linkages, structural design patterns simplify the structure. These patterns are concerned with how classes inherit from one another and how they are made up of other classes. There are mainly four design patterns that come in Structural patterns as follows:

- Facade design
- Adapter
- Bridge
- Decorator

Facade design

When working with a large number of classes, especially those that are difficult to use or comprehend, this approach is perfect. Facade designs gives complicated systems a single interface. You just offer one basic unified API to the user, rather than a variety of classes and their APIs. If the classes beneath the facade are expected to change, this is also beneficial since the facade class may keep the same API while things change behind the scenes:

```
import XCTest
class Facade {

    private var subsystem1: Subsystem1
    private var subsystem2: Subsystem2
```

```
    init(subsystem1: Subsystem1 = Subsystem1(),
         subsystem2: Subsystem2 = Subsystem2()) {
        self.subsystem1 = subsystem1
        self.subsystem2 = subsystem2
    }

    func operation() -> String {

        var result = "Facade - Sub Systems:"
        result += " " + subsystem1.operation1()
        result += " " + subsystem2.operation1()
        result += "\n" + "Facade orders Sub Systems to perform the Action:\n"
        result += " " + subsystem1.operationN()
        result += " " + subsystem2.operationZ()
        return result
    }
}
class Subsystem1 {
    func operation1() -> String {
        return "Subsystem ONE: Ready!\n"
    }
    func operationN() -> String {
        return "Subsystem ONE: Go!\n"
    }
}
class Subsystem2 {
    func operation1() -> String {
        return "Subsystem TWO: Get ready!\n"
    }
    func operationZ() -> String {
        return "Subsystem TWO: Fire!\n"
    }
}
```

```
class Client {
    static func clientCode(facade: Facade) {
        print(facade.operation())
    }
}
```

Here the **Facade** class uses other subsystem classes in it and when we want to use its internal operations, we can just pass the facade instance to the **Client** class so that it will never know what happens in the complexity of facade operations.

```
// Let's see how it all works together -
class FacadeConceptual: XCTestCase {
    func testFacadeConceptual() {

        let subsystem1 = Subsystem1()
        let subsystem2 = Subsystem2()
        let facade = Facade(subsystem1: subsystem1, subsystem2: subsystem2)
        Client.clientCode(facade: facade)
    }
}
let concept = FacadeConceptual()
concept.testFacadeConceptual()
```

Adapter

The Adapter design pattern transforms a class's interface into a client-facing interface. The adapter allows classes that would not otherwise be able to operate together due to conflicting interfaces to do so. It separates the client from the targeted object's class. You will need to incorporate the **EventKit** framework and change the **Event** model from the model framework in your iOS app, if you want to include a calendar and event management feature. An adapter wraps the framework and makes it compatible with the model of your project.

```
import Foundation
import EventKit
// Event protocol
protocol Event {
    var title: String { get }
    var startDate: String { get }
    var endDate: String { get }
}
```

```
// Adapter Wrapper Class
class EventAdapter {
    private lazy var dateFormatter: DateFormatter = {
        let dateFormatter = DateFormatter()
        dateFormatter.dateFormat = "yyyy. MM. dd. HH:mm"
        return dateFormatter
    }()
    private var event: EKEvent

    init(event: EKEvent) {
        self.event = event
    }
}
// Adapter Implementation
extension EventAdapter: Event {
    var title: String {
        return self.event.title
    }
    var startDate: String {
        return self.dateFormatter.string(from: event.startDate)
    }
    var endDate: String {
        return self.dateFormatter.string(from: event.endDate)
    }
}
```

An event protocol is implemented in the event adapter class such that if required other fields and values can be adapted by the class at a later point of time. We can set those parameters while implementing and testing that adapter as shown in the following code:

```
// Test Adapter Implementation
let dateFormatter = DateFormatter()
dateFormatter.dateFormat = "MM/dd/yyyy HH:mm"
let calendarEvent = EKEvent(eventStore: EKEventStore())
calendarEvent.title = "iOS Class Deadline"
```

```
calendarEvent.startDate = dateFormatter.date(from: "09/30/2021 10:00")
calendarEvent.endDate = dateFormatter.date(from: "09/30/2021 11:00")
// Use Adapter class as an Event protocol
let adapter = EventAdapter(event: calendarEvent)
adapter.title
adapter.startDate
adapter.endDate
```

Bridge

The Bridge pattern separates an abstraction from its implementation, allowing the two to change independently. It is quite useful when you do not know the specific business logic to implement but need to develop your abstraction due to a project deadline. When business logic is derived from a client's request, only business logic must be coded:

```
protocol Switch {
    var appliance: Appliance { get set }
    func turnOn()
}
protocol Appliance {
    func run()
}
final class RemoteControl: Switch {
    var appliance: Appliance

    func turnOn() {
        self.appliance.run()
    }

    init(appliance: Appliance) {
        self.appliance = appliance
    }
}
final class TV: Appliance {
    func run() {
        print("Television Turned ON");
```

```
    }
}
final class VacuumCleaner: Appliance {
    func run() {
        print("Vacuum Cleaner Turned ON")
    }
}
let tvRemoteControl = RemoteControl(appliance: TV())
tvRemoteControl.turnOn()
let remoteControlVC = RemoteControl(appliance: VacuumCleaner())
remoteControlVC.turnOn()
```

Decorator

A decorator is a structural design pattern that enables you to wrap new functions in helpful wrappers to dynamically fix them to an object. The Decorator design pattern is also known as the Wrapper design pattern. The basic concept behind this pattern is that you may nest a target object within a wrapper object, which then activates the target item's behavior and adds it to the result. You may mix the behavior of several wrappers by using them all at the same time. It is an alternative to subclassing in which you change the functionality of a class by wrapping it in another object. In Objective C, we can achieve this pattern by category implementation and in Swift, we can make Extensions to class to achieve this pattern.

```
protocol Transporting {
    func getSpeed() -> Double
    func getTraction() -> Double
}
final class RaceCar: Transporting {
    private let speed = 10.0
    private let traction = 10.0

    func getSpeed() -> Double {return speed}
    func getTraction() -> Double {return traction}
}
let raceCar = RaceCar()
let defaultSpeed = raceCar.getSpeed()
let defaultTraction = raceCar.getTraction()
```

```
class TireDecorator: Transporting {
    private let transportable: Transporting
    init(transportable: Transporting) {
        self.transportable = transportable
    }
    func getSpeed() -> Double {
        return transportable.getSpeed()
    }

    func getTraction() -> Double {
        return transportable.getTraction()
    }
}
class OffRoadTireDecorator: Transporting {
    private let transportable: Transporting

    init(transportable: Transporting) {
        self.transportable = transportable
    }

    func getSpeed() -> Double {
        return transportable.getSpeed() - 3.0
    }

    func getTraction() -> Double {
        return transportable.getTraction() + 3.0
    }
}
class ChainedTireDecorator: Transporting {
    private let transportable: Transporting

    init(transportable: Transporting) {
        self.transportable = transportable
    }
```

```
    func getSpeed() -> Double {
        return transportable.getSpeed() - 1.0
    }

    func getTraction() -> Double {
        return transportable.getTraction() * 1.1
    }
}
// Create Race Car
let defaultRaceCar = RaceCar()
defaultRaceCar.getSpeed() // 10
defaultRaceCar.getTraction() // 10
// Modify Race Car
let offRoadRaceCar = OffRoadTireDecorator(transportable: defaultRaceCar)
offRoadRaceCar.getSpeed() // 7
offRoadRaceCar.getTraction() // 13
```

Behavioral patterns

The Behavioral design pattern is involved with how items interact with one another. It defines how objects communicate with one another and how the phases of a task are split up across multiple objects to increase flexibility and testability. There are many design patterns that come in Behavioral patterns but due to the limits of this book, we will discuss only important patterns which are used most of the time in best architecture, which are listed as follows:

- Template pattern
- State pattern
- Observer pattern
- Mediator pattern
- Iterator pattern

Template pattern

The purpose of this Swift design pattern for iOS apps is to keep implementation-specific behavior out of the generic class. Only base classes that implement the algorithm steps are used to communicate across classes. We will utilize interface delegation in Swift to do this. The base class defines the template of an algorithm and lets the subclass implement these abstract methods in the same way they are defined in the base class without changing the overall structure.

```
protocol Office {
    func officeSchedule()
}
protocol Employee {
    func work()
    func getPaid()
}
class MyOffice: Office {
    var delegate: Employee

    init(employee: Employee) {
        self.delegate = employee
    }
    func officeSchedule() {
        delegate.work()
        delegate.getPaid()
    }
}
class Developer: Employee {

    func work() {
        print("Developer has worked 60 hours per week this month")
    }
    func getPaid() {
        print("Developer has earned Rs 80,000 this month")
    }
}
class ProjectManager: Employee {
    func work() {
        print("Project Manager has worked 55 hours per week this month")
    }
    func getPaid(){
        print("Project Manager has earned Rs 100,000 this month")
    }
```

```
}
let xyzOfficeDev = MyOffice(employee: Developer())
let xyzOfficeManager = MyOffice(employee: ProjectManager())
xyzOfficeDev.officeSchedule()
xyzOfficeManager.officeSchedule()
```

State pattern

Each application state passes through a funnel defined by ReSwift until one reducer responds to it and executes the desired behavior. The user interface would then reflect each new state.

```
protocol Human {
    func getState() -> ManState
    func set(state: ManState)
}
protocol ManState {
    func stand()
    func walk()
    func toString() -> String
}
extension ManState {
    func stand() {}
    func walk() {}
}
class Man: Human {
    var state: ManState?
    init() {state = nil}
    func set(state: ManState) {
        self.state = state
    }
    func getState() -> ManState {
        return state!
    }
}
class StandingState: ManState {
    var human: Human
```

```
    init(_ human: Human) {
        self.human = human
    }
    func stand() {
        print("The Man State is - Standing Position")
        human.set(state: self)
    }

    func toString() -> String {
        return "Standing State"
    }
}
class WalkingState: ManState {

    var human: Human
    init(_ human: Human) {
        self.human = human
    }
    func walk() {
        print("The Man State is - Walking Position")
        human.set(state: self)
    }
    func toString() -> String {
        return "Walking State"
    }
}
let man = Man()
let standingState = StandingState(man)
standingState.stand()
print(man.getState().toString())
let walkingState = WalkingState(man)
walkingState.walk()
print(man.getState().toString())
```

Observer pattern

In this design, one object notifies other objects when its state changes, that is, when one object's state changes, other objects that are subscribed to it are alerted. As a result, the connection is one-to-many. The observable or subject is the entity whose state changes, and the observers are the objects that subscribe to changes in the observable as follows:

```
protocol Observable {
    func add(customer: Observer)
    func remove(customer : Observer)
    func notify()
}
protocol Observer {
    var id: Int { get set }
    func update()
}
class  OrangeSeller: Observable {
    private var observers: [Observer] = []
    private var count: Int = 0
    var fruitCount: Int {
        set {
            count = newValue
            notify()
        }
        get {return count}
    }
    func add(customer: Observer) {
        observers.append(customer)
    }
    func remove(customer : Observer) {
        observers = observers.filter{ $0.id != customer.id }
    }
    func notify() {
        for observer in observers {
            observer.update()
        }
```

```
    }
}
class Customer: Observer {
    var id: Int
    var observable:  OrangeSeller
    var name: String
    init(name: String, observable:  OrangeSeller, customerId: Int) {
        self.name = name
        self.observable = observable
        self.id = customerId
        self.observable.add(customer: self)
    }
    func update() {
       print("Wait, \(name)! \(observable.fruitCount) Oranges arrived at shop.")
    }
}
let seller = OrangeSeller()
let james = Customer(name: "James", observable: seller, customerId: 101)
let david = Customer(name: "David", observable: seller, customerId: 102)
seller.fruitCount = 10
seller.remove(customer: james)
seller.fruitCount = 20
```

Mediator pattern

Consider a situation in which two or more classes must interact with one another. Instead of interacting directly with one another and learning about their implementation, they can communicate through a **Mediator**. When two teams compete against one other for a spot in the game's finals, the **Avatar** is on **TeamA**, and the **Bengaluru Techriders** are on **TeamB**. Instead of conversing directly with one another, they register with the mediator object and then use **Mediator** to deliver messages to one another as follows:

```
protocol Receiver {
    var name: String { get }
    func receive(message: String)
}
protocol Sender {
```

```
    var teams: [Receiver] { get set }
    func send(message: String, sender: Receiver)
}
class Mediator: Sender {
    var teams: [Receiver] = []

    func register(candidate: Receiver) {
        teams.append(candidate)
    }

    func send(message: String, sender: Receiver) {
        for team in teams {
            if team.name != sender.name {
                team.receive(message: message)
            }
        }
    }
}
struct TeamA: Receiver {
    var name: String
    init(name: String) {
        self.name = name
    }
    func receive(message: String) {
        print("\(name) Received: \(message)")
    }
}
struct TeamB: Receiver {
    var name: String
    init(name: String) {
        self.name = name
    }
    func receive(message: String) {
        print("\(name) Received: \(message)")
```

```
    }
}
let mediator = Mediator()
let teamA = TeamA(name: "The Roadies")
let teamB = TeamB(name: "The League of Extraordinary Gentlemen")
mediator.register(candidate: teamA)
mediator.register(candidate: teamB)
mediator.send(message: "Selected for final! from \(teamA.name)", sender: teamA)
mediator.send(message: "Not selected for final! from \(teamB.name)", sender:
teamB)
```

Iterator pattern

This pattern is used to repeatedly iterate over a set of items. It provides an interface that iterates through the collection of components without disclosing the underlying representation, rather than exposing the data structure used to implement it. Have you ever wondered how Swift's **for…in** loop works? Swift has a **Sequence** protocol that aids in the creation of iterators. By constructing an iterator, the **Sequence** protocol provides sequential access to its items as follows:

```
struct GreatFilms: Sequence {
    let films: [String]

    func makeIterator() -> GreatFilmsIterator {
        return GreatFilmsIterator(films)
    }
}
struct GreatFilmsIterator: IteratorProtocol {
    var films: [String]
    var cursor: Int = 0
    init(_ films: [String]) {
        self.films = films
    }

    mutating func next() -> String? {
        defer { cursor += 1 }
        return films.count > cursor ? films[cursor] : nil
    }
```

```
}
let myFilms = GreatFilms(films: ["3 Idiots", "The Great Gatsby", "Godfather Trilogy"])
for film in myFilms {
    print(film)
}
```

Here with the help of iterator protocol, you can iterate on the list of text, name or any kind of serial data which can help you to present data in a better format in a structured way.

Anti-design patterns in iOS

Anti-design patterns are patterns that are used to intentionally break good design practices. These patterns are usually used as a quick fix or as a workaround to a problem, but they often lead to negative consequences in the long run. These patterns are often used in situations where the traditional approaches to design do not fit the needs of the project, or when the cost or effort of implementing a traditional design pattern is not justified. Anti-design patterns should be avoided because they often lead to poor code quality and decreased maintainability. They can also lead to increased development time and increased costs due to the need for frequent fixes and updates. Good design patterns, on the other hand, prioritize simplicity, maintainability, and scalability in order to create efficient and effective systems. There are mainly five anti patterns as given below:

- The God Object anti pattern
- The Singleton anti pattern
- The Blob anti pattern
- The Spaghetti anti pattern
- The Golden Hammer anti pattern
- The Boat Anchor anti pattern
- The Dead Code anti pattern

The God object anti-pattern

The God object is an object that knows too much or does too much. It is an anti-pattern because it represents a design flaw that can lead to complex, inflexible, and hard-to-maintain code. The God object often serves as a central hub or controller for the rest of the code, and it is often responsible for a large number of tasks or functions. This can make it difficult to understand the responsibilities of the object and can lead to a high degree of coupling between the object and the rest of the codebase.

To avoid the God object anti-pattern, it is important to follow good object-oriented design principles, such as encapsulation, separation of concerns, and the single responsibility principle. These principles encourage the creation of small, focused objects that have a clear and well-defined set of responsibilities. This can lead to more modular, flexible, and maintainable code.

The Singleton anti-pattern

The singleton design pattern is a software design pattern that is used to ensure that a class only has one instance and provides a global point of access to it. While this can be useful in some cases, it can also lead to problems if not used properly. One problem with the Singleton pattern is that it can lead to tight coupling between classes. This means that classes become dependent on each other, which can make it difficult to change or modify the code. It can also make testing more difficult, as it can be difficult to test classes that are tightly coupled.

Another problem with the singleton pattern is that it can make it difficult to scale applications. If a singleton class is extensively used throughout an application, it can become a bottleneck when the application needs to scale to handle more users or data.

Finally, the singleton pattern can also make it difficult to maintain code. If the Singleton class is used throughout the application, it can be difficult to modify or update the code without breaking the application. In general, the Singleton pattern should be used sparingly and with caution. It is important to carefully consider whether it is the appropriate solution for a given problem before implementing it.

The Blob anti pattern

The Blob anti pattern refers to a large, monolithic software design that lacks modularity, flexibility, and reuse. It is characterized by a single, massive class or module that contains a large amount of code and functionality, often with few or no clear boundaries between different responsibilities or areas of concern. This can lead to a number of problems, including:

- Difficulty in understanding and maintaining the code
- Difficulty in identifying and fixing problems or bugs
- Difficulty in adapting the code to changing requirements or needs
- Difficulty in reusing code or integrating it with other systems

To avoid the Blob anti-pattern, it is important to focus on modularity, separation of concerns, and reuse when designing software. This can involve breaking up large classes or modules into smaller, more focused components, and defining clear boundaries between different areas of functionality. It can also involve using design patterns and software frameworks that encourage modularity and reuse.

The Golden Hammer anti-pattern

The Golden Hammer is an anti-pattern that occurs when a person or team becomes too reliant on a single solution or tool to solve all problems. This often results in the overuse of this solution, even when it may not be the most appropriate or effective option. This pattern can occur in any field, but is commonly seen in software development, where a developer may be overly attached to a particular programming language or framework. They may continue to use this tool for every problem, even when it is not the best fit for the task at hand.

The Golden Hammer can be detrimental to a project because it limits flexibility and creativity and can lead to suboptimal solutions. It can also result in technical debt, as the team becomes more and more reliant on a single tool that may become outdated or obsolete. To avoid the Golden Hammer anti-pattern, it is important to remain open to different solutions and to regularly reassess the tools and approaches being used. It is also important to continually learn and stay up to date with new technologies and best practices.

The Boat anchor anti-pattern

The Boat anchor Anti-Pattern is a term used to describe situations in which an organization becomes heavily reliant on outdated or cumbersome systems, processes, or technologies that weigh it down and prevent it from adapting to new challenges or opportunities. These *boat anchors* often take the form of legacy systems that are expensive to maintain, difficult to use, or no longer fit the needs of the organization. The Boat anchor Anti-Pattern can have serious consequences for an organization, including reduced efficiency, increased costs, and limited agility. It can also lead to a culture of resistance to change, as employees become accustomed to working with outdated systems and may fear the challenges that come with adopting new technologies.

To avoid the Boat anchor anti-pattern, organizations should regularly assess and update their systems, processes, and technologies to ensure that they are meeting the needs of the business and enabling it to adapt to changing circumstances. This may involve implementing new technologies, streamlining processes, or retiring outdated systems. It is important to involve all stakeholders in this process, including employees, customers, and partners, to ensure that the transition is successful and beneficial for all parties involved.

The Dead Code anti-pattern

The Dead Code Anti-Pattern refers to the presence of code in a program or system that is no longer used or relevant. This can occur for a variety of reasons, such as changes in requirements or functionality, updates to the system, or simply the accumulation of unnecessary code over time. Dead code can be harmful to a system in a number of ways. Firstly, it can take up unnecessary space and memory, potentially slowing down the system's performance. It can also make the codebase more difficult to read and understand, as developers have to sift through unnecessary lines of code to find the relevant sections. Additionally, dead code can be a security risk, as it may contain vulnerabilities or outdated security measures that could be exploited.

To avoid the Dead Code anti-pattern, it is important to regularly review and clean up the codebase, removing any unnecessary or outdated code. This can be done through code reviews, automated tools, or regular maintenance sessions. It is also important to have clear documentation and communication within the development team to ensure that code is not unnecessarily duplicated or left unused.

Overall, the Dead Code anti-pattern can be detrimental to the efficiency and security of a system. By regularly reviewing and cleaning up the codebase, developers can ensure that their systems are streamlined and secure.

Mobile app architecture case studies

App architecture case studies are real-time architectural issues you may come across while designing and implementing a consumer end product. Although, there is no limit to discussing such cases, we will take two problems that can be resolved with correct architectural decision-making.

Case 1

There are requirements of the iOS project, where every text of the label, content color, font name, label size should be configurable from the Server side at any point of time even after the app is uploaded to the Apple Store. Some features of this app could be offline too, and others are heavily dependent upon Server API data. What architectural approach will you take to fulfil these criteria? We will discuss answer of this question in below mentioned solution.

Case 1: Solution discussion

In the given requirements, we have a specific problem that every design text label configuration should be dynamically changed from server side. From the start of native app development, this was a challenging task because. once we upload an app on the app store all the design interfaces kept inside that package which can be changed once we upload a new version of the app with those changes due to this nature of native design developers prefers cross platform hybrid development with HTML CSS. But this problem can be easily maintained by native elements too. We have to develop a framework that takes every design component from a specific file. Let us consider a **`property list`** file (this could be an XML or JSON too). We have to keep this file in the document directory initially which will be bundled in the app package and when the first-time code gets initialized we can put those files into the document directory. Now, whenever a page design will load that will refer to those files for size, color and default text of labels.

The framework of design labels should be configured in such a way that we will keep those files on the backend side and make track of the changes. When a regular API notifies that those files have some change, only those changes can be sent to the client app via API request in XML or JSON and the app will update those files and app designs will continue as usual following the flow.

Case 2

There is an ecommerce iOS application, where users can browse the app even without login. Requirements contain - category, subcategory and featured items in every subcategory should be configured from server and dynamic (not changes frequently but may change in 15 days). There should be some featured items in each category / subcategory which should show as fast as possible even in a low network, there should be no delay due to any circumstances. The server team comes up with 14 API to call for all such data (category, subcategory and featured items with images), and data could be changed in future. During testing, the product owner of the app observed that after app download, sometime server fails, and no data (category, subcategory and featured items) will be displayed. Product owner thinks it would give a very bad impression if after download there will be blank screens even due to any reason (here reason could be either no internet or server failure as well). So, users should be able to see at least category - subcategory and featured items with images in any condition.

Case 2: Solution discussion

In the given case, there might be multiple solutions that can be implemented as per the development cost and time. If you are short on time than you can simply put all 14 APIs JSON responses in files and further you can put those files in app bundle. When an app is installed the first time, all the files responses can be provided to those development modules which were expected the response from the server and due to either no internet or low internet failed to receive that data. For long-term, a local database can be maintained which will already keep some data which will be initially shown irrespective of internet or no internet. Later on, that database can be synced to server-side data, if required.

Mobile app architectures

Mobile app architecture refers to a collection of structural components and their interfaces that make up the system, as well as their behavior within the context of all structural elements. This may be considered the skeleton of a program, and its quality determines the entire work of the mobile application. You risk the success of your project by overlooking a crucial component when designing a mobile app architecture. The difficulty of creating high-quality architecture is proportional to the application's size. In the future, appropriate architecture will allow for a significant time, energy, and cost savings. In mobile client applications whenever the user interacts with the app, the first presentation layer comes across which have UI components. The presentation layer further interacts with the business layer which has actual logic of tasks and processing uses data models which might be interacting with the local database in some cases as shown in the following figure:

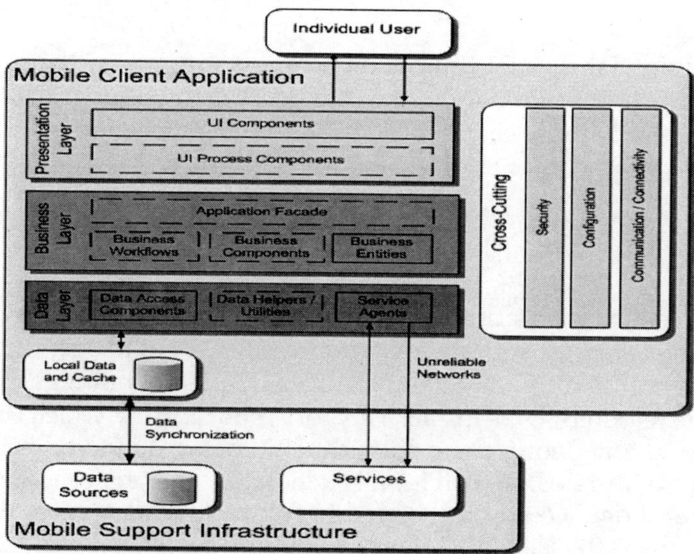

Figure 16.1: Mobile client application layer architecture

All of the successful projects with the best architecture approaches that are now operating on iOS were built entirely by hand, without the assistance of frameworks or other comparable tools. The existence of any library should not be relied upon in architecture. As a result, you may utilize frameworks as tools rather than trying to force your system to conform to their constraints. Good architecture is, first and foremost, a lucrative design that simplifies and streamlines the process of building and maintaining a program. A well-architected software is easier to grow and alter, as well as to test, debug, and comprehend. The basic building blocks of architecture start with the fundamental layers as follows:

- Data layer
- Business layer
- Presentation Layer

Data layer

All data utilities, service agents, and data access components are part of the data layer. This layer is dedicated to data maintenance security, which includes access, utilities, and service tools. It is the foundation on which you may build your business logic and presentation features. Your app's behavior is determined by the patterns you pick for the main functions.

Business layer

All of the different processes and business entities, as well as the business components themselves, are included in the business layer. This platform hides all of the management effort involved in developing the app such as logging, caching, verifying, and other technological activities that will be divided into distinct tasks. This is also where you will find complicated company procedures and corporate policies. To put it another way, you have an application facade with processes, components, and entities behind.

Presentation layer

The most essential step here is to create the customer profile so that your users are satisfied with the visuals on the screen and the layout of items. Now, your consumer is always right, even when it comes to data format decisions. This layer is not about picking the perfect data; it is about creating a format that prohibits incorrect data from being entered.

Types of mobile app architectures

Evaluation of architecture can be done on multiple parameters such as distribution, testability and ease of use. Where ease of use is given less priority in large scalable projects. A defined and structured architecture is required for a balanced distribution of responsibilities among every entity of a project. While we strive to figure out how things operate, distribution puts a considerable amount of strain on our brains. You are correct if you believe that the more you develop, the better your brain will adapt to grasping complexity. However, this talent does not scale linearly and rapidly approaches its limit. Further testability comes even with the first feature which is not an issue for those who are writing unit test cases while developing new features.

Writing a test unit can save time for those developers who might take weeks to fix bugs to deliver at the user end. However, it is worth mentioning that the finest code is that which has never been written. As a result, the less code you have, the fewer problems you will encounter. This implies that a developer's desire to write less code should never be attributed entirely to laziness, and you should never choose a better solution without considering its maintenance costs. Writing a less code architecture gives ease of use with good maintenance of overall code. When it comes to architecture design patterns, we can divide this mainly into four categories as follows:

- Model View Controller (MVC)
- Model View Presenter (MVP)
- Model View View-Model (MVVM)
- Clean architecture (VIPER)

Model View Controller

The **Controller** in Apple's MVC architecture acts as a mediator between the **View** and the **Model**, ensuring that they are unaware of one other. Cocoa MVC is so closely involved in the lifecycle of views that it is difficult to say they are independent. Although, you can still offload some of the business logic and data processing to the **Model** and you do not have much option when it comes to offloading work to the **View**. The View's primary duty is to transmit actions to the **Controller** in most cases. Apple MVC performs the view and controller related task in one module which we called **ViewController** which can handle view as well as other task handling and processing which further updates data models whenever required as shown in the following figure:

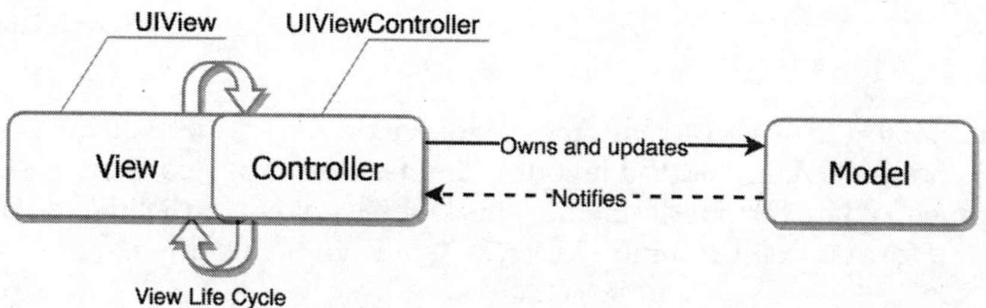

Figure 16.2: *Model View Controller*

Model View Presenter

The **UIViewController** subclasses are the Views, not the Presenters, according to the MVP. This difference provides excellent testability at the cost of development speed since manual data and event binding is required. The View's UI business logic is defined in the **Presenter**. The **Presenter** is the recipient of all invocations from the **View**. The **Presenter** is also separated from the **View** and communicates with it via an interface. This is because the View may be mocked in a unit test. In MVP, the presenter plays a major role which communicates to the model as shown in the following figure:

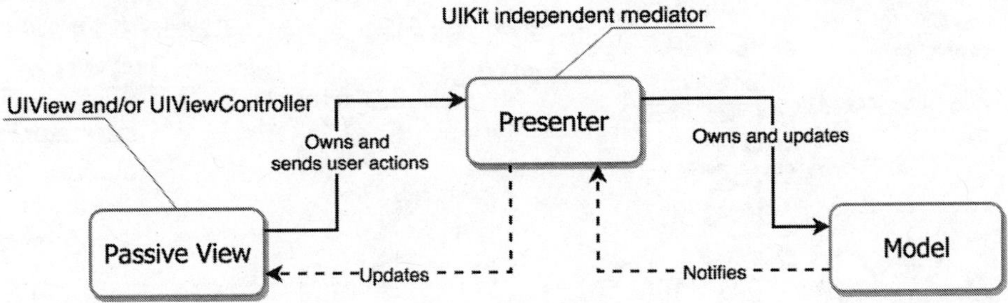

***Figure 16.3**: Model View Presenter*

Model View View-Model

In MVVM the view controller is treated as the **View**, as well as the View and the Model are not tightly coupled. It binds in the same way as the Supervising version of the MVP does, except this time between the **View** and the **View Model** rather than the View and the Model. The **View** in MVVM has additional responsibilities than the **View** in MVP. Because the first one sets up bindings to update its state from the **View Model**, whilst the second one just sends all events to the **Presenter** and does not update itself. When a user interacts with UI components the architecture flow starts from **View** which further calls the **View model** for processing and task handling, while doing this if there is any need to update the model if further call associated models as shown in the following figure:

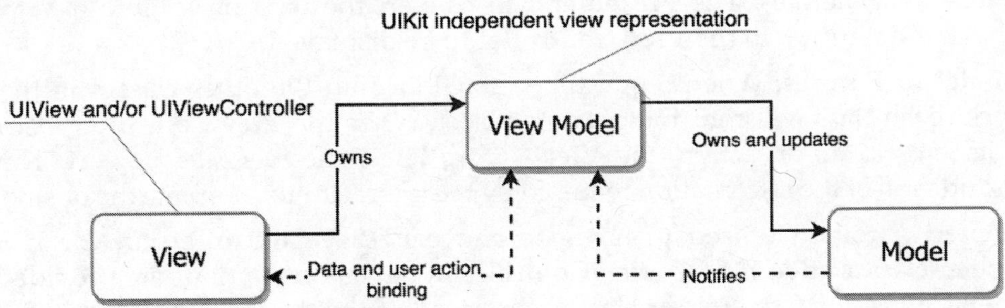

***Figure 16.4**: Model View View-Model*

VIPER clean architecture

VIPER iterates on the concept of dividing responsibilities yet again, this time with five levels. For clarity and testability, the Clean Swift design pattern separates the responsibilities of distinct entities. These elements come together to make settings. Each scene may run on its own, utilizing only the components included in that scene. All the five components play their responsibility and communicate with each other as shown in the following figure:

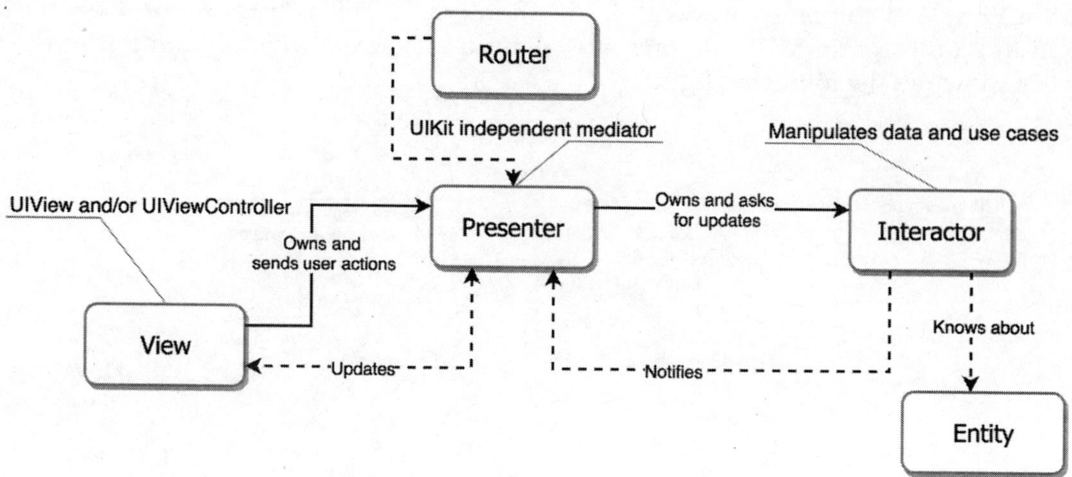

Figure 16.5: VIPER Clean Architecture

VIPER architecture can be formed with five distinct responsible components which are discussed in detail as follows:

- **View Controller**: Xcode interface or XIB controlled by the view controller.
- **Interactor**: It includes data entity or networking business logic, such as generating new instances of entities or retrieving them from the server. You will need some Services and Managers for those reasons, which are not considered part of the VIPER module but rather external dependencies.
- **Presenter**: The **Presenter** is the class that is in charge of displaying the object that the Interactor generates. The **Presenter** will convert the data object into a **ViewModel** object and return it to the **ViewController** to be displayed.
- **Model or Entities**: When requesting an action from the other classes in the VIPER cycle, each class will contribute a data object. When the **ViewController** instructs the Interactor to do an action, the **ViewController** creates a *Request* object. This object includes all of the information required by the interactor to complete the business logic.
- **Router:** A router is used to navigate between **ViewControllers** in Clean Swift. A Router class is added to the **ViewController** if navigation options are provided for the **ViewController**. The **Router** class includes all of the navigation options available to that particular **ViewController**.

MVI architecture in iOS

The **Model-View-Intent** (**MVI**) design pattern is a reactive design pattern commonly used in Android development, but it can also be implemented in iOS applications. MVI separates the responsibilities of data management and user interface updates, resulting in a more predictable and testable codebase. In this pattern, the user interface (**View**) sends intents (user actions or events) to the **ViewModel**, which updates the **Model** and emits new states to the View, triggering UI updates accordingly.

To implement the MVI design pattern in an iOS application, you can follow these steps:

1. **Define the Model.**

   The model represents the current state of your application. It should be a struct or a class that holds the relevant data for your UI. For example:

   ```
   struct CounterModel {
       var count: Int
   }
   ```

2. **Create the View.**

   The view is responsible for rendering the UI and displaying the current state to the user. It should not hold any business logic but simply reflect the data provided by the view model. For example:

   ```
   class CounterViewController: UIViewController {
       @IBOutlet weak var countLabel: UILabel!

       func render(model: CounterModel) {
     countLabel.text = "\(model.count)"
   }
   }
   ```

Implement the ViewModel

The **`ViewModel`** processes intents from the view and updates the model accordingly. It should be a class that conforms to the **`ObservableObject`** protocol from SwiftUI or the **`NSObject`** subclass with **Key-Value Observing** (KVO) for **`UIKit`**. For example:

```
class CounterViewModel: ObservableObject {
    @Published var model = CounterModel(count: 0)

    func increment() {
        model.count += 1
    }

    func decrement() {
        model.count -= 1
    }
}
```

Connect the View and ViewModel

In your view controller or SwiftUI view, create an instance of the **ViewModel** and observe changes to its model. When a user interacts with the UI, send intents to the **ViewModel** to update the state. For example:

```
class CounterViewController: UIViewController {
    private var viewModel = CounterViewModel()

    override func viewDidLoad() {
        super.viewDidLoad()
        viewModel.$model.sink { [weak self] model in
            self?.render(model: model)
        }
    }

    @IBAction func incrementButtonTapped() {
        viewModel.increment()
    }

    @IBAction func decrementButtonTapped() {
        viewModel.decrement()
    }

    func render(model: CounterModel) {
        // Update UI
    }
}
```

In this example, whenever the model in the **ViewModel** changes, the View's render function is called to update the UI. The view sends intents to the view model by calling its methods, such as **increment()** and **decrement()**. By following the MVI design pattern, you can achieve a clear separation of concerns, making your iOS codebase more maintainable and testable.

Redux architecture in iOS

Redux has a particular location for the state (the store) and where the state is updated (the reducers). The flow of data is unidirectional. This implies that your data is only handled in one direction. The idea is that your subscribers (for example, **ViewController**) just listen for updates and do not alter the data they get. The state serves as a representation of your app's current state. Substates in states can include navigation states and ones for each view of your app. The store keeps track of the full app state, and when a request to alter it comes in, it calls the reducer to make the change. It alerts the subscriber connected to the state with the new data when a change occurs.

Actions are what cause state changes. When a user begins a timer, for example, the store, where the state resides, will dispatch actions. When the store receives an action, it will notify Reducer. The reducers are in charge of carrying out the action and changing the state. Subscribers choose a certain state in which they will get notifications later. My timer-view, for example, will only subscribe to the timer state. The subscriber will not be notified if a state change happens that does not affect the timer-state.

ReSwift in iOS

Swift's ReSwift is a small redux-like implementation. It includes a store and procedures to help you get started with redux quickly. You may use your preferred package management to integrate it into your projects. Each application state passes through a funnel defined by ReSwift until one reducer responds to it and executes the desired behavior. The user interface would then reflect each new state. In Redux Architecture, when a user initiates the interaction the flow of process starts from View which triggers actions and actions might change state of variables which is managed by Store globally in the whole project as shown in following figure:

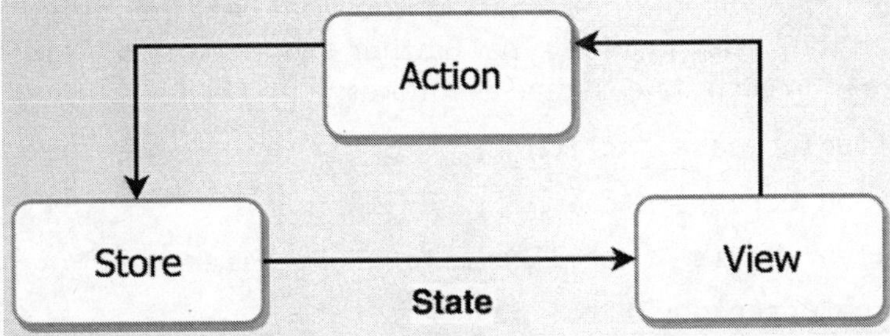

Figure 16.6: *Redux like Architecture in iOS*

Now we will understand the concept of redux with the simple implementation of counter features. Store implementation must be kept in **`AppDelegate`** so it can be started with the app start if it is not there. Reducer functionality could be triggered from the view controller which will change the app state in real time as follows:

```
import ReSwift

let mainStore = Store<AppState>(

    reducer: counterReducer,

    state: nil

)

func counterReducer(action: Action, state: AppState?) -> AppState {
```

```
    var state = state ?? AppState()

    switch action {
    case _ as CounterActionIncrease:
        state.counter += 1
    case _ as CounterActionDecrease:
        state.counter -= 1
    default:
        break
    }

    return state
}
struct AppState: StateType {
    var counter: Int = 0
}
```

The counter reducer method is designed to take actions that have the instance of app state and make the decision on the basis of action type. Further view controllers subscribe to the main store, which updates it on each state change as follows:

```
struct CounterActionIncrease: Action {}
struct CounterActionDecrease: Action {}
class ViewController: UIViewController, StoreSubscriber {
    typealias StoreSubscriberStateType = AppState
    @IBOutlet weak var counterLabel: UILabel!

    override func viewDidLoad() {
        super.viewDidLoad()
        mainStore.subscribe(self)
    }

    func newState(state: AppState) {
        counterLabel.text = "\(mainStore.state.counter)"
    }

    @IBAction func downTouch(_ sender: AnyObject) {
```

```
        mainStore.dispatch(CounterActionDecrease());
    }
    @IBAction func upTouch(_ sender: AnyObject) {
        mainStore.dispatch(CounterActionIncrease());
    }
}
```

Whenever the user increases or decreases the counter it dispatches the action to the main store and when it actually changes the counter value in the app state which reflects via the new state function, and you can use this function to view controller UI component updates.

Conclusion

Clean Architecture, MVVM, and Redux are the most popular architectures in mobile programming. MVVM and Clean architecture may both be used independently, however, MVVM only offers separation of concerns inside the presentation layer, whereas Clean Architecture divides your code into modular levels that are easy to test, reuse, and understand. Clean architecture pairs well with (Test Driven Development) because it makes the project testable and allows for easy layer replacement. It's critical not to omit to create a use case, even if the use case only calls repository. When a fresh developer looks at your use cases, your architecture will be self-explanatory. Creational and structural app patterns help developers to design and make better reusable code modules. In this chapter, we also studied two problem cases which will give you an idea about what type of problems came at your end that can be solved with the use of either patterns or architectural approaches.

Anti-design patterns are patterns that should be avoided in software development because they can lead to negative consequences such as decreased code quality, increased maintenance costs, and decreased usability. It is important for developers to be aware of common anti-design patterns and to strive to use design patterns that lead to more effective and efficient solutions. By avoiding anti-design patterns, developers can create software that is more reliable, maintainable, and user-friendly.

In the next chapter, we will discuss the process of publishing apps on the Apple App Store as well as an analysis of Apple design guidelines and App Store Review Guidelines.

Multiple choice questions

1. **Traditionally Apple supports which Architecture Implementation?**
    a. MVP
    b. MVC
    c. MVVM
    d. Clean

2. **App State and Reducer are used in:**
    a. Redux
    b. MVC
    c. MVP
    d. Clean
3. **Which patterns Notify the object when its state changes?**
    a. Observer Pattern
    b. State Pattern
    c. Mediator Pattern
    d. Template Pattern
4. **How many layers are contained by VIPER Architecture?**
    a. 4
    b. 5
    c. 6
    d. 8
5. **Which Architecture is used mostly in mobile app Programming?**
    a. MVP
    b. MVC
    c. MVVM
    d. None of the above
6. **Which Anti Pattern is related to using less code?**
    a. God Object
    b. Golden hammer
    c. Dead Code
    d. None of the above
7. **Overuse of which pattern can make a Design pattern, an Anti-design pattern?**
    a. Decorative
    b. Singleton
    c. Golden hammer
    d. None of the above

8. **Which Architecture is good for the Testability of independent components?**
   a. MVC
   b. MVP
   c. MVVM
   d. VIPER
9. **Template Design pattern uses the concept of:**
   a. Protocol
   b. Subclass
   c. Extension
   d. None of the above
10. **Which Anti Pattern is related to using a Single Solution or tool?**
    a. God Object
    b. Golden hammer
    c. Dead Code
    d. None of the above

Answers

1. b
2. a
3. a
4. b
5. c
6. c
7. b
8. b
9. b
10. b

CHAPTER 17
Publish iOS App on the Apple App Store

Introduction

Once you have developed all the necessary features for your app, the next crucial step is to publish it on the App Store, making it available for everyone to download. However, Apple imposes guidelines and restrictions to ensure an enhanced user experience. In this chapter, we will explore these guidelines and explain the step-by-step process of uploading your app. Uploading an app to the Apple App Store requires an annual fee for an Apple developer account.

Structure

In this chapter, we will cover the following topics:

- Prepare app for app store upload
- Prepare app store connect for app submission
- TestFlight
- Xcode Cloud
- Manage Apple review rejections

Objectives

By learning this chapter, you should be able to upload apps to the app store, communicate with the Apple team about app rejections, and handle Apple Developer Account and App Store Connect as per user access.

Prepare app for app store upload

There is some compliance that needs to be updated in the app with the help of the IDE, Xcode. If you complete these steps, there will be no issue at the time of app submissions:

- **Launch image:** You can use the `LaunchScreen.storyboard` file for the launch screen and design your app branding as per your requirements. Here you can experiment with your app logo, app name, or some tag line for branding and communication, which will be a first impression for your app users.

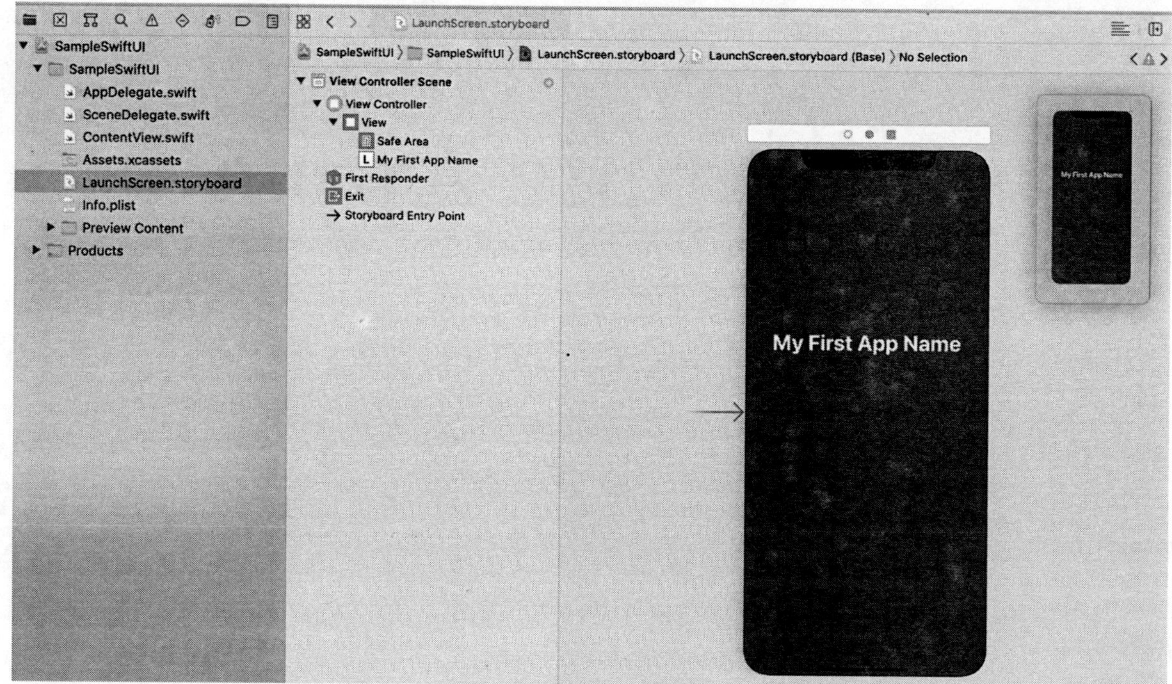

Figure 17.1: Launch image

Also, you need to add this screen name in the app target settings, as shown below:

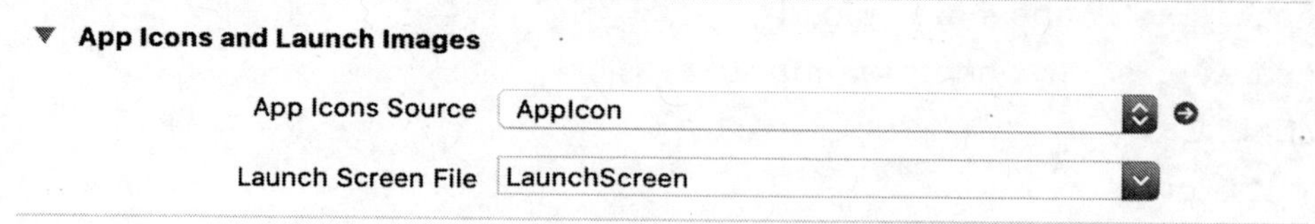

Figure 17.2: App Icon and Launch Image Settings

- **App icons:** First, you have to make a decision on whether an app is for the iPhone only or will support iPad responsive designs too. You may use the Mac software Prepo (which can be installed from the Mac store), which will help you generate all the app icons for your app. In `image.assets`, `AppIcons` image set is already there to fill with different sizes of icons.

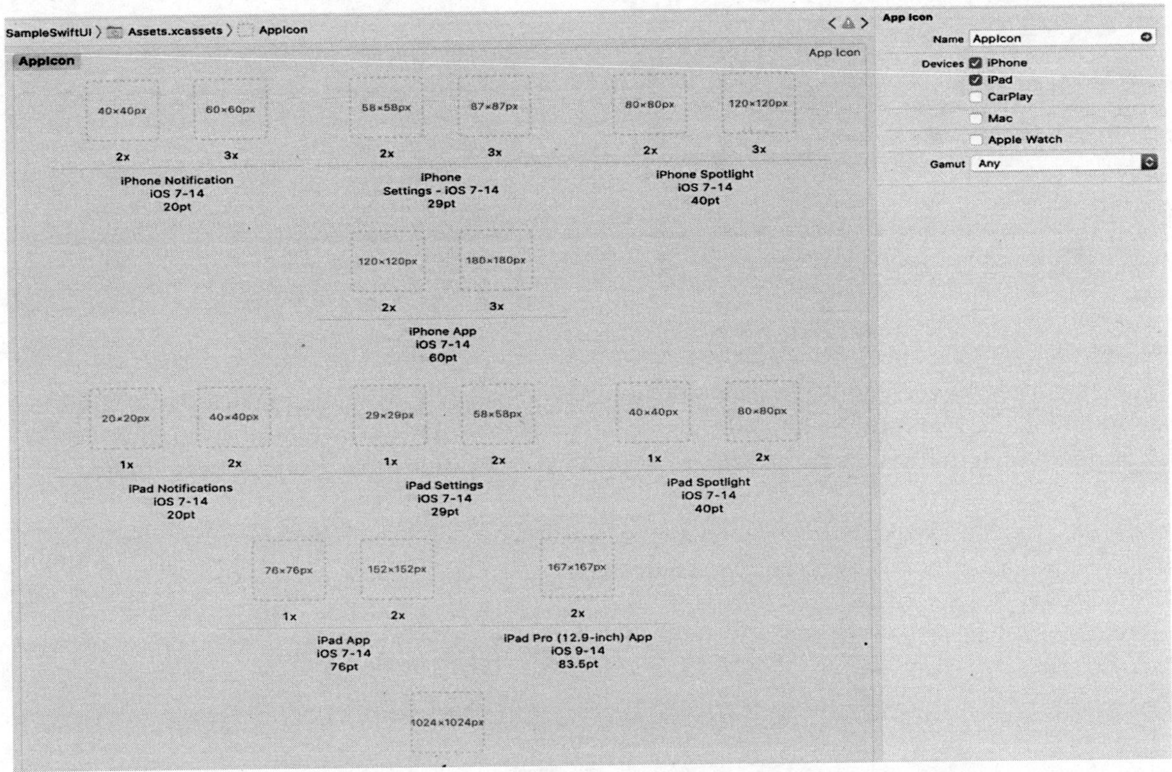

Figure 17.3: App Icons

After that you can check other app information like version number that is synced with the app store, build number, portrait and landscape modes, and so on.

Prepare to build for app store

If you want to submit your apps to the Apple App Store, you must be enrolled in the Apple Developer Program, which costs around $99 for one year of access. After successfully joining this program, you can login to your Apple Developer account via **https://developer.apple.com/account.** Now you will be able to access the section *Certificates, identifiers, and profiles.*

Create distribution certificate

We need to generate an app store certificate from the developer, which requires a private key certificate from your Mac system as input. To create a certificate, you need to open a Mac system software **Keychain Access | Certificate Assistant | Request a Certificate From a Certificate Authority....**

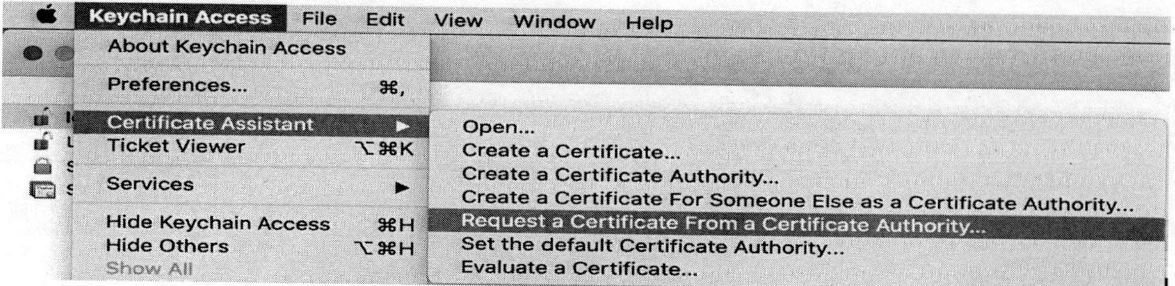

***Figure 17.4:** Request a Certificate from Certificate Authority*

Requesting a certificate from **Keychain Access** will open up a window for certificate information such as email and common name. After completing these details you should select the **Save To Disk** option which will save a certificate on your local computer in `cer` format as follows:

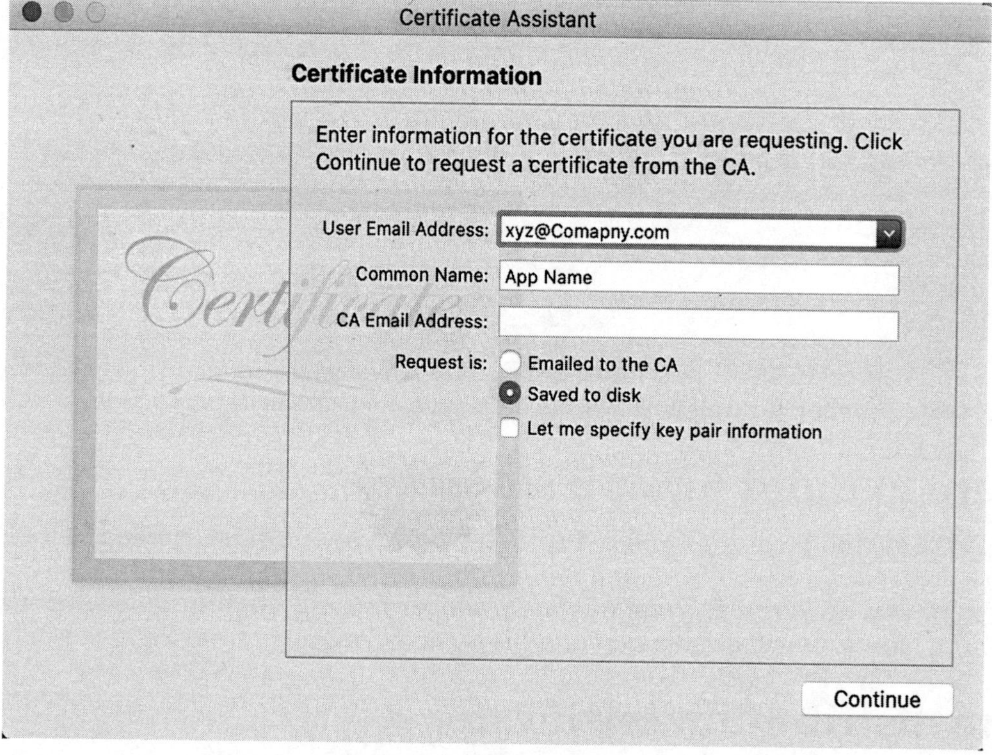

***Figure 17.5:** Certificate Assistant*

We can proceed now to create a new certificate via selecting certificate type App Store Distribution as well as selecting the private keychain certificate which we generated earlier. This will generate your App Store Distribution Certificate which can be used for any App Store Signed app required to be uploaded on your developer account. After successful creation of the distribution certificate, you will be able to view, edit and delete it from the certificate list as follows:

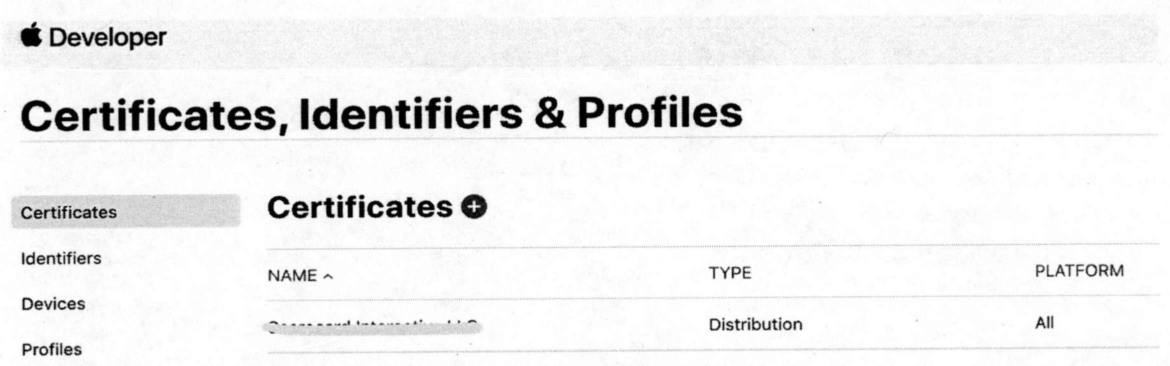

Figure 17.6: App Distribution Certificate

Create app identifier

Next, you will create an identifier that must be unique for every new app on the App Store. When you create a new identifier in the Identifiers section of the developer portal, this will open up a window to further select the option of App ID. To enable your app to use accessible services and identify your app in a provisioning profile, you must first register an App ID. When you establish an App ID, you have the option of enabling app services or changing these settings afterwards. When you move forward and continue, in the final section, you will get following option:

- Description
- App ID Prefix

In descriptions, you cannot use special characters such as **@, &, *, ', ", -, .** For the app ID, Apple suggests that you use a reverse-domain name style string like, **`com.domain name.appname`**. It cannot have an asterisk (*) in it. Although you are free to use any unique combination.

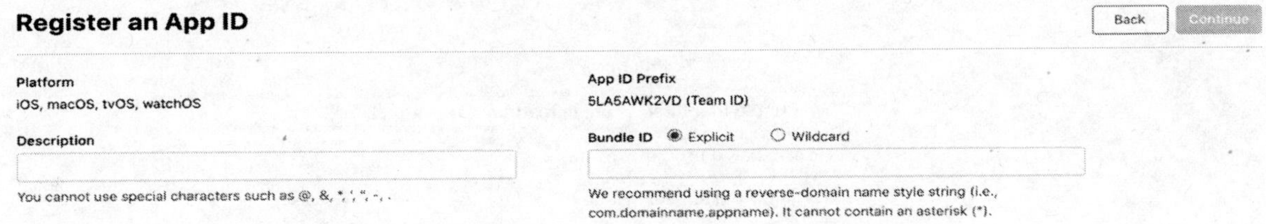

Figure 17.7: Register an App ID

Create distribution profile

Apple Distribution Profile is a signed document specific to a single app that can be used to make signed app builds for app store deployments. You can select the **Profile** section on the developer account and start creating a new profile for your app as follows:

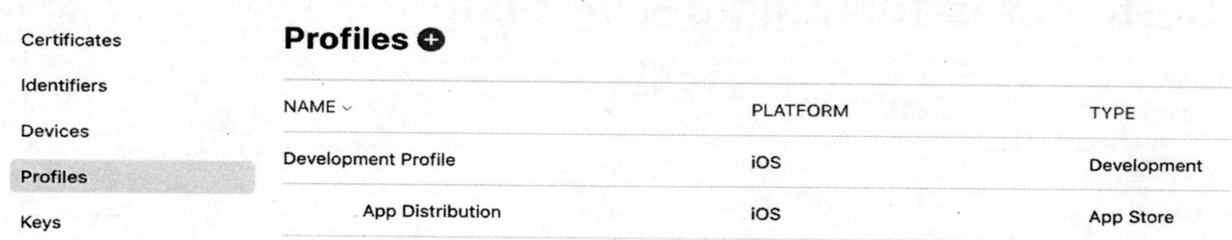

Figure 17.8: App Store Distribution Profile

In the first step of profile creation you can select the App Store and proceed further for app ID selection for this profile. You can select the app id which we created earlier. In the final step of this process there will be a list of distribution certificates and you can select one which you created from your own Mac system. That will finally create your app distribution profile.

Create app build for app store

When the whole process of creating certificate and profile gets completed you need to download both the files and install it via double clicking. For confirmation you can check **Keychain Access** if certificate and profile gets installed or not. To make build open your iOS app in Xcode and select the section **Signing & Capabilities** from the application configurations:

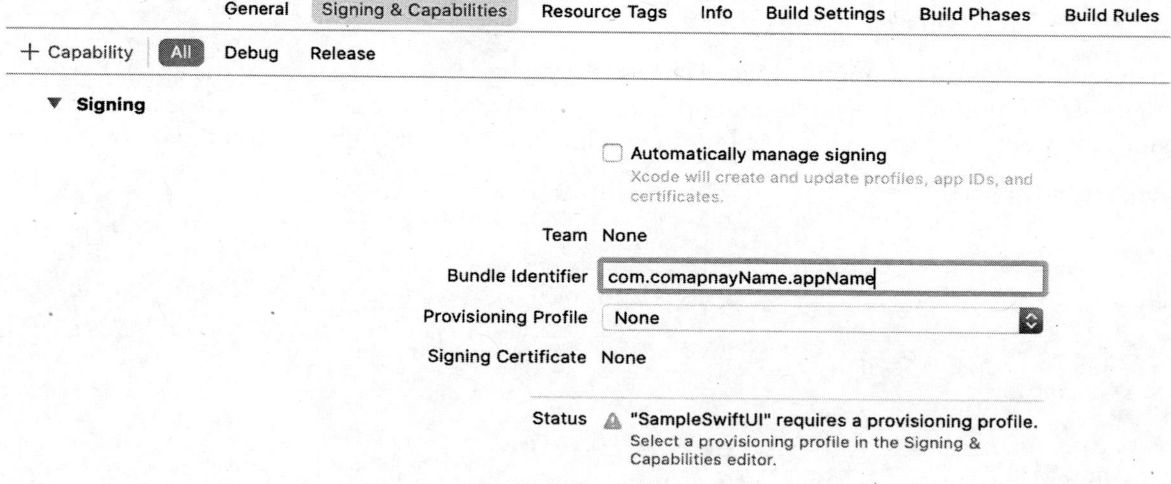

Figure 17.9: Xcode Build Signing

The app identifier which we made on the developer account must be the same as the bundle identifier of the app then you can select the installed **Provisioning Profile** from the drop-down list provided which will auto select the distribution certificate. These actions will remove the warning related to provision profile. Sometimes there might be issues to select the correct profile then you must open the signing configuration in the build setting section to select those certificates in release and debug fields.

In the Xcode select device field you need to select **Any iOS Device** to generate a generic iOS build which can run on all types of iOS devices. Further, from the product menu option select **Archive**, that will start the process of making the app build as follows:

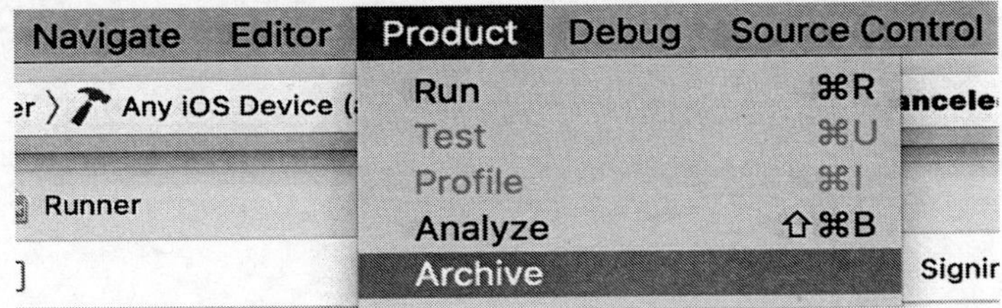

Figure 17.10: *Xcode Build Archiving*

After successfully building an app, Xcode will open App Organizer, and there you can locate the app. After selection of the build, app distribution can be started. Either you can upload that build directly from Xcode or you can just export that build and upload it from the Transporter Mac app provided by Apple specifically for app upload. Both options will require the Apple Developer login credentials with which you joined the Apple Developer Program to proceed further. Now you can see the app processing in the **TestFlight** section of App Store Connect.

Prepare app store connect for app submission

To upload an app to the Apple app store, first you have to enroll in the Apple Developer Program either as an individual or an organization. If you don't have necessary documents required for the organization account program you can continue as an individual developer program. When you login with the Admin role in the developer account you will see multiple options such as:

- My Apps
- App Analytics
- Sales and trends
- Payments and financial reports
- User and Access
- Agreements, Tax and Bankings

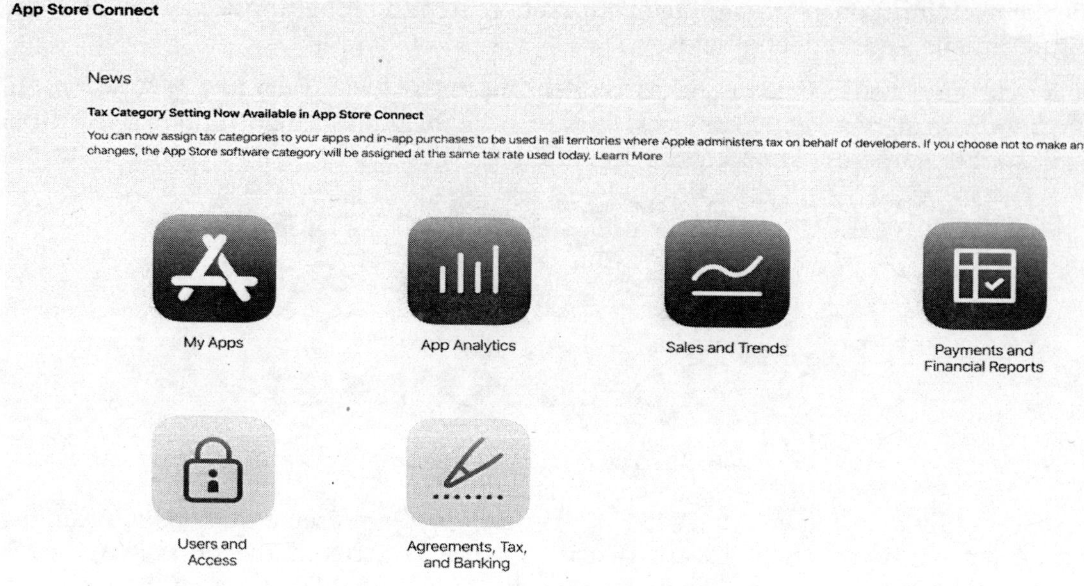

Figure 17.11: *App Store Connect Dashboard*

Further you need to add a new app in the section My Apps which will show a detailed form to fill some initial details of your app as shown here:

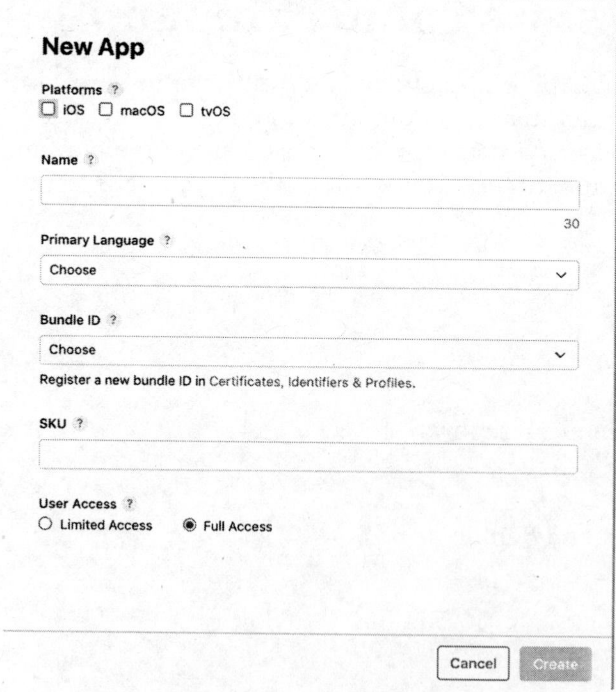

Figure 17.12: *New App Create on App Store Connect*

- **Add Platform:** Apple provides mainly three platform options of apps while creating a new app. In our case we want to upload a mobile iOS app so we will select the **iOS** option.
- **Primary Language:** Select as your preferred language from the list. If you are not sure you can select **English** as the default language.
- **Bundle ID:** First you need to create a new identifier for your app on the developer account section of **Certificates, Identifiers** and **Profiles**. We will check and learn this section in the upcoming part of this chapter. If you already have a bundle Id then you can select that.
- **SKU:** This is just a unique identifier used for your app and will not be shown in the app store. So you can provide as you like.
- **User Access:** Mostly every app is built and uploaded on the App store targeting full access to users and not limited to specific users.

Users and access

When you join the Apple Developer Program, you are automatically assigned as the Account Holder for your membership. When you're enrolled as an organization, you may expand your team by adding more members:

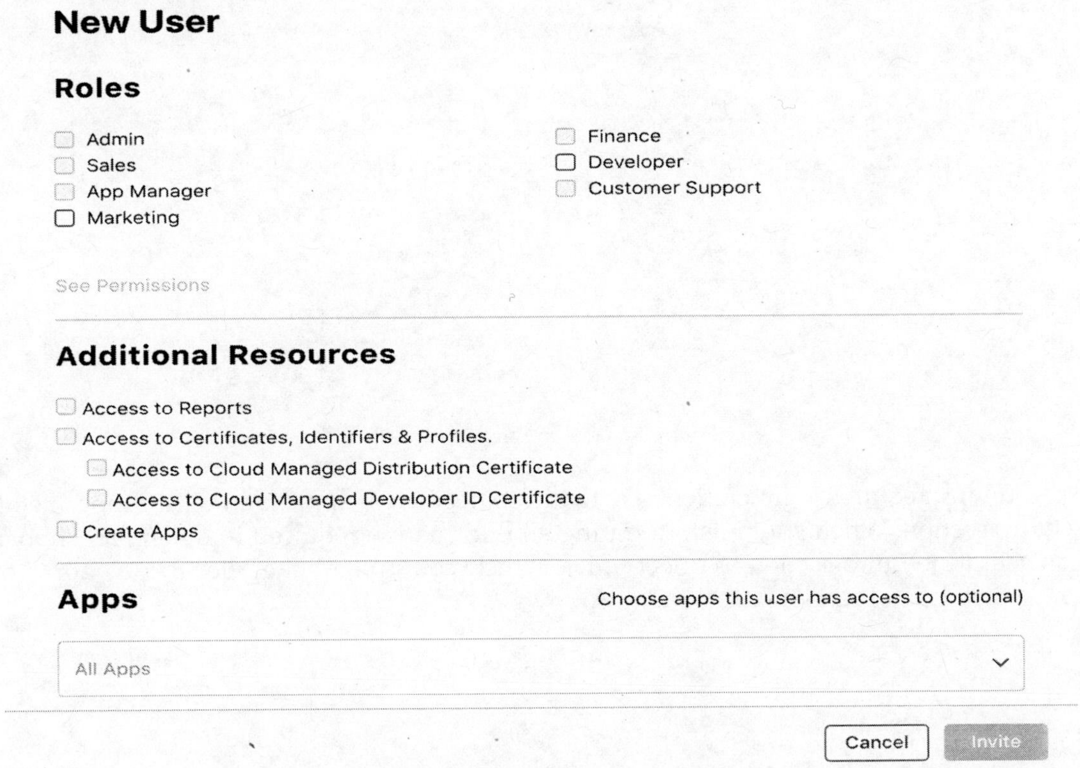

Figure 17.13: App Users and Access

Across the Apple Developer website and App Store Connect, each company has a single team with a single set of roles. App Store Connect is where users and roles are managed. The resource is a representation of an App Store Connect user. Users can be changed or deleted, but they cannot be added directly. When the user accepts the invitation, App Store Connect adds them to your team.

My Apps

In 40 languages, you may add your app's name, subtitle, keywords, description, and more. For each supported language, you may upload up to 10 screenshots and three optional app samples and pick the order in which they display as follows:

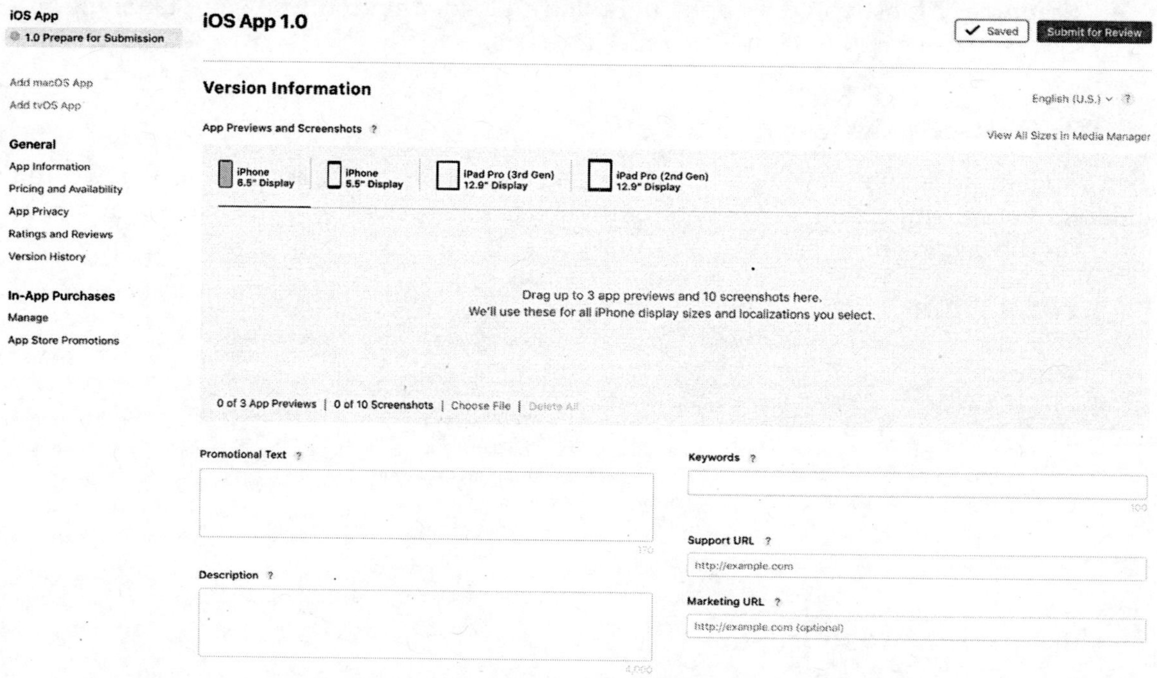

Figure 17.14: *App Product Page*

In case your app requires login credentials, that also needs to be provided with proper details in the notes section. When you finish updating all information required in the app dashboard you can select the Build section to select build, which you uploaded earlier for the app store (the one which is latest and most stable) as follows:

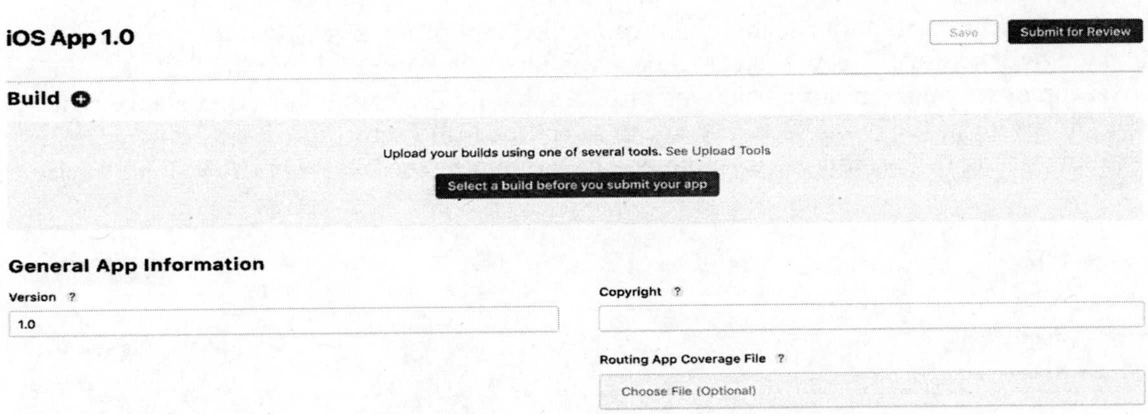

Figure 17.15: *App Product Build Section*

Other than general app information and marketing policy links in Pricing And Availability section of app pricing needs to be updated which can be either free or can be selected in terms of US dollar unit pricing. Further for location availability of the app you may choose to select some specific country or continue with all countries as follows:

iOS App
1.0 Prepare for Submission
Add macOS App
Add tvOS App
General
App Information
Pricing and Availability
App Privacy
Ratings and Reviews
Version History
In-App Purchases
Manage
App Store Promotions
Pricing and Availability
Save
Price Schedule
All Prices and Currencies
PRICE ? | START DATE ? | END DATE ?
USD 0.0 (Free) | Other Currencies | Sep 16, 2021 | No End Date
Tax Category ? Edit
Category: App Store software
Pre-Orders
Pre-orders allow customers to order your app before its release date. Once your app is released for download, customers will be notified and your app will automatically download to their device. For paid apps, customers will be charged before download. Any app that hasn't been published to the App Store can be made available for pre-order. Learn More
Make available for pre-order
Availability
All countries or regions selected Edit
Remove from sale

Figure 17.16: *App Product Pricing and Availability*

Now you can submit for review which will change the status of the app to Waiting for Review. Once the app is approved via Apple then the app will show the status as pending developer release (in case of manual release selection) or **Ready for Sale** (When you selected **Automatic Release**).

Update a new version of app

Once you are live on the App store then you might need to release new versions of the app due to either bug fixes or major feature releases. On App Store Connect portal You can add a new version of live app under section iOS App which will prompt you to enter a new version which you will submit. This will create a new version of the app with prefilled all old details such as app description and links, you may update that if you want otherwise to leave as it is. Similar to earlier in the build section you can select the build which must be properly tested before submitting to the App store. There will be a one new section **What's New in this Version?** as follows:

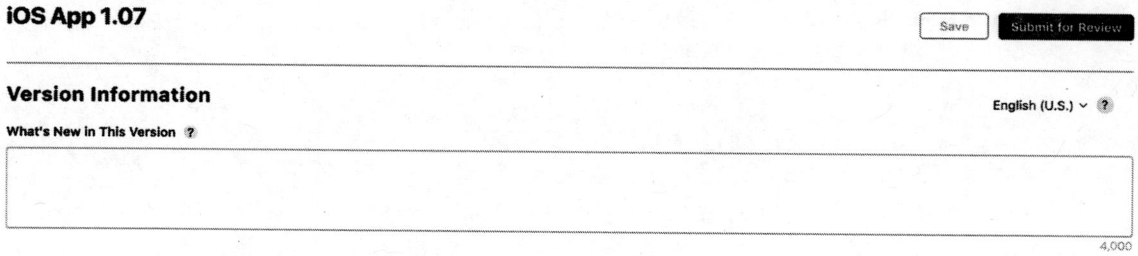

Figure 17.17: *New Version Information*

In version information you may describe new feature implementation or bug fixes and performance improvements details. So that before updating to app users would be aware about what new they will get with this version update. To better display specific features or content within your app, create many versions of your product page with varied promotional language, images, and app samples. Use a unique URL to direct targeted viewers to a specific page, and track performance in App Analytics. Improve app discovery on the App Store and offer high-quality app and in-app purchase experiences by leveraging the newest features.

TestFlight

Before publishing your apps on the App Store, TestFlight makes it simple to invite consumers to test your apps and App Clips and get vital feedback. You may invite up to 10,000 testers by simply sending them an email or posting a public link. TestFlight supports iOS, iPadOS, tvOS, watchOS, and iMessage applications, as well as automated upgrades to guarantee that testers are constantly testing the most recent release available. Internally or externally, up to 100 applications may be evaluated at once, and several builds can be checked at the same time. After being uploaded, builds are active for 90 days.

On the other side in case you want to test an app first you need to install TestFlight App from Apple App Store and then login with the apple id (in case you don't have one you need to create it first, it's simple as setting up of google or yahoo mail accounts). Now you can share your apple id with whom you will be getting an invite for testing apps. Once you receive an invite you can open that invite link in the mobile mail client so it will automatically be redirected to TestFlight App. Once you accept the invite and agree to terms and conditions, you can install that app and give feedback from the same testflight app. When you open app details you will find a section of previous build with their version number that will help you to compare or find bugs if that occurs in some specific version of the app.

Internal and external tester groups

Up to 100 people on your team with the roles of Account Holder, Admin, App Manager, Developer, or marketer can be designated as beta testers. You may even make several groups and assign various builds to each one, depending on the aspects each one should emphasize.

Invite up to 10,000 external testers through email or by activating and publishing a public link, which invites anybody to test your app. You can create a group of testers and assign them to the builds you want them to test. You may even make many groups and assign various builds to each one, based on the qualities you wish to emphasize. The initial build of your app for each version must be authorized by TestFlight App Review before testing can begin. When you add a build to a group, it is automatically forwarded for review.

Invite testers

If you have a tester's email address, you can send them an invitation along with a link to download and test your app. Email may be an efficient approach to distribute beta versions of your application with an existing group of external testers or specific persons you would like to ask to test. When you want to invite a tester to an external group first select that external group from the menu of TestFlight Dashboard, further you can add tester either via import of CSV which would have all tester's information, or you add via **Add New Testers** section as follows:

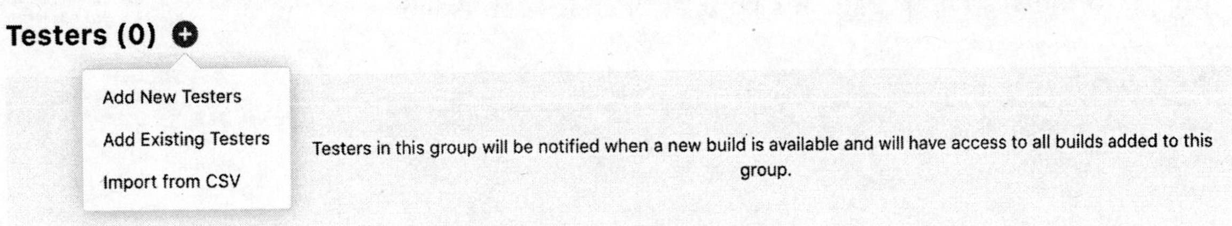

Figure 17.18: Add New Testers

This selection will open up a form that will ask for **FIRST NAME, LAST NAME** and **EMAIL** of the invitee tester. You may even continue to add multiple testers at the same time, as follows:

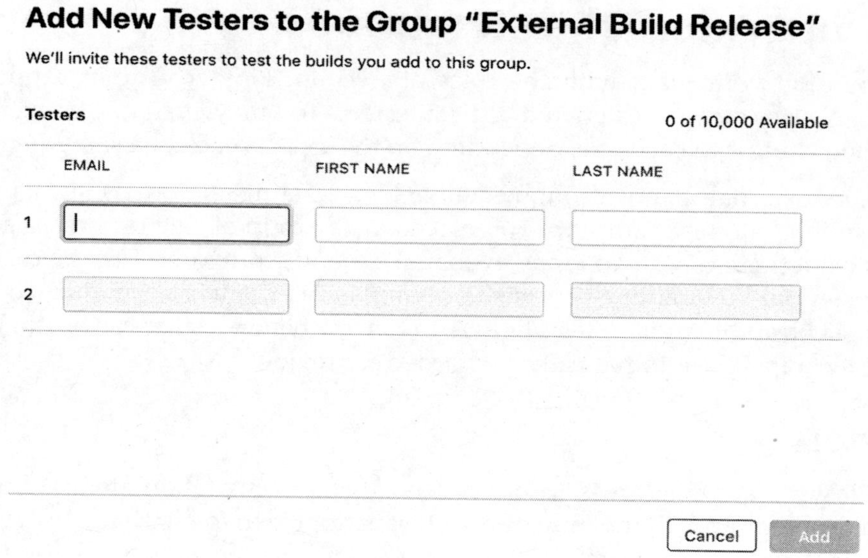

Add New Testers to the Group "External Build Release"

We'll invite these testers to test the builds you add to this group.

Testers 0 of 10,000 Available

	EMAIL	FIRST NAME	LAST NAME
1			
2			

Cancel Add

Figure 17.19: Invite New Testers with Email

If you don't have an established network of testers, public links are an efficient way to connect with people who can test your app. There is no need to provide any contact information. Simply go to the TestFlight page for your app, choose an existing group, and select Enable Public Link as follows:

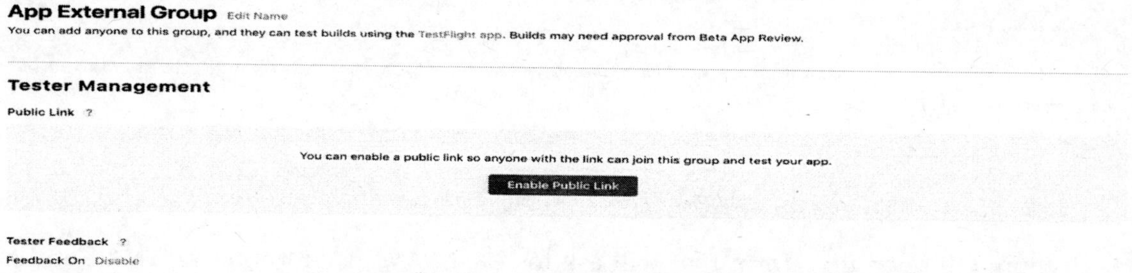

App External Group Edit Name

You can add anyone to this group, and they can test builds using the TestFlight app. Builds may need approval from Beta App Review.

Tester Management

Public Link ?

You can enable a public link so anyone with the link can join this group and test your app.

Enable Public Link

Tester Feedback ?

Feedback On Disable

Figure 17.20: App Public Link For Testing

The URL may then be copied and shared on social media, messaging platforms, email campaigns, and other platforms. You may also use the public link to limit the number of testers who can join. If the group limit is reached or your public link is disabled, anybody trying to join your beta will receive a notice stating your beta is no longer accepting new testers. Consider where you distribute your public link and when it would be appropriate to delete it to provide a positive user experience.

Test information

You will need to tell testers what to test, as well as any other pertinent information, when sharing your app with external testers. In App Store Connect, add these details to your app's

Test Information page. You should also include an email address that you check often so that you can receive and respond to tester comments. When sending your software to internal testers, test information is optional.

Beta user app feedback

Testers may provide comments straight from your app using the TestFlight app for iOS and iPadOS by capturing a snapshot. They can also give more information about an app crash right after it happens. Go to your app's TestFlight page in App Store Connect and select Crashes or Screenshots in the Feedback section to see this feedback. The email address you specify in Test Information will get feedback from testers using iOS, TVOS, or watchOS.

Manage Apple review rejections

Apple reviews all applications and app updates before submitting them to the App Store to ensure that they are reliable, perform as expected, respect user privacy, and don't contain any objectionable content. Use iOS app design standards while you develop and construct your app to make the approval process go as smoothly as possible.

iOS human interface design guidelines

A native iOS app has the best opportunity to deliver content and design rich features to enable a better user experience. Here we will discuss the design's expectations by Apple for quality and functionality:

- Text should be legible at all sizes, icons must be precise and clear, adornments should be modest and suitable, and the design must be driven by a focused focus on utility.
- People can comprehend and interact with content with fluid motion and a clear, attractive interface that never competes with it. Translucency and blurring frequently hint at more, whereas content generally cover the full screen.
- Different graphic layers and realistic motion help to express hierarchy, energy, and comprehension. Touch and discoverability contribute to enjoyment by allowing access to more functionality and material without losing context. As you move through the material, transitions give you a sense of depth.
- By employing modest, unobtrusive visuals, conventional controls, and predictable behaviors, an app that assists individuals with serious work may keep them focused. An immersive app, such as a game, on the other hand, might have a fascinating look that promises fun and excitement while promoting exploration.
- A consistent app uses system-provided interface components, well-known iconography, standard text styles, and standardized language to adopt recognized standards and conventions. The software includes features and behaviors in ways that users are accustomed to.
- To keep individuals informed, feedback recognizes activities and displays results. The built-in iOS applications provide audible feedback for every user action. When tapped,

interactive components are temporarily illuminated, progress indicators indicate the state of long-running processes, and animation and music assist in clarifying the outcomes of actions.

- By keeping interaction components familiar and predictable, confirming harmful acts, and making it easy to abort activities, even while they're already underway, an app may make consumers feel in control.
- When an app's virtual items and actions are metaphors for familiar experiences, whether in the real or digital world, people learn faster. Metaphors function effectively in iOS because users interact with the screen physically. They shift views out of the way so that the material beneath may be seen. They move material around by dragging and swiping. Switches are toggled, sliders are moved, and picker values are scrolled through.
- Direct manipulation of onscreen material fascinates viewers and aids comprehension. When users spin the device or use motions to change display content, they are directly manipulating it. They can see the immediate, tangible effects of their activities when they use direct manipulation.

Avoid common app rejection

Before you submit your app, educate yourself with the technical, content, and design criteria used by Apple to assess all apps listed in the App Store Review Guidelines. The scope of this chapter does not allow for a comprehensive discussion of all guidelines. To assist you in properly preparing your applications before submitting them for review, let's see a compiled list of the most frequent concerns that lead apps to be rejected.

Not enough features

It's possible that your app won't be accepted to the app store if it doesn't have much functionality or content, or if it only pertains to a tiny niche market. Take a look at the applications in your category on the App Store before you start developing your app and think about how you can improve the user experience.

Incomplete information

In the App Evaluation Information area of App Store Connect, fill in all of the information needed to review your app. Provide a valid demo account username and password if some functions require it. Include the specifications if there are any unique configurations to be made. Prepare to offer a demo video or the hardware if features need a difficult-to-replicate setting or specialized gear. Please double-check that your contact information is accurate and up-to-date.

Requesting permissions

You should clearly and thoroughly state how your app will utilize users or use data when asking permission to access it. Users will understand why your app is asking for access to their personal information. Let us take an example, If your app's code calls one or more APIs that access sensitive user data, the app's **`Info.plist`** file should include an **`infoPlistKey`** with a user facing purpose string that explains why the data is needed. A purpose string is required for all apps submitted to the App Store that access user data.

Crashes and bugs

You should only submit your app for evaluation after it is finished and ready to go live. Before submitting your app, be sure to properly test it on devices running the most recent version and solve any issues. Bug fixes for applications that are currently on the App Store but have minor guideline problems can be accepted as long as there are no legal issues.

Broken links and placeholder contents

All of the links in your app must work. All apps must have a link to user support with up-to-date contact information as well as a link to your privacy policy. Before sending your app in for evaluation, make sure all of the pictures and text are in place. Apps that are still in development and include placeholder content cannot be approved since they are not ready to be released.

Conclusion

Before submitting your app for review, ensure that it is prepared for public release and that your product page is optimized. The App Store evaluates all apps based on technical, content, and design criteria. Obtain valuable feedback from beta testers to refine your app before its final release. Utilize TestFlight to test your app on a smartphone and easily invite additional testers after uploading it to App Store Connect. In the previous chapter, we discussed the step-by-step processes of building an App Store app with certificates and profiles, as well as the app submission process for the product page. It is crucial for developers to carefully adhere to all App Store review and design guidelines to minimize the chances of rejection.

To ensure an excellent user interface, identify and address any UI issues before testing on a device. For the app's launch screen, Xcode storyboards must be used for updates. Additionally, new iPhone apps should support all iPhone displays, while new iPad apps must support all iPad screens. The App Store aims to offer consumers programs that fully utilize their device's capabilities. When submitting a new app that uses cutting-edge technology, ensure that your information property list (**`Info.plist`**) complies with the device requirements.

Multiple choice questions

1. **When we use What's New in this Version ?**
   a. New App Upload
   b. New Version Upload
   c. For the first time, create an app product page.
   d. None of the above

2. **Internal testers limit in app store connects ______**
   a. 10
   b. 20
   c. 30
   d. 40
3. **External testers limit in app store connects ______.**
   a. 1000
   b. 5000
   c. 10000
   d. 12000
4. **Xcode Cloud is used for _______.**
   a. Make build in cloud
   b. To Upload New Builds
   c. Manage Rejections of App
   d. None of the above
5. **Transporter Mac App is used for _______.**
   a. Make build in cloud
   b. To Upload New Builds
   c. Manage Rejections of App
   d. None of the above

Answers

1. b
2. c
3. c
4. a
5. b

Chapter 18

Continuous Integration and Delivery with Xcode Cloud

Introduction

As technology continues to advance rapidly, the demand for seamless and efficient app development workflows has never been greater. In response to this need, Apple has introduced an innovative tool that promises to revolutionize the iOS and macOS app development processes. Xcode Cloud is a cloud-based continuous integration and delivery service provided by Apple for developers working on iOS, macOS, watchOS, and tvOS applications. It allows developers to build, test, and distribute their apps in the cloud, providing a seamless and efficient development experience. With Xcode Cloud, developers can collaborate with team members, automate workflows, and easily manage their app development process.

Xcode Cloud offers several important benefits for developers. Firstly, it provides a cloud-based platform that allows developers to build, test, and distribute their apps efficiently. This eliminates the need for developers to set up and manage their own infrastructure, saving time and resources. Additionally, Xcode Cloud facilitates seamless collaboration among team members. It allows developers to easily share their code, track changes, and work together on projects. This promotes efficient teamwork and enhances productivity. Automation is another significant advantage of Xcode Cloud.

Structure

In this chapter, we will cover the following topics:

- Xcode cloud setup and maintenance
- Data Usages
- Workflows
- Source code management

Objectives

By learning this chapter, you should be able to set up a Xcode cloud, maintain it with the other team members, and design and automate your workflows and release cycles.

Key features of Xcode Cloud

The user's input highlights the benefits and advantages of using Xcode Cloud for app development. It emphasizes how Xcode Cloud eliminates the need for developers to set up and manage their own infrastructure, saving time and resources. The seamless collaboration feature allows for easy code sharing, change tracking, and teamwork on projects, promoting efficient collaboration and enhancing productivity. Additionally, automation is mentioned as a significant advantage of Xcode Cloud.

Continuous Integration and Delivery

Xcode Cloud offers powerful **continuous integration and continuous delivery** (**CI/CD**) capabilities, allowing developers to automatically build, test, and deliver their applications. This automation streamlines the development process, ensuring that code changes are thoroughly tested and deployed quickly and efficiently. With Xcode Cloud, developers can focus more on coding and less on the manual tasks involved in building and releasing their apps.

Automated testing and debugging processes

Automated testing and debugging processes are seamlessly integrated into Xcode Cloud, enabling developers to easily identify and resolve any issues in their code. By automatically running tests and providing detailed feedback, Xcode Cloud saves developers valuable time and effort, ensuring the quality and stability of their applications. Additionally, the platform offers comprehensive debugging tools that help pinpoint and fix any errors or bugs in the code, further enhancing the development process. With these automated testing and debugging processes, developers can have greater confidence in the reliability and performance of their applications.

Collaborative workflows and version control integration

Workflows are another important element of the Xcode Cloud. The technology enables developers to engage with team members in real time, making it simpler to collaborate on projects and expediting the development process. Version control integration guarantees that all changes and updates are logged, making it possible to easily roll back or compare various versions of the code. This not only increases efficiency, but also the project's general structure and management. Developers can successfully collaborate and maintain a smooth and structured working environment using Xcode Cloud's collaborative workflows and version control integration.

Parallel testing

To accelerate the testing process, Xcode Cloud uses parallel testing. It runs tests concurrently on multiple simulated devices, reducing the overall test time significantly. This helps developers identify issues faster, making it easier to iterate and deliver improvements more rapidly.

Distributed building

Xcode Cloud leverages Apple's vast cloud infrastructure to distribute the building process across multiple machines. This dramatically reduces the time required to build an app, especially for larger projects. It ensures that developers spend less time waiting and more time coding.

Xcode Editor integration

Xcode Cloud is seamlessly integrated into the Xcode IDE. Developers can access the full power of Xcode while also benefiting from Xcode Cloud's continuous integration capabilities. This allows developers to switch between coding and testing without leaving the familiar Xcode environment.

Test Flight integration

Test Flight, Apple's app testing platform, is fully integrated with Xcode Cloud. Once an app passes the automated tests, Xcode Cloud can distribute it to internal testers to Testflight. This simplifies the process of gathering feedback and performing beta testing before releasing the app to the App Store.

Secure and privacy-focused

Apple places a strong emphasis on security and privacy, and Xcode Cloud is no exception. All data is encrypted both in transit and at rest. Additionally, Xcode Cloud ensures that sensitive information, such as code signing certificates and private keys, is securely managed.

Benefits of Using Xcode Cloud

Let us dive into the various benefits of using Xcode Cloud:

Faster development cycles: With automated testing, parallel testing, and distributed building, Xcode Cloud significantly reduces the time required for each iteration in the development process. Developers can quickly identify and fix issues, leading to faster development cycles and quicker app releases.

- **Enhanced collaboration**: Xcode Cloud fosters collaboration among development teams. As the entire development process is moved to the cloud, team members can easily access the latest code changes, test results, and artifacts. This promotes better communication and teamwork.
- **Improved code quality**: Automated testing and continuous integration ensure that code changes are thoroughly tested before being integrated into the main codebase. This results in higher code quality as bugs and regressions are caught early in the development process.
- **Efficient resource utilization**: By offloading resource-intensive tasks like building and testing to the cloud, developers can use their local machines more efficiently. This is particularly beneficial for developers with less powerful hardware, as they can leverage Apple's cloud infrastructure to perform computationally intensive tasks.
- **Simplified deployment process**: Xcode Cloud integrates seamlessly with Test Flight, making it easier to distribute beta versions of the app for testing and gather feedback from internal testers. The streamlined deployment process saves time and simplifies the management of the testing phase.

SetUp Xcode cloud workflows

When you begin configuring a project or workspace to use Xcode Cloud, Xcode analyses it to identify its settings and displays the applications and frameworks it contains. The configuration for the steps you wants Xcode Cloud to execute is referred to as the workflow. A workflow comprises various settings, including:

- **General information:** This includes providing a name and description for the workflow.
- **Xcode and macOS versions:** You can specify the versions of Xcode and macOS to be used in the temporary build environment. It's important to note that Xcode Cloud may periodically update the available macOS and Xcode versions, requiring you to update your workflows accordingly for successful builds.
- **Start conditions:** These conditions determine when Xcode Cloud triggers the execution of a workflow.
- **Actions:** Xcode Cloud performs various action within a workflow. You can configure multiple actions, such as building, analyzing, testing, and archiving your app.
- **Post-actions:** These are actions that Xcode Cloud executes after completing the primary actions of the workflow. For instance, you can set up custom notifications or distribute a new version of your app to testers using TestFlight.

- **Custom build scripts**: You have the option to include custom build scripts that perform specific tasks. This could involve installing a third-party tool or executing custom actions. For detailed information on writing custom build scripts, refer to the documentation on this topic.

By configuring these settings in your workflow, you can tailor the behaviour of Xcode Cloud to meet your specific requirements and automate various stages of the app development and deployment process.

Workflow access

After completing a build, Xcode Cloud carries out the following actions:

1. Sends an email notification containing comprehensive details about the build, including links to access the build report in both Xcode and App Store Connect.
2. Stores the artifacts generated by the build and provides the ability to download them from either Xcode or App Store Connect.

The artifacts produced by Xcode Cloud include:

- **Detailed build logs**: These logs provide a comprehensive record of the build process, aiding in debugging and troubleshooting any issues that may arise.
- **Exported app archive, app binary, or framework**: Depending on the type of project, Xcode Cloud generates the relevant files necessary for distributing or deploying the app. These files can be used for submission to the App Store or for further distribution and testing purposes.
- **Test result bundle**: Xcode Cloud also generates a bundle containing the results of the automated user interface tests performed during the build process. This bundle includes valuable information such as test outcomes, logs, and any screenshots captured during the tests.

By providing access to these artifacts, Xcode Cloud ensures that developers have easy and convenient access to the build-related information and outputs necessary for further analysis, distribution, and submission of their apps.

Select the archive

Ensure that the scheme associated with each app or framework you intend to build using Xcode Cloud incorporates the archive action.

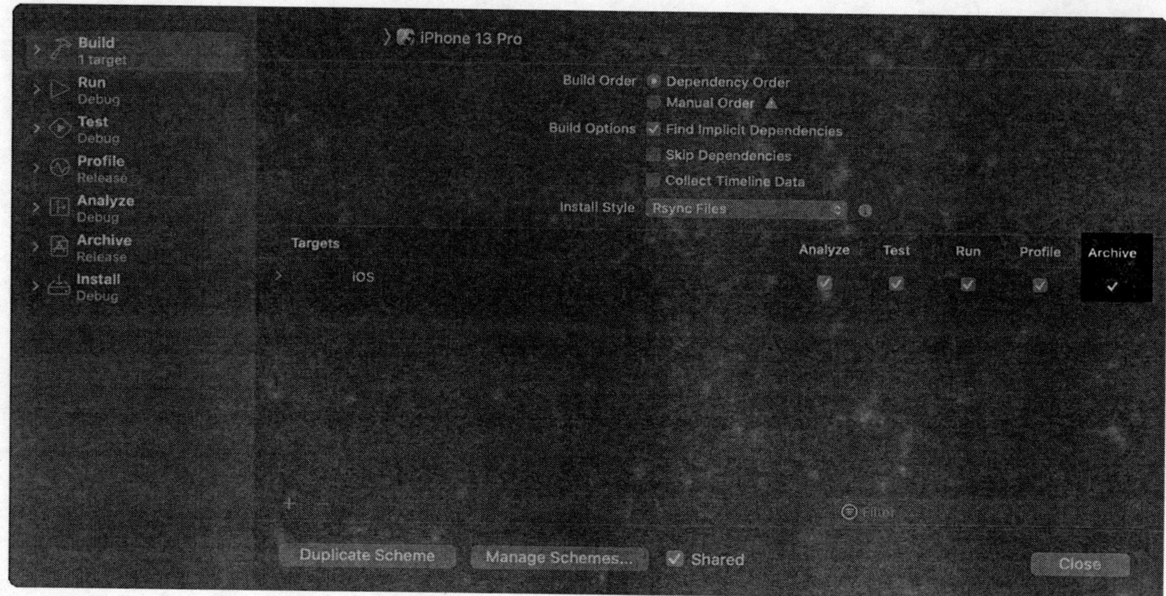

Figure 18.1: App Project Archive Options

To identify the schemes within your project that use the archive action, execute the following command in the Terminal:

```
xcodebuild -project MyApp.xcodeproj -describeAllArchivableProducts -json
```

Choose the product

To set up Xcode Cloud for your project or workspace, follow these steps within Xcode:

1. Open your project or workspace in Xcode.
2. Ensure that the Report Navigator is visible in Xcode.
3. Select the **Cloud tab** within the Report Navigator.
4. Click on the **Create Workflow** option.

Figure 18.2: *Xcode Cloud Editor*

If your project includes targets with identical bundle identifiers, Xcode Cloud treats them as a single product. It's important to note that a product can only have one bundle identifier, and each bundle identifier corresponds to exactly one Xcode Cloud product. If your workspace or project consists of multiple app targets, the following guidelines apply:

1. Whenever possible, use the same bundle identifier across different versions of your app for each platform. This means that you should use the same bundle identifier for your iOS, macOS, and watchOS versions of the app.
2. In cases where each version of your app has a distinct bundle identifier, such as **`com.example.myiosapp`** for the iOS version and **`com.example.mymacapp`** for the macOS version, Xcode recognizes multiple products. In such situations, you need to choose one of the products when creating your initial workflow. Subsequently, you can configure additional workflows for the other product.

By adhering to these guidelines, you can ensure smooth integration with Xcode Cloud, enabling effective management and deployment of your app's different versions across various platforms.

Review workflow

Based on your selected product, Xcode provides a recommended initial workflow that includes the following steps:

1. Initiates a build for every change made to the default branch of your Git repository, as well as for each pull request targeting the default branch.

2. Use the most recently released versions of macOS and Xcode for the temporary build environment.
3. Incorporates the archive action as part of the workflow.
4. Sends an email containing relevant details about the build, including links to the build report accessible in both Xcode and App Store Connect.

Prior to commencing your first build, it is advisable to review the suggested workflow. You may want to ensure that Xcode has accurately selected the appropriate scheme for your project. To review the suggested workflow, follow these steps:

1. Click on **Edit Workflow** within the **Review Workflow sheet.**
2. If necessary, make any required modifications in the displayed sheet containing the workflow information. Save the changes once you have made them.
3. Proceed to the next step by clicking **Next** in the **Review Workflow sheet.** Allow Xcode to guide you through the process of granting Xcode Cloud the necessary access to your source code.

By following these steps, you can review and tailor the suggested workflow according to your specific requirements, ensuring that Xcode Cloud operates in alignment with your project's needs.

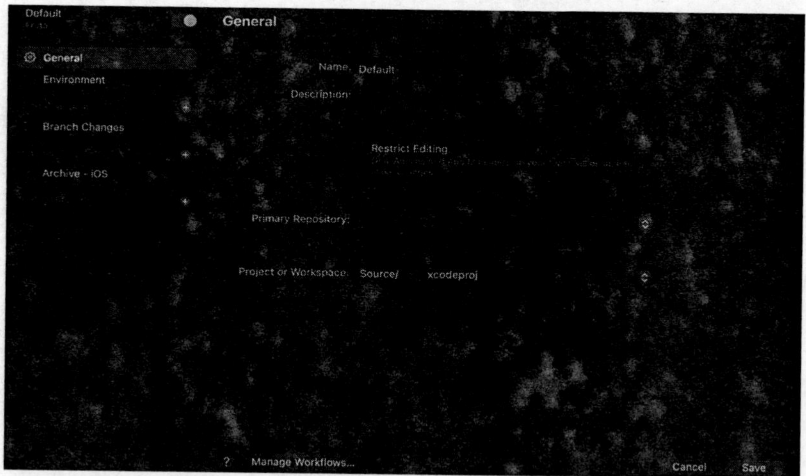

Figure 18.3: Xcode Cloud Default Configuration

Access to source code

To use Xcode Cloud, it is necessary to grant access to the Git repository that houses your code. This access enables Xcode Cloud to automatically build and test your code whenever changes are made. When configuring your project or workspace to use Xcode Cloud, Xcode examines the setup to identify the specific **Source Code Management** (**SCM**) provider being used. In the **Grant Access to Your Source Code** sheet, you can grant access by selecting the **Grant Access** option, which will initiate Xcode's guidance through the native authorization process of your SCM provider.

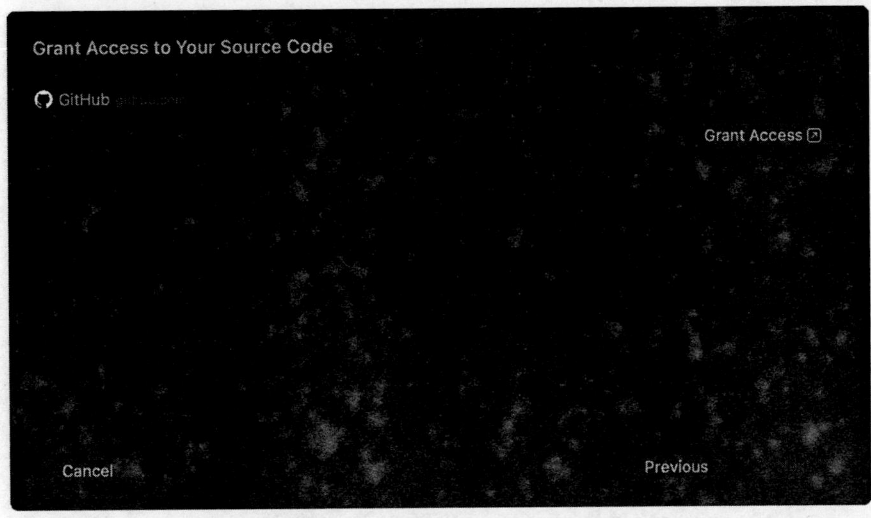

Figure 18.4: Xcode Cloud Access to GitHub Code

App record and build

Xcode Cloud integrates Xcode, TestFlight, and App Store Connect to create a robust CI/CD system. Consequently, having an app record in App Store Connect is a prerequisite for using Xcode Cloud.

If you have already established an app record in App Store Connect for your application, Xcode Cloud will seamlessly use it without any additional steps. On the other hand, if you haven't yet created an app record for your app in App Store Connect, Xcode Cloud simplifies the process for you. Once you grant Xcode Cloud access to your Git repository, Xcode assists you in creating the necessary app record, ensuring a smooth setup process.

Figure 18.5: Configured Xcode Cloud

Once you have authorized Xcode Cloud to access your Git repository and, if applicable, created an app record, you are all set to initiate your initial build. Simply select a branch and click on the **Start Build** button. Xcode Cloud will then proceed to check out the chosen branch and initiate the build process for your code.

Conclusion

In this chapter, we discussed in detail how Xcode Cloud represents a significant step forward in the world of iOS and macOS app development. Its powerful features, such as automated testing, continuous integration, and distributed building, provide developers and development teams with the tools they need to create high-quality apps more efficiently.

By leveraging the cloud and integrating seamlessly with Xcode, Xcode Cloud empowers developers to focus on writing code while automating time-consuming tasks. The benefits of Xcode Cloud, including faster development cycles, enhanced collaboration, and improved code quality, make it an invaluable tool for any iOS or macOS app development project.

As Apple continues to invest in developer tools and services, it's evident that Xcode Cloud is poised to become an essential component of the app development ecosystem, helping developers bring their ideas to life with greater speed and efficiency.

In the next chapter, we will start learning about Advance iOS's latest and most updated new frameworks, which you might use as per the requirements and use cases of mobile applications.

Multiple choice questions

1. **What is Xcode Cloud primarily used for?**
    a. Cloud storage
    b. Continuous integration and delivery
    c. Mobile device management
    d. Data analytics
2. **Which IDE is Xcode Cloud integrated with?**
    a. Android Studio
    b. Visual Studio Code
    c. Xcode
    d. Eclipse
3. **What type of testing does Xcode Cloud support?**
    a. Unit testing only
    b. UI testing only
    c. Integration testing only
    d. Unit testing, UI testing, and integration testing

4. **How does Xcode Cloud speed up the testing process?**
    a. By providing faster internet connection
    b. By running tests on multiple simulated devices in parallel
    c. By skipping the testing phase
    d. By outsourcing testing to external testers
5. **What happens when a code change is pushed to the version control system in Xcode Cloud?**
    a. Xcode Cloud triggers a build and runs automated tests
    b. The code change is rejected and rolled back automatically
    c. Xcode Cloud sends a notification to the development team
    d. Xcode Cloud archives the code change for future reference
6. **What does Xcode Cloud integrate with for beta testing and gathering feedback?**
    a. Firebase
    b. TestFlight
    c. HockeyApp
    d. App Center
7. **How does Xcode Cloud ensure the security of sensitive information?**
    a. By storing data in plain text
    b. By encrypting data in transit and at rest
    c. By sharing sensitive information with third parties
    d. By publishing sensitive information publicly
8. **What is one benefit of using Xcode Cloud for app development?**
    a. Slower development cycles
    b. Limited collaboration options
    c. Improved code quality
    d. Manual deployment process
9. **What does Xcode Cloud offer in terms of building apps?**
    a. Local buildings only
    b. Cloud-based distributed building
    c. Cross-platform building
    d. Manual building

10. Which platform is Xcode Cloud primarily designed for?

a. Android

b. Windows

c. iOS and macOS

d. Linux

Answers

1. b
2. c
3. d
4. b
5. a
6. b
7. b
8. c
9. b
10. c

Join our book's Discord space

Join the book's Discord Workspace for Latest updates, Offers, Tech happenings around the world, New Release and Sessions with the Authors:

https://discord.bpbonline.com

CHAPTER 19

Advance iOS with New Frameworks

Introduction

As technology continues to evolve at a rapid pace, the iOS development landscape is also experiencing exciting advancements. Apple, the company behind the iOS platform, consistently introduces new frameworks and updates existing ones to empower developers and enhance the capabilities of iOS applications. These frameworks serve as powerful tools for creating innovative and feature-rich apps, enabling developers to push the boundaries of what is possible on the iOS platform. We will learn about a few of the latest frameworks introduced in recent times with new updates, such as RealityKit, VisionKit, Activity Kit and Symbols.

Structure

In this chapter, we will cover the following topics:

- RealityKit
- VisionKit
- ActivityKit
- Symbols

Objectives

By learning this chapter, you should be able to learn about new and latest frameworks which are broadly based on new technology advancements such as RealityKit, VisionKit, ActivityKit and Symbols Framework.

RealityKit

RealityKit is the newest augmented reality (AR) framework from Apple. It is intended to make it simple for developers to construct immersive and interactive augmented reality experiences. RealityKit is based on Metal, Apple's high-performance graphics engine, ensuring that AR experiences run smoothly and convincingly. RealityKit represents the AR world via scenes. Entities, or the items that appear in the scene, make up scenes. Entities range from 3D models to text labels.

Components may be used to configure entities. Components improve entities' behavior and appearance. A component, for example, might be used to make an object move, rotate, or change color. RealityKit supports physics, allowing things to interact with one another and with their surroundings. A ball, for example, may bounce off a wall, or a vehicle could travel over a road. RealityKit supports haptics, which enables users to engage with AR experiences by receiving physical input. When a user taps on an item, for example, they may feel the vibration of their phone:

```
import RealityKit
class MyARExperience: ARExperience {
    override func didInitialize() {
        // Create a scene
        let scene = Scene()
        // Create an entity
       let entity = ModelEntity(mesh: .box(width: 0.1, height: 0.1, depth: 0.1))
        entity.position = .init(x: 0, y: 0, z: -0.5)
        // Add the entity to the scene
        scene.add(entity)
        // Set the scene as the root node of the experience
        self.root = scene
  }
}
```

The previous code generates a small, augmented reality experience that depicts a box floating in the air. The **ModelEntity** class, which is used to represent 3D models, is utilized to generate the box. The box is positioned in the scene at (0, 0, -0.5), which indicates it is 0.5 meters in front of the user. The box is subsequently added to the scene, and the scene is designated as the experience's root node.

Placing virtual objects in AR scene

To demonstrate the power of RealityKit, let's create a simple AR application that allows users to place virtual objects in the real world using their iOS devices. We will use Xcode and Swift to build the project:

1. **Set up the project:** Create a new Xcode project and choose the **Augmented Reality App** template. This template includes the necessary ARKit and RealityKit dependencies.
2. **Add a button to place objects:** In your View Controller, create a `UIButton` and add it to the `ARView`:

```
import UIKit
import RealityKit
class ViewController: UIViewController {
    @IBOutlet var arView: ARView!
    var virtualObject: Entity?
    override func viewDidLoad() {
        super.viewDidLoad()
        let placeObjectButton = UIButton(type: .system)
        placeObjectButton.setTitle("Place Object", for: .normal)
  placeObjectButton.addTarget(self, action: #selector(placeVirtualObject),
for: .touchUpInside)
       placeObjectButton.frame = CGRect(x: 20, y: 20, width: 120, height:
40)
        view.addSubview(placeObjectButton)
    }
    @objc func placeVirtualObject() {
        // Code to place virtual object in the AR scene
        // Create or load the virtual object entity
    }
}
```

3. **Load and place virtual objects:** In the `placeVirtualObject()` function, you can load or create the virtual object entity and set its position and rotation in the AR scene. Here's an example using a 3D model:

```
@objc func placeVirtualObject() {
    let modelEntity = try! Entity.loadModel(named: "VirtualObject.usdz")
  modelEntity.setPosition([0, 0, -1], relativeTo: arView.cameraTransform)
    arView.scene.addAnchor(modelEntity)
}
```

Ensure that you have a 3D model file named `VirtualObject.usdz` in your project's assets.

4. **Run the App:** Build and run the application on a supported iOS device. You can interact with the **Place Object** button to position the virtual object in the AR scene. The virtual object will appear based on the device's camera feed, giving the illusion of it being part of the real world.

RealityKit provides developers with a powerful framework for building immersive augmented reality experiences on iOS devices. Its high-level abstractions, rendering capabilities, and integration with tools like Reality Composer make it an ideal choice for AR development. By leveraging RealityKit's features and using the provided code example, you can begin creating your own engaging AR applications and unleash your creativity by merging the virtual and physical worlds.

VisionKit

Apple provides the VisionKit framework, which enables iOS application developers to incorporate document capture and processing capabilities. Using VisionKit, developers can create seamless document scanning experiences by leveraging the device's camera and image processing algorithms. VisionKit is developed on top of the Vision framework and offers an interface designed for document digitization and processing at a higher level. It simplifies the implementation of document scanning features by providing a user interface and image processing capabilities that are ready for use. Let's discuss the features of VisionKit in detail:

- **Document scanning user interface:** VisionKit offers a pre-built user interface component, `VNDocumentCameraViewController`, that provides a seamless and intuitive document scanning experience. It allows users to capture images of documents, automatically detects the document edges, and provides features like flash control, auto-capture, and multi-page support.
- **Image processing and enhancement:** VisionKit leverages the power of the device's camera and built-in image processing algorithms to automatically enhance the scanned documents. It adjusts the perspective, corrects distortions, and applies image filters to ensure the best possible quality of the scanned documents.
- **OCR and text extraction:** VisionKit supports Optical Character Recognition (OCR), allowing developers to extract text from scanned documents. By leveraging the Vision framework's text recognition capabilities, you can enable search, indexing, or further processing of the extracted text.
- **Document export and sharing:** Once the document scanning and processing are complete, VisionKit provides easy options for exporting and sharing the scanned documents. It supports various file formats, such as PDF, JPEG, and PNG, enabling seamless integration with other applications or cloud storage services.

Implementing document scanning with VisionKit

To demonstrate the capabilities of VisionKit, let's create a simple document scanning application that allows users to capture and save scanned documents. We will use Xcode and Swift to build the project:

- **Implement the document scanning functionality:** Create a new Xcode project and import the necessary frameworks. Create a function to present the document scanning interface and handle the captured documents.

```
import UIKit
import VisionKit
class ViewController: UIViewController,
VNDocumentCameraViewControllerDelegate {

    func scanDocument() {
      let documentCameraViewController = VNDocumentCameraViewController()
        documentCameraViewController.delegate = self
       present(documentCameraViewController, animated: true, completion: nil)
    }

    func documentCameraViewController(_ controller:
VNDocumentCameraViewController, didFinishWith scan: VNDocumentCameraScan) {
        for pageIndex in 0..<scan.pageCount {
            let image = scan.imageOfPage(at: pageIndex)
            // Perform desired processing on the scanned image
            // Save or export the scanned image as needed
        }
        controller.dismiss(animated: true, completion: nil)
    }
}
```

Handle scanned documents

Implement the delegate method to handle the scanned documents:

```
extension ViewController: VNDocumentCameraViewControllerDelegate
{
  func documentCameraViewController(_ controller: VNDocumentCameraViewController,
didFinishWith scan: VNDocumentCameraScan) {
        for pageIndex in 0..<scan.pageCount {
            let image = scan.imageOfPage(at: pageIndex)
            // Perform desired processing on the scanned image
            // Save or export the scanned image as needed
        }
```

```
        controller.dismiss(animated: true, completion: nil)
    }
}
```

Build and run the application on a compatible iOS device. Tap the scan button, and the VisionKit interface will be presented, allowing you to capture and process documents. The scanned images can be further processed, saved, or exported based on your application's requirements.

VisionKit is a powerful framework that simplifies the implementation of document scanning and processing features in iOS applications. Its pre-built user interface, image processing capabilities, and OCR support make it a valuable tool for developers aiming to create seamless and efficient document scanning experiences. By leveraging VisionKit's features and utilizing the provided code example, you can integrate document scanning functionality into your iOS app, empowering users to effortlessly digitize and manage their physical documents.

ActivityKit

ActivityKit is a powerful framework in iOS that allows developers to create engaging and interactive experiences within their applications. Whether you want to build a workout tracking app, a guided meditation tool, or a productivity tool, ActivityKit provides a robust set of tools and features to make it happen. Here, we'll explore the capabilities of ActivityKit and provide a code example to demonstrate its usage. ActivityKit is built on top of UIKit and provides a collection of classes and APIs to simplify the development of interactive experiences. It revolves around the concept of activities, which represent individual tasks or actions that users can perform within an app. These activities can range from simple actions like tapping a button to more complex workflows involving multiple steps. Let's discuss the key components of ActivityKit in detail:

- **Activity:** At the core of ActivityKit is the **`Activity`** class, which represents a single activity in your application. It encapsulates the logic and user interface elements associated with that particular activity. You can define actions, gestures, and UI elements within an activity to guide users through the interaction.
- **Activity manager:** The **`ActivityManager`** class acts as a central coordinator for managing activities within your app. It handles the presentation and dismissal of activities, tracks the progress of activities, and provides a way to navigate between different activities.
- **Activity view:** The **`ActivityView`** class is a container view that displays the content of an activity to the user. It provides a dedicated space for presenting the user interface elements associated with an activity.
- **Activity stack:** The **`ActivityStack`** class is responsible for managing the stack of activities in your app. It keeps track of the current activity, allows for pushing and popping activities onto the stack, and enables navigation between different activities.

Creating a workout tracking activity

Let's dive into a code example that demonstrates how to create a workout tracking activity using ActivityKit. In this scenario, we'll create an activity that allows users to record their running distance and time. First, we need to define our custom activity by subclassing the **Activity** class:

```
import ActivityKit
class WorkoutActivity: Activity {
    var distance: Double = 0
    var time: TimeInterval = 0
    override func viewDidLoad() {
        super.viewDidLoad()
        // Customize the UI elements for the workout tracking activity
        // e.g., Add labels, buttons, and text fields
    }
    override func completeActivity() {
        super.completeActivity()
        // Perform any necessary actions when the workout activity is completed
        // e.g., Save the workout data to a database
    }
}
```

Next, we'll create an instance of the **ActivityManager** and push our workout tracking activity onto the stack:

```
let activityManager = ActivityManager()
let workoutActivity = WorkoutActivity()
activityManager.pushActivity(workoutActivity)
let activityView = ActivityView(frame: view.bounds)
activityView.activityManager = activityManager
view.addSubview(activityView)
```

With this code in place, users can now interact with the workout tracking activity, record their distance and time, and complete the activity when finished. ActivityKit is a versatile framework that empowers developers to build engaging and interactive experiences within their iOS applications. By leveraging the power of activities, you can create dynamic workflows, guide users through specific tasks, and provide a rich and interactive user experience. Experiment with ActivityKit in your projects and explore its full potential to create unique and compelling experiences for your users.

SF symbols

SF Symbols are a set of vector icons that are available in iOS, iPadOS, macOS, watchOS, and tvOS. They are designed to be consistent with the look and feel of Apple's Human Interface

Guidelines, and they can be used in a variety of different contexts, including app icons, UI elements, and marketing materials. SF Symbols are available in a variety of styles, including filled, outlined, and stroked. They can also be rendered in a variety of colors and sizes. This makes them highly versatile and adaptable to a wide range of design needs.

To use SF Symbols in your app, you can either import the pre-made symbols from the Apple Developer website or create your own custom symbols. If you're using Xcode, you can import the SF Symbols library by opening the **Assets.xcassets** file in your project and dragging the SF **Symbols.bundle** file into the library. Once the symbols are imported, you can use them in your app by adding them to your views or controls. If you want to create your own custom symbols, you can use the SF Symbols app, which is available for free on the App Store. The SF Symbols app allows you to create and edit symbols, and it also includes a variety of tools for exporting your symbols in different formats:

```
import SwiftUI

struct ContentView: View {

  var body: some View {

    VStack {

      Text("SF Symbols")

        .font(.largeTitle)

      Image(systemSymbol: "heart.fill")

        .foregroundColor(.red)

      Image(systemSymbol: "gear")

        .foregroundColor(.blue)

    }

  }

}
```

This code will generate a straightforward display with two text labels and two photos. The **heart.fill** sign will be used in the first picture, and the gear symbol will be used in the second. Both photos will be presented in their filled condition, with red and blue backgrounds, respectively. Create a new SwiftUI project in Xcode and paste the code into the **ContentView.swift** file to execute this code. Then, in the upper left corner of Xcode, click the play button to launch the project.

Symbols framework

The Symbols framework allows you to apply symbol effects to animate SF Symbols in your AppKit, UIKit, and SwiftUI projects. These animations include a variety of characteristics, including discrete, indefinite, transition, and content transition. A symbol effect may display a variety of behaviors. For example, you may include a pulse effect with the ability to repeat a certain number of times as a distinct action. You may also include a pulse effect with the ability to loop indefinitely.

```
// Add an effect in SwiftUI.
Image(systemName: "globe")
    // Add effect with discrete image view.
    .symbolEffect(.pulse, options: .repeat(5))
Image(systemName: "globe")
    // Add effect with indefinite image view.
    .symbolEffect(.pulse)
```

Universal animation effects may be applied to symbol-based visuals shown in image views. Regardless of your UI framework or language of choice, the Symbols framework offers a uniform set of effects to employ. Consider a SwiftUI app that shows a Wi-Fi sign with a changeable color effect as the system searches for Wi-Fi networks.

```
// Add an effect in SwiftUI.
Image(systemName: "wifi").symbolEffect(.variableColor.reversing)
```

Conclusion

The advent of technologies such as RealityKit, ActivityKit, VisionKit, and Symbols has significantly transformed various domains and opened up exciting possibilities for developers and users alike. RealityKit has revolutionized the world of augmented reality (AR), enabling the creation of immersive and realistic AR experiences for iOS devices. With its advanced rendering capabilities and seamless integration with Apple's devices, developers can build interactive and visually stunning AR applications.

ActivityKit has empowered developers to design engaging and personalized fitness experiences. By leveraging the power of Apple Watch and the Health app, ActivityKit enables the creation of innovative fitness apps that can track and analyze users' activities, providing them with valuable insights and motivation to achieve their health goals. VisionKit has emerged as a powerful tool for incorporating computer vision capabilities into iOS applications. By leveraging machine learning and image recognition algorithms, VisionKit enables developers to build apps that can analyze images and extract valuable information. From text recognition to object detection, VisionKit expands the possibilities of what developers can achieve in the realm of visual intelligence. Symbols, with its vast library of customizable and scalable icons, has streamlined the process of designing visually appealing user interfaces. By providing a standardized set of symbols, Symbols simplifies the design process and ensures consistency across different iOS apps. Developers can easily integrate these symbols into their applications, saving time and effort while delivering polished and user-friendly interfaces.

As these technologies continue to evolve and improve, we can expect even more exciting developments in the future. The combination of RealityKit, ActivityKit, VisionKit, and Symbols provides developers with a powerful toolkit to create innovative, immersive, and visually captivating experiences across various domains. With Apple's commitment to pushing the boundaries of technology, the possibilities for creating exceptional user experiences are boundless.

Multiple choice questions

1. **What is the purpose of RealityKit in iOS development?**
    a. To create 2D user interfaces
    b. To develop augmented reality (AR) experiences
    c. To build machine learning models
    d. To design virtual reality (VR) games

2. **Which framework is used in conjunction with RealityKit for ARKit integration?**
    a. Core ML
    b. SpriteKit
    c. Metal
    d. ARKit

3. **Which component of RealityKit allows developers to place virtual objects in the real world?**
    a. Reality Composer
    b. Reality Converter
    c. ARView
    d. Entity

4. **Which type of rendering does RealityKit utilize for realistic 3D graphics?**
    a. Ray tracing
    b. Rasterization
    c. Vector graphics
    d. Wireframe rendering

5. **Which framework in iOS allows developers to integrate document scanning and processing capabilities?**
    a. ARKit
    b. Core ML
    c. VisionKit
    d. RealityKit

6. **Which functionality does VisionKit provide in iOS development?**
    a. Image recognition and classification
    b. Facial recognition and tracking
    c. Document scanning and processing
    d. Natural language processing

7. **Which object is used to present the document scanning interface using VisionKit?**
    a. VNDocumentCameraViewController
    b. AVCaptureSession
    c. VNImageRequestHandler
    d. AVPlayerViewController
8. **Which feature of VisionKit allows users to capture multiple pages and create a scanned document?**
    a. Text recognition
    b. Image stabilization
    c. Multi-page support
    d. Barcode scanning
9. **What is the primary purpose of ActivityKit in iOS development?**
    a. To create user interfaces for activity tracking apps
    b. To integrate with external fitness devices and sensors
    c. To manage and monitor user's physical activity data
    d. To provide workout routines and exercise plans
10. **Which permission is required from users to access their activity data using ActivityKit?**
    a. Camera permission
    b. Location permission
    c. Motion and Fitness permission
    d. Microphone permission

Answers

1. b
2. d
3. d
4. a
5. c
6. c
7. a
8. c
9. c
10. c

Index